F
697
.I74
M3

Irving   10458

The western journals
of Washington Irving

F
697
.I74
M3

Irving   10458

The western journals of
Washington Irving

D1064141

The Western Journals of

WASHINGTON IRVING

THE

WESTERN JOURNALS

OF

WASHINGTON IRVING

Edited and Annotated by

JOHN FRANCIS McDERMOTT

NORMAN

UNIVERSITY OF OKLAHOMA PRESS

By John Francis McDermott

Collected Verse of Lewis Carroll (Editor) (New York, 1929)
The Russian Journal and Other Prose of Lewis Carroll (Editor) (New York, 1935)
Private Libraries in Creole Saint Louis (Baltimore, 1938)
Tixier's Travels on the Osage Prairies, translated by Albert J. Salvan (Editor) (Norman, 1940)
A Glossary of Mississippi Valley French (St. Louis, 1941)
The Western Journals of Washington Irving (Editor) (Norman, 1944)
Old Cahokia: A Narrative and Documents Illustrating the First Century of Its History (Editor) (St. Louis, 1949)
Travels in Search of the Elephant: The Wanderings of Alfred S. Waugh, Artist, in Louisiana, Missouri, and Santa Fe, in 1845–1846 Editor) (St. Louis, 1951)
Up the Missouri with Audubon: The Journal of Edward Harris (Editor) (Norman, 1951)
Indian Sketches, by John Treat Irving (Editor) (Norman, 1955)
A Tour on the Prairies, by Washington Irving (Editor) (Norman, 1956)
Prairie and Mountain Sketches, by Matthew C. Field (Editor, with Kate L. Gregg) (Norman, 1957)
The Lost Panoramas of the Mississippi (Chicago, 1958)
George Caleb Bingham: River Portraitist (Norman, 1959)
Seth Eastman: Pictorial Historian of the Indian (Norman, 1961)
Streaks of Squatter Life, by John S. Robb (Editor) (Gainesville, 1962)
Audubon in the West (Editor) (Norman, 1965)

To My Son
John F. McDermott IV

Preface to the Second Edition

The original publication of The Western Journals of Washington Irving *was a war casualty: a critical short-age of paper in 1944 limited the printing to some fifteen hundred copies. Now the strong revival of interest in Irving, exhibited in part by the masterfully annotated editions of* The Adventures of Captain Bonneville *and* Astoria *pre-pared by Edgeley W. Todd, also published in The American Travel and Exploration Series by the University of Oklahoma Press, warrants the re-issue of Irving's on-the-spot observations of the frontier.*

On reviewing this volume I am content to let it stand except for the correction of a few typographical and other errors. Having mellowed somewhat in the intervening years and having grown more understanding of Irving as a literary artist, I would not now be quite so stern in my comments on the Tour on the Prairies. *My present position is better indicated by my introduction to the University of Oklahoma Press's Western Frontier Library edition of that narrative (1956) and by the introduction to a volume of selections from the writings of Irving published by Laurel Editions (Dell, 1965) with the title of* The World of Washington Irving. *But I am of the same opinion still about the value of the journals as historical documents and as pictures of the frontier world.*

JOHN FRANCIS MCDERMOTT

St. Louis, March 28, 1966

Preface

The five extant Journals kept by Washington Irving on his trip west from Cincinnati in 1832 are reproduced here as faithfully as possible. In preparing the text I have made use of a microfilm of the originals and the Trent-Hellman edition published by the Bibliophile Society of Boston in 1919. The circumstances in which Irving made many of his notes and the extreme badness of his handwriting have made some passages difficult to decipher. Where a word or a phrase proved illegible, it is so noted in square brackets. Such brackets have also been used for occasional editorial purposes and for the expansion of abbreviations, the meaning of which might not always be immediately clear. Otherwise (with the exception of the long s) Irving's copy—spelling, punctuation, mechanics, paragraphing—has been followed as exactly as possible.

The map accompanying the text shows Irving's route from St. Louis to the mouth of the Arkansas River. For the tour of the Oklahoma prairies the location of camps can only be approximate. Statements of direction and reports of mileage by Irving, Ellsworth, and Latrobe are too contradictory, vague, or incomplete to permit positive reconstruction of their route.

I am indebted to many persons and institutions for courteous and valuable assistance: to the New York Public Library for a microfilm of the Irving Journals and for photostats of other material; to the Bibliophile Society of Boston for per-

mission to make use of their text published in 1919; to the Harvard-Andover Theological Library for material from the records of the American Board of Commissioners of Foreign Missions; to the National Archives for materials from the Office of Indian Affairs, the Adjutant General's Office, and the Surgeon General's Office; to the Library of Congress; to the Kansas State Historical Society; to the Arkansas Historical Commission; to Mr. Floyd C. Shoemaker and the State Historical Society of Missouri; to Mr. Clarence E. Miller and the Mercantile Library of St. Louis; to the Library of Washington University; to Mr. George D. Vaill of Yale University. Above all I am grateful to my wife for her skill and patience in preparing the manuscript and working with me.

JOHN FRANCIS McDERMOTT

St. Louis, August 23, 1944

Contents

EDITOR'S INTRODUCTION : *Washington Irving as*
Western Traveler   3

JOURNAL   I : *Cincinnati, September 3—St. Louis,*
September 14, 1832   69

JOURNAL   II : *Independence, September 26—*
Cabin Creek, October 6, 1832   89

JOURNAL   III : *Cabin Creek, October 6—On the*
Red Fork, October 17, 1832   107

JOURNAL   IV : *On the Little River, October 31—*
Fort Gibson, November 10, 1832   139

JOURNAL   V : *Fort Gibson, November 11—*
Stack Island, November 17, 1832   155

APPENDIX   I : *The Creole Village*   171

APPENDIX   II : *Roster of Bean's Rangers*   181

BIBLIOGRAPHY   187

INDEX   195

Illustrations

Washington Irving   *facing page*   16

St. Louis in 1832   32

"A Buffalo Hunt on the Southwestern Prairies"   48

Buildings in Cincinnati   64

Carondelet or Vide Poche   112

Le Soldat du Chene   128

Encampment near the Red Fork   144

Mouth of the Arkansas River   160

Map Showing Irving's Route   176

Editor's Introduction

Washington Irving as Western Traveler

I

ON April 11, 1832, Washington Irving boarded the New York packet *Havre* at Havre de Grace to return to America. For seventeen years—more than one-third of his life—he had lived in Europe. At first as a reluctant businessman, then as a highly successful writer, and at last as a minor diplomat, he had become the most Europeanized American of his time. But he was sensitive to an increasing coldness and indifference on the part of his countrymen, and during his long absence he had felt a growing desire to see once more the city and the country of his earlier years. Like other expatriates, he wanted to sink roots in his native soil. The attractions of the Old World which had drawn him across the Atlantic—the quaintness, the picturesqueness, the security of dwelling in a fixed society, and the excitement of working in a colorful and not too real past—no longer could satisfy him completely. New York was still home to Irving, and he became the more excited the nearer he drew to his homeland, which he was now going to discover, to explore. When, at a public dinner in New York, he was asked if he could be content to live in America and how long he intended to remain, he replied with much feeling:

Whoever asks that question, must have but an inadequate idea of its blessings and delights. What sacrifice of enjoyments have I to reconcile myself to? I come from gloomier climes to one of brilliant sunshine and inspiring purity. I come from countries lowering with doubt and danger, where the rich man trembles, and the poor man frowns—where all

3

repine at the present and dread the future. I come from these, to a country where all is life and animation; where I hear on every side the sound of exultation; where every one speaks of the past with triumph, the present with delight, the future with growing and confident anticipation. Is this not a community in which one may rejoice to live? Is this not a city by which one may be proud to be received as the son? Is this not a land in which one may be happy to fix his destiny, and his ambition—if possible—to found a name? I am asked how long I mean to remain here? They know but little of my heart or feelings who can ask me this question. I answer as long as I live.[1]

Washington Irving had come home at last—eager to see, to know, and to live in the land that the United States had become during his long years of absence.

The voyage to the United States had been uneventful, but two of the passengers on the *Havre* were to be Irving's traveling companions for the greater part of seven months. Charles Joseph Latrobe, nephew of the architect Benjamin Henry Latrobe, who had settled in America in 1796, was going to America apparently as tutor to the young Count de Pourtalès. "Mr. Latrobe," Henry L. Ellsworth later wrote in his *Narrative*, "has travelled much in Europe[,] has read a vast deal, attended the fashionable circles. . . ." At this time he was visiting America "on a tour of curiosity and information," and the parents of Pourtalès had "requested his supervisorship & assistance." He was, Ellsworth decided after two months' companionship, "a gentleman deserving the highest estimation . . . well informed, judicious, and moral in his example. . . ."[2]

[1] P. M. Irving, *The Life and Letters of Washington Irving*, II, 227.

[2] All quotations above in this paragraph are from Henry Leavitt Ellsworth, *Irving on the Prairies, or a Narrative of a Tour of the Southwest in the Year 1832*, edited by Williams and Simison, 67–69. Hereafter this book will be referred to as *Narrative*. All unidentified quotations from Ellsworth below are from it. Latrobe's account of his and Pourtalès's travels in the Western Hemisphere will be found in his *The Rambler in North America* and *The Rambler in Mexico*. For a sketch of the life of Latrobe (1801–75), English traveler and government official in Australia, consult *Dictionary of National Biography*, XI, 623–24. All quotations from Latrobe in this book are from *The Rambler in North America*, hereafter referred to as *Rambler*.

Irving, before their adventure was over, decided that Latrobe, having traveled in many countries, "had become, to a certain degree, a citizen of the world, easily adapting himself to any change. He was a man of a thousand occupations; a botanist, a geologist, a hunter of beetles and butterflies, a musical amateur, a sketcher of no mean pretentions, in short, a complete virtuoso; added to which, he was a very indefatigable, if not always successful, sportsman. Never had a man more irons in the fire, and, consequently, never was man more busy nor more cheerful."[3]

Albert-Alexandre de Pourtalès was to prove something of a trial to the three older men on the tour of the prairies. Ellsworth, in the fall of 1832, spoke of Pourtalès as being "19 nearing 20" and declared that Latrobe was expected to keep him in America until the boy was twenty-one. "From a hint dropped one day, I infer the parents wish to have the child absent from Switzerland to change some previous attachments, and to sow his wild oats in a foreign country—Whether the first object named will be accomplished I know not—The last I am sure will be done, unless his wild store is beyond measurement." Ellsworth found Pourtalès "a curious compound of character, brilliancy & fun mixed with frivolity and base sensuality" and was repeatedly annoyed or shocked by the young man's conduct.[4] The truth seems to be that he was lively, im-

[3] *A Tour on the Prairies*, 4; hereafter referred to as *Tour*.

[4] The principal sources of information about Pourtalès are the two works of Latrobe described in n. 2, above. Unofficial but highly interesting are the various references in Irving's two accounts and in the Ellsworth *Narrative*, from which the quotations in this paragraph are taken.

Albert-Alexandre Pourtalès, Comte de Pourtalès, was born in Neuchâtel, Switzerland, October 10, 1812, and died in Paris, December 18, 1861. In 1850 he was Prussian ambassador to Constantinople and in 1859 to Paris. In the fall of 1833, among other points, Fort Snelling "was visited by Count Portales, a young Swiss some twenty years of age, in company with an Englishman named Latrobe, and an American named Ewing [M'Euen] or something like it. They came in a fine birch-bark canoe, with a crew of Canadian voyageurs. My father invited them to dinner, and they proved to be uncommonly bright and pleasant men" (John H. Bliss, "Reminiscences of Fort Snelling," *Minnesota Historical Society Collections*, VI [1894], 347).

pulsive, and filled with romantic notions—youthfully irritating to middle-aged men, but hardly more than that. Irving was to describe him later as being "full of talent and spirit, but galliard in the extreme, and prone to every kind of wild adventure."[5]

The crossing, Irving wrote to his brother Peter, "was rather boisterous and wintry, excepting the latter part, when we ran to the south into the latitude of the Bermudas, and found smooth seas and summer weather."[6] Latrobe wrote admiringly of the captain and amusedly of the mates. He and his companions found interest in the usual shipboard amusements, in the French and German emigrants seeking a new land, in the adventures of the ship's cat and a caged mockingbird, and in the everlasting subject of the weather.

Finally, on May 21, the *Havre* arrived off Sandy Hook, and Irving was stirred by the sight of his native city:

We had scarce descried the land, when a thousand sails of all descriptions gleaming along the horizon, and all standing to or from one point, showed that we were in the neighborhood of a vast commercial emporium. As I sailed up our beautiful bay, with a heart swelling with old recollections and delightful associations, I was astonished to see its once wild features brightening with populous villages and noble piles, and a seeming city, extending itself over heights I had left covered with green forests. But how shall I describe my emotions when our city rose to sight, seated in the midst of its watery domain, stretching away to a vast extent—when I beheld a glorious sunshine lighting up the skies and domes, some familiar to memory, others new and unknown, and beaming upon a forest of masts of every nation, extending as far as the eye could reach. I have gazed with admiration upon many a fair city and stately harbor, but my admiration was cold and ineffectual, for I was a stranger, and had no property in the soil. Here, however, my heart throbbed with pride and joy as I admired—I had a birthright in the brilliant scene before me: "This was my own, my native land."[7]

[5] *Tour,* 5.
[6] P. M. Irving, *Washington Irving,* II, 223.
[7] *Ibid.,* 226–27.

Whatever anticipations he had as he approached his birthplace were fulfilled, for, soon after landing, he wrote to Peter that he was "continually in the midst of old associates" whose "good health, good looks, and good circumstances" with "the increased beauty, and multiplied conveniences and delights of the city [have] rendered my return home wonderfully exciting. I have been in a tumult of enjoyment ever since my arrival."[8]

But enjoyable as New York was, Irving did not remain there long. He was eager to see more of America, and he had two European companions who were quite as interested as he was. The acquaintance that Latrobe and Pourtalès had formed with him on shipboard "led to a series of common projects and common wanderings." In June they visited Washington, Baltimore, and Philadelphia. Early in July Irving wrote from New York to his brother Peter, ". . . I have been for a few days up the Hudson. I set off in company with James Paulding, Mr. Latrobe, and the Count de Pourtales, whom I have found most agreeable traveling companions. We left New York about seven o'clock, in one of those great steamboats that are like floating hotels, and we arrived at West Point in about *four hours.*" They visited Gouvernour Kemble at his cottage in the highlands and then went on to the Catskills before returning to New York.

The next joint excursion was to the White Mountains in New Hampshire. Irving went to Boston alone; the other two followed by steamer to New Haven, then up the Connecticut Valley and across to Boston, admiring the natural scenery and the towns and villages through which they passed. They found Irving at the Tremont Hotel awaiting their arrival, and they now arranged to go northward immediately. The first day's travel brought them to Concord, New Hampshire; the second,

---

[8] *Ibid.*, 224. The account of Irving's wanderings before setting out on his western tour is taken from Latrobe, *Rambler*, and P. M. Irving, *Washington Irving*.

to Lake Winnepesaukee. "The journey through the centre of New Hampshire," wrote Irving to Peter, "was delightful—the roads good, the inns good, and the country beautiful beyond expectation. A fine medley of lakes and forests, and bright, pure running streams." They climbed Mount Washington and crossed the White Mountains. Latrobe and Pourtalès then went on into Vermont to Montpelier and south through the Green Mountains to Bennington, while Irving returned to New York.

Early in August the two Europeans moved on to the rendezvous at Saratoga Springs, where Irving rejoined them. By the fifteenth they had reached Trenton Springs, on a branch of the Mohawk River, sixteen miles from Utica. "Range all the world over," wrote Latrobe, "and you will never see a more lovely valley than that of the Mohawk throughout its whole extent." Irving, too, found the excursion a pleasant one:

My tour thus far has been through a continued succession of beautiful scenes; indeed the natural beauties of the United States strike me infinitely more than they did before my residence in Europe. . . . The murmur of the neighboring falls lulls me to a delicious summer nap, and in the morning and evening I have glorious bathing in the clear waters of the little river. In fact, I return to all the simple enjoyments of old times with the renovated feelings of a schoolboy, and have had more hearty homebred delights of the kind since my return to the United States, than I have ever had in the same space of time in the whole course of my life.

Presently they moved on to Niagara Falls, and at Buffalo they boarded a lake steamer for Detroit. Irving proposed to leave the boat at one of the Ohio ports, cross the state of Ohio, and return east by way of the Ohio River. The others intended to travel from Detroit through Canada to Montreal and Quebec. A chance meeting with Henry L. Ellsworth, however, changed the plans of all three, and in the words of Latrobe "it was now—hurra! for the Far West!"

On July 14, 1832, Lewis Cass, secretary of war, sent to Governor William Carroll of Tennessee, Governor Montfort Stokes of North Carolina, and Roberts Vaux of Philadelphia their appointments as Indian commissioners and their instructions "to visit and examine the country set apart for the emigrating Indians, west of the Mississippi," to make themselves acquainted with Indian claims, to adjust difficulties between tribes, to report on places for the location of tribes yet to emigrate, and to make necessary treaties. Carroll and Vaux declined their appointments; Henry L. Ellsworth was named in place of Vaux and, after Dr. Felix Robertson and William E. Anderson, both of Nashville, Tennessee, and William Jay of West Chester, Pennsylvania, had all declined, the third place was accepted by John F. Schermerhorn of Utica, New York.

Ellsworth's appointment was dated July 23, 1832. In his letter of acceptance four days later he asked about the "most eligible route to Fort Gibson" and was informed by the Acting Secretary of War that "General Gratiot will desire Colonel Chouteau, the gentleman named at the close of your instructions, who is now in Philadelphia, and about to proceed to his station within four miles of Fort Gibson, to write to you, and give the requisite information, as to the route, and the outfit it will be expedient for you to provide." It was presently understood that the commissioners would meet Chouteau at St. Louis and that he would conduct them to Fort Gibson.

It was toward the end of August that the three tourists had the luck to meet Ellsworth on the Lake Erie steamer. They

learned from him [Latrobe wrote] that from this point [Fort Gibson] it was contemplated to dispatch expeditions to various parts of the unexplored region to the West. . . . To the solicitation made that Mr. Irving would join company, and connect himself with the Commission, so far as he might find it agreeable, a prompt acquiescence was yielded

9

on his part, as so doing merely entailed an extension of his plans; and as far as my comrade and myself were concerned, the frank promise of hearty welcome, if we would also form part of the expedition to further our own projects, offered too much temptation to be resisted or rejected.[9]

Irving likewise had a few words to say of this meeting in a letter to his brother Peter:

> After I wrote to you in August, from, I think, Niagara, I proceeded with my agreeable fellow travellers, Mr. L. and Mr. P., to Buffalo, and we embarked at Black Rock, on Lake Erie. On board of the steam-boat was Mr. E. one of the commissioners appointed by government to superintend the settlement of the emigrant Indian tribes, to the west of the Mississippi. He was on his way to the place of rendezvous, and on his invitation, we agreed to accompany him in his expedition. The offer was too tempting to be resisted: I should have an opportunity of seeing the remnants of those great Indian tribes, which are now about to disappear as independent nations, or to be amalgamated under some new form of government. I should see those fine countries of the "far west," while still in a state of pristine wilderness [wildness], and behold herds of buffaloes scouring their native prairies, before they are driven beyond the reach of a civilized tourist.[10]

Ellsworth, a Connecticut man forty years of age, was to be pleasantly spoken of by two of his traveling companions. By the time they had reached Independence, Missouri, Latrobe could write of him that "his kindliness of spirit won our regard; and we all did justice to the singleness of purpose with which

---

[9] *Rambler*, I, 82.

[10] This letter, dated Washington City, December 18, 1832, was first published, apparently, in the London *Athenaeum* for 1833 (pages 137–38); it was republished in the New York *Commercial Advertiser*, the Little Rock *Arkansas Gazette* (June 26, 1833), and the Columbia *Missouri Intelligencer* (May 11, 1833). The copy used here is from the *Arkansas Gazette*; here and elsewhere in the present work variants from the *Athenaeum* are in square brackets. Pierre M. Irving identified this letter as addressed to Peter Irving; at least, he quoted several paragraphs from a letter to Peter which are essentially the same as those in the published letter *(Washington Irving, II, 252)*. All versions of the letter show annoying excisions; the original is not known to exist.

he, a happy husband and parent, and truly a lover of quiet, had left his family and the comforts of an Eastern home, to become a peace-maker among the rude tribes and inhabitants of the West." Irving, who never liked Yankees, was agreeably surprised to find him "a man in whom a course of legal practice and political life had not been able to vitiate an innate simplicity and benevolence of heart," and he, too, romantically saw in Ellsworth one who had been called from the "bosom of his family and the society of deacons, elders, and selectmen . . . to mount his steed, shoulder his rifle, and mingle among stark hunters, backwoodsmen, and naked savages, on the trackless wilds of the Far West."[11]

The four travelers soon left the steamboat and struck out across Ohio for Cincinnati by way of Cleveland, Newark, and Columbus. Irving described this stretch of the journey in a letter to his sister, Mrs. Paris:

Cincinnati, September 2, 1832

My dear Sister:–

You have no doubt heard from our brother E[benezer] I. of the alteration, or rather extension of my travelling plans, in consequence of which I shall accompany the Commissioners on their expedition into the territories west of the Mississippi, to visit and hold conference with the emigrating Indian tribes. The Commissioner, Mr. Ellsworth, who invited me to this journey, and whom I accidentally met on board of a steamboat on Lake Erie, is a very gentlemanly and amiable person, and an excellent travelling companion. I have also my old fellow-travellers, Mr. Latrobe and the young Count Pourtales, who are delighted with the idea of travelling on horseback through the forests and prairies, camping in tents at nights, and hunting deer, buffaloes, and wild turkeys. We have made a very interesting tour through Ohio.

---

[11] *Rambler*, I, 146; *Tour*, 4. For Henry Leavitt Ellsworth (1791–1858), consult the *Dictionary of American Biography*, VI, 110–11; and Ellsworth's *Narrative*. Not everyone, however, who came into contact with Ellsworth approved so thoroughly of him; S. C. Stambaugh, secretary to the Commissioners West, Governor Stokes, Colonel A. P. Chouteau, Colonel Matthew Arbuckle, commandant, and most of the other officers at Fort Gibson were far from finding Ellsworth an adequate person for dealing with the Indians.

We landed at Ashtabula, a small place on the shore of Lake Erie. From thence we proceeded along the ridge road parallel to the lake to Cleveland, and thence through the centre of the State to this city, where we arrived last evening. I have been greatly delighted with the magnificent woodland scenery of Ohio, and with the exuberant fertility of the soil, which will eventually render this State a perfect garden spot. When the forests are cleared away, however, the country will be a vast plain, diversified here and there by a tract of rolling hills; and nothing will compensate for the loss of those glorious trees, which now present the sublime of vegetation.

In the course of our journey we diverged from the direct route, to visit one of those stupendous and mysterious antiquities which are among the wonders of the land. Immense ramparts and mounds of earth extending for miles, that must have required the united labors of a vast multitude, and have been intended to protect some important city or some populous region. These works are now in the depths of thick forests, overgrown with trees that are evidently the growth of centuries. Nothing relative to them remains in Indian tradition, nor is the construction of such vast works in any way compatible with the habits and customs of any of our aboriginal tribes. You may imagine what a subject for speculation and reverie the sight of such monuments presents in the silent bosom of the wilderness.[12]

We shall leave Cincinnati very probably the day after to-morrow. Indeed, I remain as brief a time as possible in towns and cities, for the attentions I meet with are often rather irksome and embarrassing than otherwise. I went into the theatre, last evening, to see the acting of Mrs. Drake, with which I was wonderfully delighted, when, to my astonishment and dismay, the manager came out between the acts, and announced that I was in the house. As you partake of the nervous sensibility of the family, you may conceive how I felt on finding all eyes thus suddenly turned upon me. I have since had a note from the manager, requesting me to visit the theatre on Tuesday evening, and to permit him to announce it. I have declined it, of course, and have induced my companions to hasten our departure, that I may escape from all further importunities of the kind.

[12] The mounds referred to were apparently those at Newark. For a description of them, see Caleb Atwater, *Writings*, 25–29.

I hope my countrymen may not think I slight their proffers of kindness and distinction; no one can value their good opinion more highly; but I have a shrinking aversion from being made an object of personal notoriety, that I cannot conquer. . . .[13]

Latrobe had little to add to Irving's remarks about Cincinnati. They "found the good citizens of that rising and flourishing city busily ruminating over the first edition of a well-known picture of their domestic manners, which the English press had just sent forth for their special benefit."[14] The only large hotel was crowded because two other hotels had been burnt that spring, and the travelers were glad, after two days' stay, to leave, on September 3, on the steamboat *Messenger* for Louisville. Although Irving made no mention of the visit in his Journal, Timothy Flint was among the persons who had come to call upon him in Cincinnati.

At Louisville the party immediately took passage in the steamboat *Illinois* for St. Louis, but engine trouble held them up for two days. They now made a leisurely progress towards the mouth of the Ohio River, and Irving had many opportunities for word sketches of quaint, picturesque, romantic sights in this new world. Latrobe wrote little about the cities in which they stopped, but the scenery, the boat, and the river proved of constant interest.

For many miles below the Rapids, the river scenery continued fine but monotonous: the shores were often hilly and always forested, but never rose to any prominent outline; while every object on the banks was diminished to the eye by the vast breadth of the stream. . . . We used to sit for hours in a little group on the high roof of the cabins, far removed from the heat of the fires and the boilers, the chatter of the passengers, or the jar of the engine; while the lapse of each second was marked by

---

[13] P. M. Irving, *Washington Irving*, II, 245–46. The account of the journey is taken mainly from Latrobe, *Rambler*; Ellsworth, *Narrative*; and Irving's letters in P. M. Irving, *Washington Irving*.

[14] *Rambler*, I, 99. Latrobe referred, of course, to Mrs. Trollope's *Domestic Manners of the Americans*.

the sonorous rush of the white puff of steam from the pipe above our heads. Each little settlement we passed had its own peculiar interest, and each tributary stream no less—and there were scenes incident to the river which were always pleasing. The frequent landing-places, over-shadowed by fine sycamores; the relics of ancient and whimsical craft still met with here and there—now a square or oblong box, floating along with the current, with the outline and the party-coloured vestments hung upon the shaft of the rudder-oar brightly reflected in the water;—then the broad-horn of an emigrant family, lying in some sheltered cove, while the hetrogeneous crew of all ages and colours were passing an hour of activity and relaxation on shore.[15]

The *Illinois* ran aground several times and gave the passengers even more hours than they wanted for shore excursions, but at last they reached the Mississippi and started north. Irving continued to note down the odd and the strange scenes and persons he encountered during these leisurely days. The most interesting town to him was Ste Genevieve. The most exciting event was a collision, on September 12, with the steamboat *Yellowstone*, which was making a run down-river after its famous record-breaking trip to Fort Union at the mouth of the Yellowstone River earlier in the summer. "We were nearly wrecked and sent to the bottom," Irving wrote to Peter, "by encountering another steam-boat coming with all the impetus of a high pressure engine, and a rapid current. Fortunately we had time to shear a little so as to receive the blow obliquely, which carried away a part of a wheel, and all the upper works on one side of the boat."[16] It is a bit amusing to recall that the boat which might have caused Irving's death was in good part owned by John Jacob Astor (the principal stockholder in the American Fur Company, which owned the boat), who later was to induce Irving to write an account of Astor's fur-trading enterprise in the Northwest.

[15] Latrobe, *Rambler*, II, 111–12.
[16] Washington Irving to [Peter Irving], December 18, 1832, *Arkansas Gazette*, June 26, 1833.

The steamboat reached St. Louis late that night, but the passengers did not go ashore until the next morning. Their few days in town were largely taken up with preparations for the frontier expedition, but Irving, at least, found time to pay a visit to General Clark at his farm, and the two Europeans went with him to see Black Hawk at Jefferson Barracks. The latter excursion, on September 14, gave the travelers an opportunity to see the old village of Vuide Poche or Carondelet as well as the post. Irving found the Sauk chief a "meagre old man" with a "fine head, a Roman style of face, and a prepossessing countenance."[17]

Writing to Mrs. Paris from St. Louis on the day of their arrival, Irving mentioned briefly their leaving Cincinnati on the third, their repeated running aground, and the collision. He then continued:

We made shift to limp through the remainder of our voyage, which was but about twelve miles. I have been charmed with the grand scenery of these two mighty rivers. We have had splendid weather to see them in —golden sunshiny days, and serene moonlight nights. The magnificence of the Western forests is quite beyond my anticipations; such gigantic trees, rising like stupendous columns—and then the abundance of flowers and flowering shrubs. . . .

I am writing late at night, and with difficulty, for I have unluckily strained the fingers of my right hand a few days since, so that I can scarcely hold a pen. Good night.

September 16th—Since writing the foregoing, I have been to Fort Jefferson, about nine miles from this, to see the famous Black Hawk, and his fellow chiefs, taken in the recent Indian war. This redoubtable Black Hawk, who makes such a figure in our newspapers, is an old man, upward of seventy, emaciated and enfeebled by the sufferings he has experienced, and by a touch of cholera. He has a small, well-formed head, with an acquiline nose, a good expression of eye; and a physician present who is given to craniology, perceived the organ of benevolence strongly developed, though I believe the old chief-

17 *Ibid.*

tain stands accused of many cruelties.[18] His brother-in-law, the prophet, is a strong, stout man, and much younger. He is considered the most culpable agent in fomenting the late disturbance; though I find it extremely difficult, even when so near the seat of action, to get at the right story of these feuds between the white and the red men, and my sympathies go strongly with the latter.

Colonel Chouteau had arrived in St. Louis before the others, and so had Dr. O'Dwyer, who was in some way connected with Ellsworth's official business. All were anxious to move, and it was finally determined that "each should travel, as it best suited his convenience or fancy" to another rendezvous at Independence, Missouri, the last settlement up the Missouri River. Chouteau apparently set off alone overland with his servants. The commissioner and the doctor decided to wait a few days and then go up river in a steamboat. But Irving, Pourtalès, and Latrobe "at once determined to purchase horses and a light waggon to transport our baggage, and travel as a trio, as heretofore, by easy day's journies to the place of rendezvous."[19] They procured blankets and bearskins from the American Fur Company and with difficulty obtained horses.

Another important character was now added to the group. Latrobe wrote briefly: "We had secured the services of a French Creole, accustomed to the country and the mode of travelling, who was to serve us in the several capacities of guide, groom, driver, valet, cook, interpreter, hunter, and jack-of-all-trades."[20] This was the Antoine Deshetres of the

[18] P. M. Irving, *Washington Irving*, II, 247–48. Latrobe wrote: "the fine old warrior then seemingly near his end. . . . Little did I then think that six months after I should see him alive and in freedom, on his 'progress' through the Atlantic cities after being set at liberty." (*Rambler*, I, 116). The physician was probably the Dr. O'Dwyer whom Irving met in St. Louis on September 13.

[19] *Ibid.*, 117. Irving said nothing in his notebook about the outfitting; in the letter to Peter (December 18, 1832) he wrote briefly that "At St. Louis, we bought horses for ourselves, and a covered waggon for baggage, tents, provisions, &c., and travelled by land to Independence" (*Arkansas Gazette*, June 26, 1833).

[20] *Rambler*, I, 117. Antoine Deshetres had recently returned to St. Louis after serving as a guide to Major H. C. Brish and a party of emigrating Senecas on a trip to their lands above Fort Gibson, from April 26 to July 26.

WASHINGTON IRVING
from the portrait by C. R. Leslie

Journals whom Irving romanticized into the "Tonish" of the *Tour on the Prairies.*

Late on September 15 Irving and his companions left St. Louis and traveled, according to Latrobe, "about twelve miles over a horrible road to the Missouri, opposite St. Charles, where we found a shelter for the night in a little French inn, which, with its odd diminutive bowling-green, skittle-ground, garden-plots, and arbours to booze in, reminded us more of the Old World than any thing we had seen for many weeks." Tonish had gone home to say good-bye to his family at Florissant, and the next day they waited for him at their inn until noon. It was not until they had crossed the river that the Creole at last "made his appearance, fully equipped, and gave us the first specimen of that dexterous effrontery with which we became at a later period extremely familiar." Tonish took charge of the wagon, and the three friends "were left at perfect liberty to saunter, halt, hunt, or do what they would."[21]

They left St. Charles by the Boonslick Road[22] and for days their route was "over an undulating country, the lower parts of which were thickly covered with forest, and the upper spread out into open prairie. Over these the decline of the year was beginning to shed those gorgeous and brilliant hues, which none can fancy or form an idea of, but those who have beheld them."[23]

They enjoyed the easy and hearty hospitality of the settlers along the way. The houses at this time were mostly "built substantially of round or square logs, all the interstices being neatly filled with white plaster, and they presented two quadrangular apartments, distinct from each other, with a wide open space in the centre, all covered by one common roof. . . . The

[21] Latrobe, *Rambler*, 1, 119–20.
[22] For the first stage of this road see Kate L. Gregg, "The Boonslick Road in St. Charles County," *Missouri Historical Review*, XXVII (1933), 307–14; XXVIII (1933), 9–16.
[23] Latrobe, *Rambler*, I, 120.

central division of the dwelling formed the ordinary sitting apartment of the family, and from its being open on both ends, was a pleasant, cool retreat." The kitchen was generally in a separate building in the rear, and the clearing "surrounded by a zig-zag fence of chesnut rails, beyond which might be seen many an acre of tall Indian corn, rising from the girdled trees of the forests. Here the settler apparently lived in peace and plenty; cattle, swine, poultry, being abundant, and costing little or no toil or expense in raising. . . ."[24]

The arrival of the travelers was always the opportunity for lavish expression of hospitality. It was a poor farm, Latrobe wrote, "which did not enable the good woman, with half an hour's notice, to spread before her guests a plentiful meal of ham, fried chicken, eggs, milk, honey, delicious butter, boiled maize, and hot wheaten bread." The catching of the fowls presented a lively scene: ". . . as soon as the black Clorinda, or blacker Juno in the kitchen received her orders, a strong detachment of the little woolly-headed urchins of every hue, which swarmed like musquitoes in this land of corn-bread and pumpkins, was upon the alert to secure two or three of the long yellow-legged cacklers within the fence. They were generally aided by a big dog, and not unfrequently backed by one of those noisy, garrulous, busy old negroes, who are to be met with every where, as privileged inmates of the family, in consequence of having known and cared for the master or mistress when children, and followed their fortunes from the Old States."[25]

In this fashion they traveled on, advancing about thirty miles a day, enjoying the strangeness and the roughness, the beauty and the generosity of the frontier life. On the fourth day Latrobe recorded that they crossed the "Thirty Mile Prairie." That night they slept in Columbia, where their stay called for a paragraph in the newspaper:

[24] *Ibid.*, 121–22.   [25] *Ibid.*, 122–23.

This gentleman [Irving] arrived in Columbia on Wednesday the 19th inst. and remained here until the next day, when he resumed his journey for the Osage country. From the notice in one of the St. Louis papers, announcing his arrival there, that he was on his way to the Upper Mississippi, we did not anticipate the honor of seeing him here. His destination, however, for the present at least, is different. He expressed the greatest surprise and admiration of what he had already seen of Missouri—having previously formed somewhat different views of the country. In his manners, Mr. Irving is unostentatious, affable and gentlemanly. He will no doubt acquire a valuable fund of materials in his progress, for interesting works or Sketches, which, ere long, we may have the gratification of perusing.[26]

The next day they arrived at Franklin. On the sixth day they made a side excursion to Boon's Lick and then crossed the Missouri at Arrow Rock ferry. Their road now was across the prairie until they struck the Missouri River once more, as they entered Lafayette County. Apparently on September 22 they spent the night at the house of John J. Heard,[27] and on the following day they reached Lexington.

When we were within a few miles of that town we met the long train of Trappers, which annually crosses the great western desert towards New Mexico, returning from the Rocky Mountains and Santa Fe; their mules laden with the skins for which they had dared that long and perilous pilgrimage. They were about seventy in number; men worn with toil and travel, bearing in their garb and on their persons evident marks of the adventurous passage of those immense prairies which lie to the Westward. Seven of their number had fallen in combat with the Indians on their return. These expeditions, however,

[26] Columbia *Missouri Intelligencer and Boon's Lick Advertiser*, September 29, 1832.

[27] The county historian reported that Washington Irving "immortalized the section of country near Dover and Waverly, this county"; he "enjoyed the hospitality of Squire John J. Heard . . . at whose house he remained several days in 1819"; in *Astoria*, the historian concluded, Irving paid "a glowing tribute to the kindness of pioneer Heard" (William Young, *History of Lafayette County, Missouri*, I, 47). In spite of the obvious errors here, it is probable that Irving did spend one night at Heard's.

hold out the expectation of such enormous profit, that adventurers are never wanting to fill their ranks.[28]

On the afternoon of the twenty-fourth Irving, Latrobe, and Pourtalès found themselves at Independence, "a small frontier hamlet of log houses, situated between two and three hundred miles up the Missouri, on the utmost verge of civilization."[29] Colonel Chouteau arrived the same evening, but they all had to wait three days for Ellsworth and O'Dwyer.

The days of waiting for the commissioner were passed in savoring the frontier at this interesting point and preparing for the next stage of their journey. On September 26, Irving found time to write to Mrs. Paris:

My dear Sister:—

We arrived at this place day before yesterday, after nine days' travelling on horseback from St. Louis. Our journey has been a very interesting one, leading us across fine prairies and through noble forests, dotted here and there by farms and log-houses, at which we found rough but wholesome and abundant fare, and very civil treatment. . . .

The fertility of all this Western country is truly astonishing. The soil is like that of a garden, and the luxuriance and beauty of the forests exceed any that I have seen. We have gradually been advancing, however, toward rougher and rougher life, and are now at a little straggling frontier village, that has only been five years in existence. From hence, in the course of a day or two, we take our departure southwardly, and shall soon bid adieu to civilization, and encamp at night in our tents. My health is good, though I have been much affected by the change of climate, diet, and water since my arrival in the West. Horse exercise, however, always agrees with me. I enjoy my journey exceedingly, and look for still greater gratification in the part which is now before me, which will present much greater wildness and novelty. The climax will

[28] Latrobe, *Rambler*, I, 126. Lexington and the road between that place and Independence were described a few years later by Victor Tixier (J. F. McDermott, [ed.], and A. J. Salvan, [trans.], *Tixier's Travels on the Osage Prairies*, 102–103).

[29] Washington Irving to [Peter Irving], December 18, 1832, *Arkansas Gazette*, June 26, 1833.

be our expedition with the Osages to their hunting-grounds, and the sight of a buffalo hunt.[30]

Irving did not write any description of Independence in his Journal, but Latrobe set down observations which were probably the impressions of all the newcomers:

The town of Independence was full of promise, like most of the innumerable towns springing up in the midst of the forests in the West, many of which, though dignified by high-sounding epithets, consist of nothing but a ragged congeries of five or six rough log-huts, two or three clap-board houses, two or three so-called hotels, alias grogshops; a few stores, a bank, printing office, and barn-looking church. It lacked, at the time I commemorate, the three last edifices, but was nevertheless a thriving and aspiring place, in its way; and the fortune made here already in the course of its brief existence, by a bold Yankee shop-keeper who had sold sixty thousand dollars' worth of goods here in three years,—was a matter of equal notoriety, surprise, and envy. It is situated about twenty miles east of the Kansas River, and three miles south of the Missouri, and was consequently very near the extreme western frontier of the State. A little beyond this point, all carriage roads ceased, and one deep black trail alone, which might be seen tending to the southwest, was that of the Santa Fe trappers and traders.[31]

To Latrobe fell "the perplexing but honourable offices of Commissary-general, and minister of finance to our mess." He was doubtful whether his two companions had recognized his "superior skill and activity" or had imposed those duties on him "from the simple and pure intention of sparing themselves extraordinary trouble of mind or body." At any rate he found plenty to do. He remarked, "I purchased bacon and knives and forks, salt, sugar and flour, coffee and camomile-flowers, pepper and potatoes, and a multitude of sundries, according to my own judgment, or their fancies and wants." The difficult and amusing business of horse-buying he spent three pages in de-

[30] P. M. Irving, *Washington Irving*, II, 248–49.
[31] *Rambler*, I, 128.

21

scribing. Then, after all was done, on the afternoon of September 27 they were ready to leave Independence.

The three-hundred-mile trip to Fort Gibson, with its camping experiences and its scenery, had much interest for Latrobe. "Clearings were few in number, and of rare occurrence; the general character of the country being that of wide open prairies with long lines of timber trees skirting the course of the creeks and rivers, many of which rose in this elevated corner of the country. The road was merely a track over the natural sod of the prairie."[32] They would travel about fifteen or twenty miles in the morning, and after an hour's halt for dinner do another ten or twelve miles, generally stopping about an hour before sundown to make camp. The spot chosen would, if possible, be in a belt of forest near a stream. "Each unsaddles his steed, hobbles it, as the term is, by tying the two fore-feet close together, and sends it hopping into the forest like a kangaroo, crashing and scrambling through the gigantic and entangled brushwood . . . [to] feed upon the pea-vine. . . . While the half-breed and the black cut wood, Tonish makes a fire against some fallen tree or log, and flits to and fro in the smoke, like a goblin, while preparing his poles and spits for cookery. Meanwhile other hands are employed in pitching the tent, and laying down the bear skins and blankets within or without, as suits convenience." After feasting, they would sit around the fire, "listen to each other's tales, and, between whiles, to the distant howl of the prairie wolf, the shriek of the owl, the chirp of innumerable grasshoppers and crickets, the cry of the bustards going to sleep in the neighbouring marsh . . ." until fatigue and sleep overtook them.

Irving's Journal is so rich in detail about this stage of the journey that there is no need to discuss it here.[33] They passed

[32] *Ibid.*, 148. For the first stage of this journey compare Tixier's account in 1840 (McDermott and Salvan, *Tixier's Travels*, 105–15).

[33] In the letter to Peter (December 18, 1832) he wrote briefly: "From Independence, we struck across the Indian country, along the line of Indian mis-

from Missouri westward into the Osage country, and they began to meet parties of Osage out on hunting expeditions. The night of October 3 they spent at Boudinot Mission, on the Neosho River. On the sixth they had noon dinner at the Hopefield Mission (Requa's), some ninety miles further south on the Neosho,[34] and that evening they reached Colonel Chouteau's establishment at the Grand Saline.

The next afternoon Irving and Ellsworth set out in the dearborn[35] for Fort Gibson. They slept at Union Mission, and the following morning, Ellsworth wrote, they "came in site of the numerous little log buildings, that compose Fort Gibson lying on the opposite side of the [Neosho or Grand] river. . . . The officer on 'ferry detachment' soon brought us the flat owned by Gov^t, and we were safely landed without any pay for ferriage."[36] Introductions were performed, and Irving's anxiety to visit the buffalo country brought forth Colonel Arbuckle's regret that a detachment of rangers had just gone out

sions; and arrived, on the 8th of October, after ten or eleven days' tramp, at Fort Gibson, a frontier fort in Arkansas. Our journey lay almost entirely through vast prairies, or open grassy plains, diversified occasionally by beautiful groves, and deep fertile bottoms along the streams of water. We lived in frontier and almost Indian style, camping out at nights, except when we stopped at the Missionaries, scattered here and there in this vast wilderness. The weather was serene, and we encountered but one rainy night and one thunder storm, and I found sleeping in a tent very sweet and healthy repose. It was now upwards of three weeks since I had left St. Louis and taken to travelling on horseback, and it agreed with me admirably" (*Arkansas Gazette*, June 26, 1833).

[34] "One of the U. S. Commissioners Henry L. Ellsworth Esq. of Hartford Connecticut has arrived in this country[,] has been here since the sixth ultimo. He is in company with the celebrated Washington Irvine who has lately returned from Europe; also a Mr. Latrobe an English Botanist & a young Count from Switzerland & also a physician of the U. S. Army called upon us, and dined with us while on their way from Missouri across the Prairie to Fort Gibson. . . ." (William C. Requa to David Green, Hopefield, Neosho, West of Arkansas Territory, November 27, 1832, ABCFM Records, Harvard-Andover Theological Seminary, LXXIII, No. 200).

[35] Colonel Samuel Stambaugh, writing to Colonel Matthew Arbuckle, Fort Gibson, May 3, 1834, declared that this dearborn was a public conveyance which, with its two horses, Ellsworth had obtained from McCoy, surveyor in the Indian Country (Letters Received, 1826–1834, Office of Indian Affairs, Records of the Department of the Interior, National Archives).

[36] *Narrative*, 2.

to explore that region. Ellsworth made clear to Arbuckle that the War Department had intended to place the rangers at the disposal of the commissioners. The rest of the day was spent in examining the fort and discussing plans.

Ellsworth now made a report to the Secretary of War and began to exercise his full authority:

Fort *Gibson*, October 9, 1832

Sir:

I have the honor and pleasure to inform you of my safe arrival at this post last evening, in company with Mr. Irving. The other commissioners have not arrived, and I learn, by Gov. Houston, that they cannot be expected for two weeks. On my arrival, I found Col. Arbuckle had ordered all the rangers to explore the southwestern section, and that they had been gone two days. Desirous to employ my time to the best advantage, I requested Col. Arbuckle to despatch an express to detain the troops and furnish us an escort to join them in safety, which he very promptly has done; and myself and Mr. Irving start to-morrow morning, expecting to return in about three weeks, which will be as soon, probably, as Gov. Stokes will arrive and get rested for business. Col. Chouteau took us, by way of Independence, which is situated at the mouth of Kanzas river, which I now find is not the shortest way; [37] but I had an opportunity to see Gen. Clark, agent of the Kanzas, and Col. Cummins; [38] also the Osages, the Requais' band,

[37] Certainly Ellsworth, in traveling from Hartford by Buffalo and Cleveland, had not chosen the shortest way of reaching Cincinnati and the West. His instructions were specific enough: "The most direct course will be through this city [Washington] to Guyandot, on the Ohio; and thence to the mouth of the White River. A more lengthened route will be to St. Louis, where a steamboat conveyance may possibly be obtained to Little Rock. There is much uncertainty, however, as to the time when the fall of the waters of the Arkansas will prevent the passage of boats. At my request, General Gratiot will desire Colonel Chouteau . . . who is now in Philadelphia, and about to proceed to his station within four miles of Fort Gibson, to write to you, and give the requisite information as to the route, and the outfit it will be expedient for you to provide" (John Robb, acting secretary of war, to H. L. Ellsworth, Esq., War Department, August 2, 1832; in Twenty-third Congress, first session, *Senate Document* 512, II, 983). Furthermore, it must be remembered that Chouteau was acting without compensation; Ellsworth was drawing $8.00 for every twenty miles of travel.

[38] Richard W. Cummins, Delaware and Shawnee agent. For the other persons named in this letter see the notes for the corresponding entries in the Irving Journals.

the Harmony mission, Dwight [Union] mission, and the northeastern section generally. I also visited Mr. McCoy at his house, by his special request, who, I find, cannot complete his returns and surveys in time for us;[39] and as he has public conveyances, and is under per diem pay, I requested him to come to Fort Gibson to explain to the commissioners some particulars to expedite our mission. I have earnestly requested the agents to urge the chiefs to suspend hostile operations for the present, and I am sorry to add that there is much general hostility against the Pawnees. I rejoice that my health is good. I shall use every exertion, and be deterred by no ordinary difficulty or danger in lending my efforts to advance the benevolent designs of the administration.

With the highest respect,
I am yours sincerely,
Henry L. Ellsworth.

Hon. Lewis Cass, *Secretary of War.*

P.S. Col Arbuckle says he has had no instructions respecting the commissioners, and being ignorant of the wishes of the Government, despatched the Rangers to keep them in activity, and to overawe the Pawnees. I read him a part of my instructions, and he is satisfied with my requisitions.[40]

Ellsworth was upset, not only by the failure of his fellow commissioners to arrive and by the commanding officer's thoughtlessness in dispatching a portion of the military without waiting to consult him, but also by the nonarrival of Colonel Samuel C. Stambaugh, secretary of the commission. However, this last annoyance gave the lone commissioner the opportunity to make Irving's position official. "Permit me to say," he wrote to the Secretary of War, "that on my arrival here I found no secretary of our board and requested Mr. Irving to accompany me in that capacity, in my expedition to the West."[41]

[39] A report of the activities of Isaac McCoy and John Donelson, Jr., dated Neosho River, Indian Territory, September 12, 1832, is to be found in *Senate Document* 512, III, 446–51. The report to the Commissioners West was dated Creek Nation, Indian Territory, October 15, 1832; it is printed in *ibid.*, 486–98.

[40] *Senate Document* 512, III, 481.

[41] Fort Gibson, November 18, 1832 (Office of Indian Affairs, Department

Until he arrived at Fort Gibson, Irving apparently had not known definitely what he would do in the frontier country, but circumstances had now arranged themselves conveniently for him. Plans and prospects were summed up in a letter to his sister:

On arriving at this post, I found that a mounted body of rangers, nearly a hundred, had set off two days before to make a wide tour to the West and South, through the wild hunting countries, by way of protecting the friendly Indians who have gone to the buffalo hunting, and to overawe the Pawnee Indians, who are the wandering Arabs of the West, and continually on the maraud. Colonel Ellsworth and myself have determined to set off to-morrow in the track of this party. We shall be escorted by a dozen or fourteen horsemen, so that we shall have nothing to apprehend from any straggling gang of Pawnees; and we shall have three or four Indians with us as guides and interpreters, besides the servants that have accompanied us hitherto. A couple of Creek Indians have been dispatched by the commander of this fort to overtake the party of rangers, and order them to await our coming up with them, which we expect in the course of three days; and to find them in the buffalo range on the Little Red River. . . . I am in hopes that we may be able to fall in with some wandering band of Pawnees in a friendly manner, as I have a great desire to see some of that warlike and vagrant race. We shall have a Pawnee captive woman with us as an interpreter.

You see I am completely launched in savage life, and am likely to continue in it for some weeks to come. I am extremely excited and

of Interior, National Archives, Washington, D. C.). Ellsworth added: "He does not desire the appointment as it would detain him from his literary pursuits." Irving, of course, could not have had the permanent appointment as secretary, even if he had wanted it, for Stambaugh had been officially appointed on July 14. On their return Irving declined to accept the secretary's pay of $5.00 per day (just what kind of secretarial work he performed cannot be discovered), but he did allow the commissioner to "remunerate him for some losses he has sustained" (Ellsworth, *Narrative,* 9). On November 9, Ellsworth, as attorney for Irving, received payment from the Commissioners on Indian Affairs for one saddle and stirrups ($13), one bridle ($2.00), one pair blue Mackinaw blankets ($11), one large bearskin ($3.00), and one India mat ($1.00)—(Letters Received, 1826–1834, Office of Indian Affairs, Records of the Department of the Interior, National Archives).

interested by this wild country, and the wild scenes and people by which I am surrounded.

I am uncertain whether Mr. Latrobe and Pourtales will accompany me on this further tour. I left them about forty miles behind, at one of the agencies, and they have not yet arrived here, though they probably will in the course of the day. I am writing in great haste, having all my preparations to make.[42]

Hasty preparation had now to be made for the journey beyond the frontier. Ellsworth bought some rough clothes and obtained a large pack horse for himself and Irving. A gray horse was bought for Irving to ride but he did not like its gait, and the next day at the Verdigris he paid Colonel Chouteau $125 for a "fine looking bay horse." Ellsworth was to ride a pony he had purchased at Independence. For provisions the travelers took salt pork, flour, coffee, sugar, and salt—enough for three men for fifteen days. Ellsworth now hired Pierre Beatte, or Billet, as the Yankee generally wrote the name of his employee.[43]

At the Verdigris River they met Latrobe and Pourtalès

---

[42] Dated Fort Gibson, Arkansas, October 9, 1832 (P. M. Irving, *Washington Irving*, II, 249–50). The first part of this letter, omitted here, is almost word for word that of the letter to Peter, quoted in n. 33, above.

[43] Irving called Pierre Beatte a halfbreed of French and Osage parentage (*Tour*, 17). Ellsworth described him as a Quapaw Indian (*Narrative*, 7, 32). Latrobe thought him the son of a French Creole by a Quapaw mother (*Rambler*, I, 178). He figures frequently and at length in all three of these narratives. Catlin, however, declared that he met the parents of Beatte and that they were both French; Beatte complained bitterly of Irving's calling him a half-breed (George Catlin, *Letters and Notes . . . on the North American Indians*, II, 92–93). Beatte was a guide to the dragoon expedition of 1834; in his journal Wheelock described him as "Beatte—A Frenchman who has lived nearly all his life among the Osages" (Twenty-third Congress, second session, *Senate Document* 1, 74). It is fairly certain that the travelers were wrong. Beatte was a Frenchman, not a half blood.

Beatte was paid, for his services as guide and interpreter, $1.50 a day (for himself and his horse) for thirty-four days. In this account his name is given as Pierre Beatte (Letters Received, 1826–1834, Office of Indian Affairs, Records of the Department of the Interior, National Archives). Irving's principal account of him is in the *Tour*, 197–205. He apparently died between 1834 and 1837; see page 52 ff. below. In the *Tour* Irving wrote his name Beatte; in the Journals, like Ellsworth, he wrote Billet.

once more. These two had remained a day or so at the Saline and then moved down to Chouteau's other post, where they had each bought a riding horse and a race horse for hunting wild horses and buffaloes. For pack animals they used the wagon horses bought in St. Louis, and one of these Pourtalès loaded "with shawls blanketts & presents to the squaws," for he "was fixed upon the Osage trail and could not be diverted."[44] The Europeans started to follow the Osage hunting party; Irving and Ellsworth set out to overtake the rangers.

The rangers to whom the Ellsworth-Irving party was attaching itself were a recent addition to the United States Army. An act of Congress, approved June 15, 1832, authorized the President to raise a battalion of six hundred mounted rangers to serve on the frontiers, each company of which was to consist of four commissioned officers, fourteen noncommissioned officers, and one hundred privates.[45] Jesse Bean, of Independence County, Arkansas, was chosen to raise one company. The *Arkansas Gazette* declared that:

In the selection of a Commander of the Arkansas corps, we think the President has been quite fortunate. A more experienced woods-man, or one better acquainted with the Indian mode of fighting, can hardly be found in any country, than Capt. Bean.—He took a gallant part in most of the principal engagements at New Orleans, while that city was invested by the British Army, in 1814–15, and was with Gen. Jackson in some of the subsequent Indian wars in Florida, where he commanded a company of Spies, and rendered important services for which he was highly complimented by the Commanding General.[46]

[44] Latrobe, *Rambler*, I, 173–76; Ellsworth, *Narrative*, 6–7.

[45] *Arkansas Gazette*, July 18, 1832. Privates were enlisted for one year; compensation of $1.00 a day included the use of horses and equipment. Officers served under the same conditions as those of corresponding rank in the regular service.

[46] *Ibid.* Bean continued for several years in the military service. "Captain Jesse Bean, of Independence County, passed through Batesville, about a week ago, with a full company of U. S. Dragoons, which he has recently recruited in Tennessee. We understand they are a fine looking body of young men" (*Arkansas Gazette*, June 3, 1834).

Bean was allowed thirty days to recruit, and was permitted to choose his own subalterns. Only active men under forty, "capable of enduring all the fatigues of an arduous service," were to be enlisted. They were to provide their own rifles, horses, and horse equipment, but pistols and swords would be furnished by the government. A "plain, cheap uniform" to be prescribed later would be provided by the members themselves. As soon as sufficient men had been raised, Bean was to march to the Illinois frontier for service in the Black Hawk troubles.[47] Three weeks after the first orders were issued, however, the Adjutant General instructed him: "As it will be in all probability too late before you arrive with your company at Chicago, it is the desire of the Secretary of War that you proceed to Fort Gibson with your Company, where it will be inspected and mustered by the Commanding Officer at that Post, and should it be accepted, you will be placed under his command."[48]

The War Department need not have been too much concerned over the possibility that the Arkansas rangers might make a belated march to northern Illinois. Bean, away from home during the early part of the summer, did not receive his

[47] Lewis Cass to Jesse Bean, Department of War, June 16, 1832 (*Arkansas Gazette*, July 18, 1832). Ellsworth makes clear, however, that uniforms had not been devised by the time of this expedition, nor were side arms issued before the rangers set out (*Narrative*, 9).

[48] R. Jones, Adjutant General to Captain Jesse Bean, Washington, July 7, 1832 (Adjutant General's Office, Records of the War Department, National Archives). On the same day Jones wrote to Colonel Arbuckle: "Capt. Bean . . . has been ordered this day to repair to Fort Gibson and to receive your orders. You will muster and inspect them . . . the horses are not to be above 8 years of age, and not under 14½ hands. . . . The men are not to be above 40 years. They are to be equipped with a good rifle each; with saddles and bridles and every thing necessary to enable them to perform their duty. After receiving the Rangers, you will order them into the Indian country where you may judge their presence will be of the most importance, and keep them ranging the frontier to preserve peace and order. . . ." (Adjutant General's Office, Records of the War Department, National Archives). The swords and pistols were to be issued at Fort Gibson. Again, Ellsworth informs us that the side arms had not been issued before this first tour of duty (*Narrative*, 9).

instructions until July 27. Immediately he announced that he would be at Batesville, Arkansas, on the thirtieth to receive recruits, and on that day he enrolled fifty, "nearly all of whom are active and intelligent young men." He named Joseph Pentecost first lieutenant; Robert King, second lieutenant; and George Caldwell, third lieutenant. In the first week in August, King visited Little Rock and then Pope County on a recruiting tour, and he gave notice of a rendezvous at Batesville for August 22.[49] The *Arkansas Gazette* on the twenty-ninth was "gratified to learn, by a gentleman from Batesville, that Capt. BEAN has succeeded in raising his Company of Rangers, and that the members of it were to rendezvous at Batesville on Monday last [August 27], preparatory to taking up their line of March for Fort Gibson. . . ." On September 12 the *Gazette* said, "We forgot to mention in our last that Capt. Bean's Company of Mounted Rangers paraded at Batesville on the 25th ult."

Bean did not reach his destination without some difficulty. On September 15, Colonel Arbuckle reported to the Adjutant General the arrival at Fort Gibson the previous day of the captain, the first and second lieutenants, and seventy-seven noncommissioned officers and privates. "The Captain reports his Company is complete and that they would have been now present had they not been prevented by sickness. Their complaint (with one or two exceptions) is the Measles and his 3ᵈ Lieuᵗ is detained on the way by the same disease." The commandant therefore decided not to muster the company for some days so that the absent would have an opportunity to join the main body. "The men present," he wrote, "have a good appearance and as far as I have observed are well mounted and equipped."[50]

It was three weeks longer, however, before the rangers

[49] *Arkansas Gazette*, August 8, 1832.
[50] Adjutant General's Office, Records of the War Department, National Archives.

were officially brought into the national service. On October 6 Arbuckle informed the Adjutant General:

> I have the honor herewith to transmit a Muster Roll of Captain Jesse Bean's company of Mounted Rangers.
>
> The Company with very few exceptions is composed of very active young men raised on the Western Frontier and are well accustomed to the use of the Rifle,—In fact, I have not noticed a single individual of the company who I do not consider well qualified for active service.
>
> Two of the company who were absent at the time of muster have not yet joined (viz.) Privates Wiley Taylor & Christopher Meacham, they had arrived within eighteen miles of this Post, when Meacham lost his horse; which they have been in search of. Should they not join shortly their names will be omitted on the next Muster Roll of the Company.
>
> You have enclosed a copy of Instructions to Captain Bean who marched for the West today with his Company except the sick.[51]

Colonel Arbuckle had been a little surprised earlier in the summer to hear that the rangers were then being dispatched to him, but he had acknowledged that the company "may be usefully employed in protecting the Indian Tribes in this quarter (who have treaties with the United States) from depredations by the Comanchee and Pawnee Indians. And the company will be so employed as soon as it arrives."[52] As soon, therefore, as the company was in the proper strength, he drew up the following instructions for Captain Bean—instructions of particular interest because they give us the plans for the rangers' expedition, even though the journey was cut short in the Cross Timbers.

Head Quarters 7th Inf.

Fort Gibson 5th Octob^r 1832

Sir,

You will proceed with the company under your Command to the

---

[51] *Ibid*. The muster roll of Bean's rangers will be found in Appendix II, page 181 ff.

[52] Colonel Matthew Arbuckle to Colonel R. Jones, Adjutant General (Arbuckle Letters, 1830–1836, National Archives).

West, keeping near the Arkansas river until you arrive at the mouth of Little Red River; which enters on the south side about sixty or seventy miles from this post; from thence you will ascend the Little Red River, about sixty miles west from its junction with the Arkansas.—And then proceed due South to the Red River: which, it is presumed you will arrive on, about twenty five miles or more, West of the mouth of Faux Ouachita: from thence you will pass down between the Red River and Faux Ouachita, until you arrive near the mouth of the latter, when you will pursue a north East course until you arrive on the water of L'eau Bleu, which you will ascend to the western borders of the Cross Timbers, and from thence you will keep near the border of that Timber, until you arrive on the North Fork of the Canadian river, when you will take a course North East by East for this Post. The principal object of your command is to preserve peace between the different Tribes on this Frontier with which the United States have Treaties: and between these and our Citizens: and you will, as far as may be in your power, protect our Citizens and the Indian Tribes refered to, from injury from the Pawnee and Commanchee Indians.

Yet should you meet with any of the Tribes last refered to, you will not commit any act of hostility on them; unless they attack you, on the contrary should they visit you in a friendly manner and express a wish for peace with the Red people on this Frontier, you will assure them that if they will make an arrangement through their Traders, that a few of their principal Chiefs, due notice having been given by their Traders of their wish [,] will be received at this post or Fort Towson; next spring, and that the white people will assist them to make a peace with the Indian Tribes in this quarter.

It is not believed that you will have occasion to resort to force, to preserve peace between the Indian Tribes with which the United States have Treaties. Yet in the event any one of these Tribes should have resorted to acts of unprovoked hostility against another; you will redress the injured party as far as may be in your power: but if acts of hostility have ceased between the parties, you will not interfere as it will be best that the difficulty should be settled between the parties by a Council of their Chiefs assembled at this post or at such place as may be found most convenient.

You will on your march not permit your men to straggle or leave

ST. LOUIS IN 1832

from a painting by George Catlin

the company; and will advance with such Guards and Flankers as will at all times give you timely notice of an Indian or body of Indians that may happen to be near to you, and you will keep your camp well guarded at all times: and see that your horses are so secured as to prevent danger of their loss, and keep your command in readiness to punish assailants in the event you should be attacked.

You will keep a journal, in which you will note the course and distance of each day's march, the character of the soil, timber, water minerals and whatever else you may judge worthy of particular remark.[53]

I am, Sir,

very respectfully

y^r Ob. Servt

M. Arbuckle,

Col. 7th Infy Comd^{g54}

To Captain Jesse Bean

Comd^g a company of Rangers

Present

In accordance with these instructions, then, the rangers had left Fort Gibson on October 6. When Ellsworth arrived two days later, "determined to proceed at once to the West," Arbuckle sent a messenger to halt Bean until the commissioner could join him. He instructed him "then to govern his movements by the wishes of that Gentleman." On the tenth, "accompanied by a Lieutenant and thirteen non Com^d officers & privates of Capt. Bean's company," Ellsworth "with several Gentlemen who arrived here in company with him" set out to join the rangers on the Little Red River.[55]

On October 10 Irving and Ellsworth, escorted by Arbuckle and Sam Houston, rode from Fort Gibson to the Verdigris Trading Post. There they found Latrobe and Pourtalès who,

[53]. This journal has not been found.

[54] National Archives. This itinerary was considerably modified during the actual march.

[55] Colonel M. Arbuckle to Colonel R. Jones, Adjutant General, Fort Gibson, October 11, 1832 (Arbuckle Letters, 1830–1836, National Archives).

accompanied by a clerk of Chouteau's and an Osage interpreter, proposed to ride with them as far as the Osage trail.[56] The party made about ten miles the first day, the chief incidents being the loss of one of his boots by Pourtalès and the discovery by Ellsworth that they had forgotten to bring plates, knives, and forks. Before noon the next day the two Europeans struck off for an Osage encampment of which they had been informed, but they reappeared at evening, having given up all hope of overtaking the Osage. The eating comfort of the travelers was increased by three wooden bowls which Pourtalès bought from some Indians, and by several clam shells which Latrobe found in a near-by creek and contributed for use as plates and saltcellars. One night they were amused by three Osage who came into the camp and, after feasting, sang[57] and drummed upon their bare bellies, keeping "excellent time" and, "though their drums were stuffed full," making a "loud sound." The young Count began to practice: "he would strike up an Indian song & rub, a dub, dub, on his belly —He even got so completely master of the art as to imitate the native drum, with much accuracy."[58]

On October 13 they came up with Captain Bean and the main body of the rangers.[59] The days were now filled with

[56] Tonish was now clearly with Ellsworth and Irving. For his services as guide and interpreter from October 10, 1832, to March 1, 1834, at $1.00 per day, he was paid $537 (Twenty-third Congress, first session, *Senate Document* 512, V, 292).

[57] "This chant, we were told by our interpreter, Beatte, related to ourselves, our appearance, our treatment of them, and all that they knew of our plans. In one part they spoke of the young Count, whose animated character and eagerness for Indian enterprise had struck their fancy, and they indulged in some waggery about him and the young Indian beauties, that produced great merriment among our half-breeds" (Irving, *Tour*, 42).

[58] Ellsworth, *Narrative*, 21–22.

[59] In addition to the rangers and their officers, the party now consisted of Ellsworth, Irving, Latrobe, Pourtalès, Brailey (Chouteau's clerk), Dr. David Holt (surgeon of the expedition), Beatte, Tonish, and a half blood named Antoine Lombard. Since Irving's Journal for this portion of his western trip is very full, I shall merely summarize events and draw occasionally on Latrobe, Ellsworth, and the *Tour*. Comparison of the four accounts will be made when desirable in the annotations for the Irving Journals.

novelty for the travelers. A bee hunt one day, the crossing of the Arkansas River the next, the killing of a skunk, making camp and breaking camp, rifle competitions and camp games— activity and scenery were varied enough for the most romantic among them. The coffee pot lost its spout and had a few holes knocked in it, but the versatile Tonish drew deer thongs through the holes, knotted them on both sides, cut the ends, and the pot was good as new. Ellsworth was so impressed with this repair job that he decided "to stop one of my teeth with a leather thong—for I had the bad luck to loose the gold foil from a decayed tooth, and the nerve was exposed to the weather —The leather with which I filled my tooth soon swelled to the full size of the cavity and yet remains—What would Doct Crane our dentist say to this?"[60]

On the eighteenth Irving took advantage of the return of some rangers to Fort Gibson on sick leave to write his sister from "Greenpoint, near the Red Fork of the Arkansas."

I wrote to you when about to start from Fort Gibson, under an escort, to join the exploring party of rangers. We came up with them, in the course of three or four days, on the banks of the Arkansas. The whole troop crossed that river the day before yesterday, some on rafts, some fording. Our own immediate party have a couple of half-breed Indians as servants, who understand the Indian customs. They constructed a kind of boat or raft out of a buffalo skin, on which Mr. Ellsworth and myself crossed at several times, on the top of about a hundredweight of luggage—an off way of crossing a river a quarter of a mile wide.

We are now on the borders of the Pawnee country, a region untraversed by white men, except by solitary trappers. We are leading a wild life, depending upon game, such as deer, elk, bear, for food, encamping on the borders of brooks, and sleeping in the open air under trees, with outposts stationed to guard us against any surprise by the Indians.

We shall probably be three weeks longer on this tour. Two or

[60] Ellsworth, *Narrative*, 37–38.

35

three days bring us into the buffalo range, where we shall have grand sport hunting. We shall also be in the range of wild horses.

I send this letter by a party of the men who have to return to escort two or three sick men, who have the measles and fevers. The rest of the camp is well, and our own party in high spirits. I was never in finer health, or enjoyed myself more, and the idea of exploring a wild country of this magnificent character is very exciting.

I write at the moment of marching. The horses are all saddled, and the bugle sounds for mounting. God bless you. I shall not have another opportunity of writing until I return to the garrison of Fort Gibson. We are far beyond any civilized habitation or even an Indian village.[61]

Unfortunately there is no Irving Journal for the latter part of October, and two of the most interesting events—the buffalo hunt and the capture of the wild horses—are recorded only in the *Tour on the Prairies*. The moment of greatest excitement, too, occurred on the twenty-second. At mess time a cry of fire ran through the camp, and hardly had the burning prairie grass been extinguished when the alarm of "Pawnees!" sounded.

What *consternation!* I cannot describe it—my horse had gone down the Creek—no servile labour now—charity began at home—every one took care of himself—Some horses were soon ready, and Rangers seen riding with a *quick* gallop to the brow of the hill, where the Pawnees might be seen—Oh! the confusion! the cooking dishes were upset as matters of no moment, for many a poor soul, thought he should need no more nourishment—some actually shed *tears*—Mr Irving could find only one *Leggin,* and he was calling through the camp loud, and louder still, for his off leggin, of mighty little consequence in a battle—He was as *pale* as he could be, and much terrified—Latrobe seized his saddle and put it on wrong side before and girted it in this manner—Pourteles wanted to know, whether it was best to take saddle bags or not? One young chap went running around, wringing his hands, crying, "Lord jesus help me find my bridle"![62]

[61] P. M. Irving, *Washington Irving,* II, 250–51.

On October 22 they forded the Red Fork (Cimarron) and the next day entered the Cross Timbers, a region that found favor with none of the travelers. Through this difficult belt of forest they moved southwestwardly, passing near the site of Oklahoma City, and by the thirtieth reached the plains of the Canadian. It was now decided that the expedition should attempt to go no deeper into the Indian country. Accordingly, they re-entered the Cross Timbers near the site of Norman and, to the pleasure of all, pitched camp on the eastern edge of that forest on the first of November.

In spite of inconveniences, the rest of the trip was anticlimax. Irving could write to his sister with pride and pleasure of the difficulties faced:

Our tour was a very rough but a very interesting and gratifying one, part of the time through an unexplored country. We led a complete hunter's life, subsisting upon the produce of the chase, camping by streams or pools, and sleeping on skins and blankets in the open air; but we were all in high health; and, indeed, nothing is equal to such a campaign, to put a man in full health and spirits. . . . We got out of flour, salt, sugar, etc., and had to eat our meat without bread or seasoning, and drink our coffee without sweetening. Our horses were tired down by the pasturage being withered, and by their having been coursed after buffaloes and wild horses. Some of them had to be left behind; and those of us who brought back our horses to the fort, had to walk, and lead them for the greater part of the three or four last days.[63]

On November 8 they once more crossed the Verdigris River, and "Mr Braley ... piloted us through the Creek woods —we heard the supper horn of Mr Chouteaus boarding house —a delight[ful] sound, expecially to our fellow Trencher

[62] Ellsworth, *Narrative*, 93–94. In the *Tour* Irving drew a somewhat milder picture (pages 156–65).

[63] Washington Irving to Mrs. Paris, Montgomery's Point, Mouth of the Arkansas, November 16, 1832 (P. M. Irving, *Washington Irving*, II, 251–52).

men Latrobe, Pourteles & Braley, who had eaten nothing since morning."[64]

Latrobe and Pourtalès stayed at Chouteau's post until November 23, when they started down the Arkansas in a dugout with two discharged soldiers as a crew. The commissioner and Irving, however, rode over to Fort Gibson early on the morning of the ninth. There Irving planned to rest for a few days, but a steamboat arrived during the night and he seized the chance to start home the next day. Little Rock had been hoping that it would be "honored with a visit from this distinguished American novelist,"[65] and on October 14 the *Arkansas Gazette* announced that "The steam-boat Little Rock, Capt. Rudd, arrived here last evening, from Fort Gibson . . . among the passengers on board of her, is our distinguished countryman WASHINGTON IRVING, Esq. the accomplished author . . . on his return to New-York, from a tour among the Indian tribes west of Arkansas." Although Irving left Little Rock the next afternoon, there was time for an interview which appeared in the *Gazette* a week later:

The citizens of Little Rock were gratified, a few days since, by the presence of this justly celebrated individual. He is on his way from a visit to some of the Indian tribes on our borders, to the State of New-York. He acknowledges himself amazed at the fertility of the soil and the immense resources of the west. His highest expectations have been far more than realized. He dwells with rapture on the scenery afforded by our south-western *prairies*. When entering upon them, he says, he could scarcely divest himself of the belief that he was approaching the mansion of some European Nobleman. He was still looking out for the dome of a castle or the spire of a church, to rise upon his view. He expresses a full intention, if spared, to revisit these regions in the approaching Spring, when the prairies are in bloom. Should he favor the world with a description from his glowing pen, which is more than

[64] Ellsworth, *Narrative*, 144.
[65] *Arkansas Gazette*, October 31, 1832.

probable, it will excite emotions of unmingled delight in the bosom of thousands, and unfold unnumerable beauties in nature, which, to the majority of travellers, remained unnoticed and unknown.

The last dated entry in the Irving Journals is for November 17, when the steamboat was dropping down the Mississippi River a day's journey below the mouth of the Arkansas. Before long Irving was at New Orleans, where he stayed for some days. That city, he wrote to Peter, "is one of the most motley and amusing places in the United States; a mixture of America and Europe. The French part of the city is a counterpart of some French provincial town; and the levee, or esplanade, along the river, presents the most whimsical groups of people of all nations, castes, and colors; French, Spanish, Indian, Half Breeds, Creoles, Mulatoes, Kentuckians, & c."[66] While in Louisiana he had the good fortune to spend "a couple of days with Judge M——, Mrs. McLane's brother, on his sugar plantation, just at the time they were making sugar."[67]

From New Orleans, Irving took passage in the mail stage for Mobile, Alabama, and points east and north. It was a "long and rather dreary journey, travelling frequently day and night, and much of the road through pine forests in the winter season." At Columbia, South Carolina, however, he found an old friend, William C. Preston, with whom he and Peter had traveled in Scotland and England in 1817. Preston was then a member of the legislature and a leader of the nullifiers, Irving said. "I passed a day most cordially with him, talking and laughing over old times, and recalling the scenes and personages of our rambles. . . . I dined with him at Governor Hamilton's, the nullifying Governor, whom I had known as a

---

[66] *Ibid.*, June 26, 1833.

[67] P. M. Irving, *Washington Irving*, II, 253. The McLane referred to was Louis McLane (1786–1857) who married Catherine Mary, the eldest daughter of Robert Milligan of Louisiana, and served as Minister to England and in other public offices. The Milligan plantation was probably the one near Jackson's battlefield. Tixier visited there in 1840 (McDermott and Salvan, *Tixier's Travels*, 71–72).

young man at New York, and who is a perfect gentleman, but a Hotspur in politics. It is really lamentable to see such a fine set of fellows as these leading nullifiers are, so madly in the wrong." When Irving left, the Governor invited him to come soon to see him again. Irving's playful reply was, "I'll come with *the first troops*."[68]

He now went on through North Carolina and Virginia to Washington, where he intended to stay only a few days before he proceeded to New York. He arrived at the capital about the end of the first week in December and soon was so "very pleasantly situated" that he had little inclination to leave. "I have a very snug, cheery, cosey room in the immediate neighborhood of McLane's," he wrote, "and take my meals at his house, and, in fact, make it my home."[69] Here Irving can be left, for his tour of the West is completed, and his repatriation certain: "It is absolutely my intention to make our country my home for the residue of my days, and the more I see of it, the more I am convinced that I can live here with more enjoyment than in Europe."[70]

II

The direct literary result of Irving's western travel was *A Tour on the Prairies*, published in 1835 as the first volume of the *Crayon Miscellany*.[71] It had been awaited with eagerness

[68] P. M. Irving, *Washington Irving*, II, 253. Preston (1794–1860) in 1831 had married Louise Penelope (his second wife), daughter of Dr. James Davis of Columbia, South Carolina.

[69] *Ibid.*, 254.

[70] Washington Irving to [Peter Irving], Washington, December 18, 1832 (*Arkansas Gazette*, June 26, 1833).

[71] "The Creole Village" (which is reprinted in the Appendix to this volume) is also based upon his Arkansas travels. *Astoria*, of course, and *Captain Bonneville* are important results of the western experience, but they do not actually make use of any material in the Journals except that his description of St. Louis in *Astoria* and his general impressions of the French and frontiersmen are probably derived from the observations made in 1832.

The English edition of the *Tour* was published in March and the American edition in April. John Murray gave Irving £400 for the English rights—"The price is not so high as I used to get, but there has been a great change in the book-

from the moment he had started west, and it was greeted with praise when it appeared. "Irving possesses, in the highest degree," said one reviewer, "the gift of the poet, *the maker*. And delightful it is to reflect, as in a case like this, how little it imports to the man, to whom this divine gift is imparted, what materials he shall take in hand to employ it upon, or where he shall lay the scene of his creations."[72] There is truth in this statement as well as in other remarks by the same writer: "His style is sprightly, pointed, easy, correct, and expressive, without being too studiously guarded against the opposite faults. It is without affectation, parade, or labor . . . it is . . . marked with an expressive elegance."[73] Yet in spite of the pleasant, urbane, and often amusing style, the book proves to be "a sort of sentimental journey, a romantic excursion."[74]

Here was a man who in the course of travels "from the White Mountains of New-Hampshire to the plains of the Arkansas . . . will have seen more of American scenery, and had better opportunities of observing American character during one active summer, than ninety-nine hundredths of his countrymen with every advantage got in the whole course of their lives." But we can hardly agree that the results expected are "every way gratifying."[75] The Irving of the *Tour on the Prairies* proved to be the same Irving who had chosen to write a comical history of New York in which the Dutch of the seventeenth century appear in practically every guise save that of Dutchmen, the same Irving who had written so understandingly of himself in *The Sketch Book:* "I longed to wander over

selling trade of late years." Carey, the American publisher, paid $1,500 for the right to publish 5,000 copies and agreed to pay $300 more for each additional thousand—on November 10, 1835, he paid for the eighth thousand (P. M. Irving, *Washington Irving*, II, 271–72).

[72] *North American Review*, XLI (July, 1835), 12.

[73] *Ibid.*, 1.

[74] *Ibid.*, 5. The conclusion expressed in this sentence is mine, not the reviewer's. His attitude was entirely laudatory.

[75] The *New York American* as quoted in the *Arkansas Gazette*, January 30, 1833.

the scenes of renowned achievement—to tread, as it were, in the footsteps of antiquity—to loiter about the ruined castle— to meditate on the falling tower—to escape, in short, from the commonplace realities of the present, and lose myself among the shadowy grandeurs of the past." From first to last Irving was the sentimental romanticist who found a distant time or a distant place more interesting than the scene about him. In the *Tour* he was still the "humble lover of the picturesque . . . caught sometimes by the delineations of beauty, sometimes by the distortions of caricature, and sometimes by the loveliness of landscape." He had now merely turned his attention to American "nooks and corners and by-places."[76] He had great opportunities for observation during this western tour; he had the freshness of a first view and the soundness of a middle-aged and trained writer. We have some reason to be disappointed, then, that he gave us in the *Tour* no more than a smooth piece of romantic reporting.

The characteristic response of Irving to the stimulus of the new scene can be noted occasionally in his letters and Journals, and repeatedly in the published *Tour*. Writing from Independence to his sister, he declared that:

Many parts of these prairies of the Missouri are extremely beautiful, resembling cultivated countries, embellished with parks and groves, rather than the savage rudeness of the wilderness.

Yesterday I was out on a deer hunt in the vicinity of this place, which led me through some scenery that only wanted a castle, or a gentleman's seat here and there interspersed, to have equalled some of the most celebrated park scenery of England.[77]

Even the most enthusiastic person would not think of placing Latrobe on the same plane with Irving as a writer, but Latrobe's account is frequently the more satisfying because he

[76] These quotations are from "The Author's Account of Himself," the first selection in *The Sketch Book*.

[77] P. M. Irving, *Washington Irving*, II, 248.

presents frontier scenes, not as the amusing quaintness of a strange people, not as a picturesque vision to be interpreted through a superficial European romanticism, but as an interesting variation in culture worth examining in its own right. This, for instance, is his description of a frontier farm:

Having rounded a noble and expanded bend of the river, in about an hour's time, we heard by the barking of dogs, and the chattering of many voices, that we were approaching the farm in question. The tall leafless boughs of a few girdled trees then appeared, and as we entered the opening on the bank of the river, we descried the rough log-huts forming the usual habitation of a squatter or backwoodsman. From the prominent appearance of a long table covered with dinner apparatus, which appeared arranged in the open air, a few steps from the door, a number of dogs whining and snuffling around it, and the unusual bustle among the negro dependants [*sic*] toiling about a small fire in advance, we suspected that something extraordinary was going on. A young negro took our horses with that affectation of extreme politeness and good breeding, which is so amusing in many of his colour, and which inclines me to think that they appreciate the character of a "fine gentleman," more than any other part of the community. The principal log-hut was built on a little level, half way up the steep bank impending over the swift and turbid river below. In immediate proximity to it, I noticed the broad, solid stump of a magnificent oak, which had just been felled, and lay prostrate, with his crown of foliage hanging over the bluff . . .[78]

It was Irving's easy habit to interpret the new scene by reference to the old or by some commonplace romantic allusion. The western scenery, which he so honestly and completely admired, was linked, whether he was in serious or humorous mood, to the European: "Scale a hill—limestone rock & stones full of shells and miniature basalt like Giant's Causeway—boundless view of silent Prairies—distant hill like Paté de Strasbourg."[79] When, on the prairies, he described

[78] *Rambler*, I, 134–35.
[79] Journal, September 30. See page 94 below.

"one of the characteristic scenes of the Far West," he could not do so without a Gothic touch:

An immense extent of grassy, undulating, or, as it is termed, rolling country, with here and there a clump of trees dimly seen in the distance like a ship at sea; the landscape deriving sublimity from its vastness and simplicity. To the southwest, on the summit of a hill, was a singular crest of broken rocks, resembling a ruined fortress. It reminded me of the ruin of some Moorish castle, crowning a height in the midst of a lonely Spanish landscape. To this hill we gave the name of Cliff Castle.[80]

The camp of rangers did not look to Irving like a military camp, but took on the light opera appearance of a "robber's retreat." Old Ryan was the "Nestor of our camp." Tonish was "a kind of Gil Blas of the frontiers." Sunshine in the forest reminded Irving of the "effect of sunshine among the stained windows and clustering columns of a Gothic cathedral."

Irving's method of work merely intensified the romantic character of his observations. Ellsworth reported that "his mode of recording events, is not to confide much to the memory, but to sketch in a little book every occurence [*sic*] worthy of remembrance and especially *dates & facts*—These he says are his foundations—he makes additional rooms when he builds his fabric and adds the rest which he terms '*filligree work*.' . . . He cultivates the imagination and gives it wings."[81] The chief fault one finds with the *Tour on the Prairies* is the filigree, the writer's giving wings to imagination.

Irving had a hard time reporting simple things simply; anything worth including in the book apparently had to be blown up beyond life size and colored vividly. On October 11 for example, the party met "a tall, red haired, lank, leather faced settler with one eye habitually closed when he winks— says some of the Osages are near. They had stolen one of his

[80] *Tour*, 127.
[81] *Narrative*, 71.

44

horses—says they will steal horses and bring them home, pretending to have found them and claiming a reward." Later in the same day Irving noted, "Just then we meet old lanthern jawd man who had lost his horse—had just met with Osage leading him back, who said he had wandered to their camp. Lanthern jawd man was for tying him up & giving him a swing with rushes, but we interfered."[82]

These few phrases served as the "foundation" for a considerable "fabric":

. . . a tall, rawboned old fellow, with red hair, a lank lantern visage, and an inveterate habit of winking with one eye, as if everything he said was of knowing import. He was in a towering passion. One of his horses was missing; he was sure it had been stolen in the night by a straggling party of Osages encamped in a neighboring swamp; but he would have satisfaction! He would make an example of the villains. He had accordingly caught down his rifle from the wall, that invariable enforcer of right or wrong upon the frontiers, and, having saddled his steed, was about to sally forth on a foray into the swamp; while a brother squatter, with rifle in hand, stood ready to accompany him.

We endeavored to calm the old campaigner of the prairies, by suggesting that his horse might have strayed into the neighboring woods; but he had the frontier propensity to charge everything to the Indians, and nothing could dissuade him from carrying fire and sword into the swamp. . . .

We had not long regained the trail, when, on emerging from a forest, we beheld our rawboned, hard-winking, hard-riding knight-errant of the frontier, descending the slope of a hill, followed by his companion in arms. As he drew near to us, the gauntness of his figure and ruefulness of his aspect reminded me of the description of the hero of La Mancha, and he was equally bent on affairs of doughty enterprise, being about to penetrate the thickets of the perilous swamp, within which the enemy lay ensconced.

While we were holding a parley with him on the slope of the hill, we descried an Osage on horseback issuing out of a skirt of wood about

[82] Journal, October 11. See page 113 below. These are the only lines concerning this person.

a half mile off, and leading a horse by a halter. The latter was immediately recognized by our hard-winking friend as the steed of which he was in quest. As the Osage drew near, I was struck with his appearance. He was about nineteen or twenty years of age, but well grown, with the fine Roman countenance common to his tribe; and as he rode, with his blanket wrapped around his loins, his naked bust would have furnished a model for a statuary. He was mounted on a beautiful piebald horse, a mottled white and brown, of the wild breed of the prairies, decorated with a broad collar, from which hung in front a tuft of horsehair dyed a bright scarlet.

The youth rode slowly up to us with a frank open air, and signified by means of our interpreter Beatte, that the horse he was leading had wandered to their camp, and he was now on his way to conduct him back to his owner.

I had expected to witness an expression of gratitude on the part of our hard-favored cavalier, but to my surprise the old fellow broke out into a furious passion. He declared that the Indians had carried off his horse in the night, with the intention of bringing him home in the morning, and claiming a reward for finding him; a common practice, as he affirmed, among the Indians. He was, therefore, for tying the young Indian to a tree and giving him a sound lashing; and was quite surprised at the burst of indignation which this novel mode of requiting a service drew from us. Such, however, is too often the administration of law on the frontier, "Lynch's law," as it is technically termed, in which the plaintiff is apt to be witness, jury, judge, and executioner, and the defendant to be convicted and punished on mere presumption; and in this way, I am convinced, are occasioned many of those heart-burnings and resentments among the Indians, which lead to retaliation, and end in Indian wars. When I compared the open, noble countenance and frank demeanor of the young Osage with the sinister visage and high-handed conduct of the frontiersman, I felt little doubt on whose back a lash would be most meritoriously bestowed.

Being thus obliged to content himself with the recovery of his horse, without the pleasure of flogging the finder into the bargain, the old Lycurgus, or rather Draco, of the frontier, set off growling on his return homeward, followed by his brother squatter.[83]

[83] *Tour*, 25–29.

It is important to notice in this passage not merely the very considerably enlarged treatment of the frontiersman, but also the description of the gallant Osage. Concerning the latter Irving continued:

As for the youthful Osage, we were all prepossessed in his favor; the young Count especially, with the sympathies proper to his age and incident to his character, had taken quite a fancy to him. Nothing would suit but he must have the young Osage as a companion and squire in his expedition into the wilderness. The youth was easily tempted, and with the prospect of a safe range over the buffalo prairies, and the promise of a new blanket, he turned his bridle, left the swamp and the encampment of his friends behind him, and set off to follow the Count in his wanderings in quest of the Osage hunters. . . . The Count had prevailed upon his protégé and esquire, the young Osage, to continue with him, and still calculated upon achieving great exploits, with his assistance, on the buffalo prairies. . . .

In mounting our steeds, the young Osage attempted to throw a blanket upon his wild horse. The fine, sensitive animal took fright, reared and recoiled. The attitudes of the wild horse and the almost naked savage would have formed studies for a painter or a statuary.

I often pleased myself, in the course of our march, with noticing the appearance of the young Count and his newly enlisted follower, as they rode before me. Never was preux chevalier better suited with an esquire. . . .

The young Osage would ride up close behind him on his wild and beautifully mottled horse, which was decorated with crimson tufts of hair. He rode, with his finely shaped head and bust naked; his blanket being girt round his waist. He carried his rifle in one hand, and managed his horse with the other, and seemed ready to dash off at a moment's warning, with his youthful leader, on any madcap foray or scamper. . . .

In the morning . . . the young Osage who was to act as esquire to the Count in his knight-errantry on the prairies, was nowhere to be found. His wild horse, too, was missing, and, after many conjectures, we came to the conclusion that he had taken "Indian leave" of us in the night. We afterwards ascertained that he had been persuaded to do so by the Osages we had recently met with; who had represented to him the

47

perils that would attend him in an expedition to the Pawnee hunting grounds, where he might fall into the hands of the implacable enemies of his tribe; and, what was scarcely less to be apprehended, the annoyances to which he would be subjected from the capricious and overbearing conduct of the white men, who, as I have witnessed in my own short experience, are prone to treat the poor Indians as little better than brute animals. Indeed, he had had a specimen of it himself in the narrow escape he made from the infliction of "Lynch's law," by the hardworking worthy of the frontier, for the flagitious crime of finding a stray horse.

The disappearance of the youth was generally regretted by our party, for we had all taken a great fancy to him from his handsome, frank, and manly appearance, and the easy grace of his deportment. He was indeed a native-born gentleman. By none, however, was he so much lamented as by the young Count, who thus suddenly found himself deprived of his esquire. I regretted the departure of the Osage for his own sake, for we should have cherished him throughout the expedition, and I am convinced, from the munificent spirit of his patron, he would have returned to his tribe laden with wealth of beads and trinkets and Indian blankets.[84]

The excellence of Irving's memory or the magnificence of his imagination becomes clear when one looks in the Journal for the sketches from which this vivid Indian portrait was constructed:

[October 11] had just met with Osage leading him [the horse] back. . . . Pourtales was not to be dissuaded. He & Latrobe procured an Indian guide & set off in their quest. . . . Latrobe & Pourtales arrive, finding it impossible to get on with their slender attendance—determine to continue with us. Their Indian agrees to accompany them for a blanket and cloak . . .

[October 12] Osage Indian & his wild horse—attempts to put blanket of ours on him—fine scene—figure of Indian—naked bust—blanket—with piebald horse—wild eyes—collar with tuft of horsehair. . . . Young Osage leaves us clandestinely in the night.[85]

[84] *Ibid.*, 29, 35–37, 44–46.
[85] See pages 113–16 below.

"A BUFFALO HUNT ON THE SOUTHWESTERN PRAIRIES"

from a painting by John Mix Stanley, 1845

Courtesy Bureau of American Ethnology

Irving has introduced a real character but has chosen to present him as a composite. His noble savage may have been everything that the *Tour* informs us he was, but there is almost nothing in the Journal to justify the portrait. As a "maker," Irving may be successful, but as a historian and a travel reporter his method is questionable.[86]

There were frequent other examples of transposed material, too. On October 15 he wrote in his Journal: "Fires lit in dell—looks like a robbers' retreat—groups of men round fires —rifles—powder horns &c. leaning ag[ain]st trees beside them—horses grazing around with bells tinkling—baggage, blankets &c. hanging on horizontal poles to dry." This bit, however, he chose to place three days earlier in the *Tour* and to use it again on the thirteenth when he described how the party came up with the main body of the rangers.[87] A story credited to Colonel Chouteau in the Journal (October 4) is placed on October 29 in the *Tour*, and is described as "a little story, which I picked up in the course of my tour through Beatte's country."[88]

It is hardly necessary to multiply instances of this sort, but there is one more conventionalized romantic element which certainly calls for comment. Antoine Deshetres[89]— Tonish—the "Gil Blas of the frontiers"—is in Irving's hands

[86] Latrobe failed to report this episode. Ellsworth, writing privately, merely mentioned Pourtalès's hiring the Osage who had been leading the stray horse and later gave a few lines explaining how visiting Osage Indians had talked with the Osage servant and induced him to leave (*Narrative*, 13, 15, 22–23).

[87] *Tour*, 41–47.

[88] *Ibid.*, 205–207.

[89] The name has been spelled Deshetres, Dehetre, De Hetre, Dehatre, De Hatre; I have chosen the first as the most correct form. Antoine was born in Florissant, October 19, 1791, the son of Hyacinthe Deshetres and Françoise Normandeau *dit* Deslauriers. In 1812 he married Camille Mercier of Florissant. Not many of the details of his life are available, but those show the typical wide wandering of the hunter and guide: In 1822 he was with A. P. Chouteau in the Arkansas country; in 1827 he was at Paul L. Chouteau's trading post among the Osage on the Neosho River; between April 26 and July 26, 1832, he was serving as guide to a party of Senecas being moved to the lower Neosho. For his services

not a frontier Frenchman but merely a representative of that hoary literary type, the comic servant. Irving is not a traveler reporting what he sees; he is ever the self-conscious literary man, the feature-story writer who, by the ready use of his imagination, makes a little fact go a long way. One of the easiest devices for a writer is the one he follows here—the reduction of persons to stock types.

I present Tonish first as he is painted in the *Tour*. Irving's intentions become clear in the first chapter of the narrative when, having introduced the three traveling companions, he devotes quite as much space to the Frenchman as to all three of his friends:

in furnishing the public table and council room of the Commissioners West from January 1, 1833, to March 31, 1834, he was paid $1,904.94—at least one Antoine de Hetz was so paid. For his services as guide and interpreter for the Commissioners West from October 10, 1832, to March 1, 1834, he was paid, at $1.00 per day, $537; also, (if he was Antoine de Hoit) he was paid $50 for "one mare given to the Pawnees at Fort Gibson" (Twenty-third Congress, first session, *Senate Document* 512, V, 109).

On his return to St. Louis in the fall of 1833, Latrobe did not see Tonish, but "we heard enough of him from a gentleman who had been on the spring expedition with our good friend the Commissioner. He had survived the winter in doors,—had recovered his spirits, volubility, and effrontery, and had sent his son to be his aide-de-camp during the ensuing expedition" (*Rambler*, II, 236–37). This is a confusing statement since the government document cited above makes it clear that Tonish was continually in the service of the Commissioners West. The gentleman referred to was probably John T. Irving, nephew of Washington Irving, and companion of Ellsworth on the expedition mentioned. John T. Irving described this son of Tonish and, following the lead of his uncle, called the boy's mother a thorough squaw, although it is not clear or certain that he saw her (*Indian Sketches* . . ., 6–7). Edmund Flagg looked for Tonish at Florissant in 1836: "The old worthy himself was, as usual, in the regions of the Rocky Mountains: when last seen he could still tell the stoutest lie with the steadiest muscles of any man in the village, while he and his hopeful son could cover each other's trail so nicely that a lynx-eye would fail to detect them" (*The Far West*, I, 262).

Antoine Deshetres made his will on September 14, 1854; his son Joseph gave bond as administrator of his estate on October 7, 1854. Antoine left the following children: Antoine, Auguste, Edward, Joseph, Adeline, Rose, Ellen Bush, Mary Aubuchon, Sylvinia Aubuchon, Hyacinthe, and Sarpy. His property consisted of a house and lot (150 x 300), in Florissant, about thirty-two acres in the common field there, and the horses, cows, hogs, and the usual household furniture of a farmer (St. Louis Probate Court, File No. 4356).

The most interesting single document concerning Tonish is the letter printed on pages 60–62 below.

I must not pass over unnoticed a personnage of inferior rank, but of all-pervading and prevalent importance,—the squire, the groom, the cook, the tent-man, in a word, the factotum, and, I may add, the universal meddler and marplot of our party. This was a little, swarthy, meagre, French creole, named Antoine, but familiarly dubbed Tonish, —a kind of Gil Blas of the frontiers, who had passed a scrambling life, sometimes among white men, sometimes among Indians; sometimes in the employ of traders, missionaries, and Indian agents; sometimes mingling with the Osage hunters. We picked him up at St. Louis, near which he has a small farm, an Indian wife, and a brood of half-blood children. According to his own account, however, he had a wife in every tribe; in fact, if all this little vagabond said of himself were to be believed, he was without morals, without caste, without creed, without country, and even without language; for he spoke a jargon of mingled French, English, and Osage. He was, withal, a notorious braggart, and a liar of the first water. It was amusing to hear him vapor and gasconade about his terrible exploits and hairbreadth escapes in war and hunting. In the midst of his volubility he was prone to be seized by a spasmodic gasping, as if the springs of his jaws were suddenly unhinged; but I am apt to think it was caused by some falsehood that stuck in his throat, for I generally remarked that immediately afterwards there bolted forth a lie of the first magnitude.[90]

The idea of going with the Osage on a buffalo hunt had excited the very young Count, and he was full of anticipations about adventure in the savage life. But

it was still more amusing to listen to the gasconading of little Tonish, who volunteered to be his faithful squire in all his perilous undertakings; to teach him how to catch the wild horse, bring down the buffalo, and win the smiles of Indian princesses;—"And if we can only get sight of a prairie on fire!" said the young Count. "By Gar, I'll set one on fire myself!" cried the little Frenchman.[91]

Tonish appears in the *Tour* at least thirty times and occupies more space than any other character, with the possible excep-

[90] *Tour*, 5–6. The Indian wife at Florissant is apparently a creation of Irving's; see n. 89 above.
[91] *Ibid.*, 7.

tion of his foil, Beatte. He is repeatedly characterized as "our loquacious and ever-meddling Frenchman," "our vaporing, chattering, bustling little Frenchman," "our wild-fire Jack-o'-lantern little Frenchman," "little Scaramouch Tonish," and (ironically) as "the faithful and veracious Tonish." The pictures of him are sometimes amusing but they are never flattering.[92]

Our little Frenchman, Tonish, brought up the rear with the pack-horses. He was in high glee, having experienced a kind of promotion. In our journey hitherto he had driven the wagon, which he seemed to consider a very inferior employ; now he was master of the horse.

He sat perched like a monkey behind the pack on one of the horses; he sang, he shouted, he yelped like an Indian, and ever and anon blasphemed the loitering pack-horses in his jargon of mingled French, English, and Osage, which not one of them could understand.

I . . . transferred the silver-gray to Tonish, who was in such ecstasies at finding himself so completely *en cavalier*, that I feared he might realize the ancient and well-known proverb of "a beggar on horseback."

Our little Frenchman, Tonish, was in an ecstasy, and tucking up his sleeves to the elbows, set to work to make a display of his culinary skill, on which he prided himself almost as much as upon his hunting, his riding, and his warlike prowess.

Tonish, however, with his usual buoyancy, consoled himself by vociferous eulogies on the richness and delicacy of a roasted polecat, which he swore was considered the daintiest of dishes by all experienced Indian gourmands. It was with difficulty I could silence his loquacity by repeated and peremptory commands. A Frenchman's vivacity, however, if repressed in one way, will break out in another, and Tonish now eased off his spleen by bestowing volleys of oaths and dry blows on the pack-horses.

Some were evidently excited and elated with the idea of an encounter with the Indians. . . . On the other hand, little Tonish, who

[92] *Ibid.*, 13, 22, 185, 187, 8.

was busy cooking, stopped every moment from his work to play the fanfaron, singing, swearing, and affecting an unusual hilarity, which made me strongly suspect that there was some little fright at bottom, to cause all this effervescence.

As to little Scaramouch Tonish, who had marred the whole scene by his precipitancy, he had been more successful than he deserved, having managed to catch a beautiful cream-colored colt, about seven months old, which had not strength to keep up with his companions. The mercurial little Frenchman was beside himself with exultation. It was amusing to see him with his prize. The colt would kick, and struggle to get free, when Tonish would take him about the neck, wrestle with him, jump upon his back, and cut as many antics as a monkey with a kitten.

Our little Frenchman, Tonish, also, by his incessant boasting and chattering, and gasconading, in his balderdashed dialect, had drawn upon himself the ridicule of many of the wags of the troop, who amused themselves at his expense in a kind of raillery by no means remarkable for its delicacy; but the little varlet was so completely fortified by vanity and self-conceit, that he was invulnerable to every joke.[93]

Particularly ridiculous did Tonish become when he attempted to act the hunter—if we are to believe the frequent reports Irving made of his hunting exploits on this expedition:

No one, however, was more unmanageable than Tonish. Having an intense conceit of his skill as a hunter, and an irresistible passion for display, he was continually sallying forth, like an ill-broken hound, whenever any game was started, and had as often to be whipped back.

Tonish came back without any game, but with much more glory,— having made several capital shots, though unluckily the wounded deer had all escaped him.

Our two men, Beatte and Tonish, likewise went out. The former returned with a deer athwart his horse, which, as usual, he laid down by our lodge, and said nothing. Tonish returned with no game, but with his customary budget of wonderful tales. Both he and the deer

[93] *Ibid.*, 12, 19, 49–50, 73, 161, 187, 70.

had done wonders. Not one had come within the lure of his rifle without being hit in a mortal part, yet, strange to say, every one had kept on his way without flinching. We all determined that, from the accuracy of his aim, Tonish must have shot with charmed balls, but that every deer had a charmed life.

Tonish arrived, all glorious, from his hunting match; his white horse hung all around with buffalo meat. According to his own account, he had laid low two mighty bulls. As usual, we deducted one half from his boastings; but, now that he had something real to vaunt about, there was no restraining the valor of his tongue.

The most important intelligence brought by him, however, was, that he had seen the fresh tracks of several wild horses. He now considered himself upon the eve of great exploits, for there was nothing upon which he glorified himself more than his skill in horse-catching.[94]

This sort of characterization might be acceptable in fiction, even though we would still be inclined to dismiss Tonish as a pale and trite imitation of a not very satisfactory literary tradition. Putting aside the question of reality, however, we can see blunders and faults which surprise us in a practiced writer. For one thing, there is a notable lack of concrete detail. Irving is satisfied with the frequent repetition of such blanket phrases as "the incessant boasting and chattering and gasconading" of Tonish, but he never gives anything more than the most generalized summary of such characteristic talk. Furthermore, he missed some of his best opportunities both for creating the frontier atmosphere and for vivifying Tonish. Here was a Frenchman who, in one capacity or another, had wandered much over the prairies and who was always talking about his adventures. But instead of letting him talk freely, instead of reporting his tales as literally as possible—and the taller the tale the more characteristic, whether the teller be French or American—Irving merely mentioned that Tonish had much to say:

[94] *Ibid.*, 93–94, 115, 132, 156–57, 132.

the stories that the little Tonish told him [the young Count] of Indian braves and Indian beauties, of hunting buffaloes and catching wild horses, had set him all agog for a dash into savage life.

I found Tonish making himself a complete oracle among some of the raw and inexperienced recruits, who had never been in the wilderness. He had continually a knot hanging about him, and listening to his extravagant tales about the Pawnees, with whom he pretended to have had fearful encounters. His representations, in fact, were calculated to inspire his hearers with an awful idea of the foe into whose lands they were intruding. According to his accounts, the rifle of the white man was no match for the bow and arrow of the Pawnee. When the rifle was once discharged, it took time and trouble to load it again, and in the meantime the enemy could keep on launching his shafts as fast as he could draw his bow. Then the Pawnee, according to Tonish, could shoot, with unerring aim, three hundred yards, and send his arrow clean through and through a buffalo; nay, he had known a Pawnee shaft [to] pass through one buffalo and wound another. And then the way the Pawnees sheltered themselves from the shots of their enemy: they would hang with one leg over the saddle, crouching their bodies along the opposite side of their horse, and would shoot their arrows from under his neck, while at full speed!

Beatte bore his honors in silence, and closed with none of the offers. Our stammering, chattering, gasconading little Frenchman, however, made up for his taciturnity by vaunting as much upon the subject as if it were he who had caught the horse. Indeed he held forth so learnedly in the matter, and boasted so much of the many horses he had taken, that he began to be considered an oracle; and some of the youngsters were inclined to doubt whether he were not superior even to the taciturn Beatte.[95]

But to return to the apparently unimportant matter of

[95] *Ibid.*, 6–7, 108–109, 147. This overlooking of effective detail is characteristic not only in the treatment of Tonish but elsewhere as well. The night of October 13 they were with the main body of the rangers. Around the captain's fire "were a number of the prime hunters and leaders of the camp, some sitting, some standing, and others lying on skins or blankets before the fire, telling old frontier stories about hunting and Indian warfare" (*ibid.*, 63). These stories are not repeated.

reality and truth in the portrait of Tonish. First of all, how much can be found in the Journals to justify the enlargement in the *Tour?* The passages are not so many or so lengthy that they cannot all be quoted.

[September 29] plan for Antoine to go deer hunting while we journey this afternoon. . . . Antoine returns without game.

[October 2] Antoine towards the conclusion of chase [wolf hunt] leaves his waggon, mounts his stallion, & comes thundering along bringing up a corps de secours of bull-dog, cur &c. . . . Story of Antoine and the two kegs of powder behind him on horse with which he dashed thro prarie on fire.

[October 3] We spread our skin beds on the floor of room in house. Antoine &c light a fire—cook their supper & sleep under trees. ["]Every one has his caprice ["] said Antoine, ["]for my part I think it much better to camp here.["]

[October 7] Leave the Saline at 2 oclock with Mr Ellsworth in dearborn for Fort Gibson. Antoine drives the dearborn.

[October 15] After dark see glow of fires in western heavens . . . Antoine thinks them Osage fires on the other side of the Arkansas.

[In the undated notes at the close of the third Journal] Antoine thorough Frenchman—vaunts, exults, sings, boasts

[October 31] Billet [Tonish?] & Antoine set off in pursuit of wild horses, but in vain

[November 5] Antoine arrives pretty late bringing up the tired horses.

[In the undated notes at the close of the fourth Journal] Tonish says when he was about 15 years of age he was one day hunting in his neighbourhood & he saw a white deer. After a little while another white deer got up & so to the number of seven. He fired but missed— fired again and missed—could not hit the deer—went home and told the circumstance to ——, an old hunter or half breed—["]They're hard to hit,["] says he, ["] & can only be shot by a particular bul- let,["] He cast balls but would not let Tonish see how he cast them—

went out—shot—missed—but at length killed one—the rest ran off
& were never seen again.[96]

From such slender materials was Irving able to create the
Tonish of the *Tour!*[97]

It is apparent that Irving greatly extended his notebook information. This question then arises: How far he could be
drawing upon his memory of events and characters? The first
witness to be called is Latrobe. He, too, was a bookish man,
conventionally educated and conventionally read, and the
concept of the comic servant occurred to him as quickly as to
Irving. At parting, Latrobe could write, "We all looked upon
Beatte as a friend, and Tonish as a scaramouch." Again, he
could speak of the "egotistical rhapsodies of Tonish, which
always ended with a huge indefinite promise for the future,
couched in the words: '*Ah-qu-qu-que vous verrez!*'" and of
Tonish's habit of spreading "the tidings of his own going forth
to the chase throughout the camp, with hugh predictions of
extraordinary success, which were very rarely fulfilled."[98]

But although thus far Latrobe seems to agree with Irving,
not everything the Englishman had to say was in disparage-
ment. Tonish had come to them "upon strong recommenda-
tions from impartial people, who knew his super-excellent
qualities and testified to his being an undaunted buffalo hunter," and on his first appearance at St. Charles he gave them
a "specimen of that dexterous effrontery with which we became at a later period extremely familiar." Later he was called
by Latrobe "the indispensable Tonish" and "the sharp-witted
Tonish."[99] Finally, there is the principal description of the
Frenchman, somewhat anticlimactic in form but an excellent

[96] See pages 93, 96, 99, 110, 127, 138, 140, 146, and 152 below.

[97] It is true that no Journal exists for two periods of Irving's acquaintance
with Tonish: September 15–25, and October 18–30, both inclusive. But the
slightness of references in the existing Journals suggests that not much more
material about him would be found in the missing sections.

[98] *Rambler*, I, 149, 205, 178.

[99] *Ibid.*, 119–20 and 175, 177.

passage, nevertheless, because it emphasizes not merely his defects but also his notably good qualities:

Light, active, in the prime of life, no horse could take him by surprise; no inclined plane could throw him off his balance. He was a man of no mean qualifications. Full of make-shifts, and unspeakably useful in the woods, they were his home. A house was an abomination to him, and he was at a loss what to do with himself when he got within one. He possessed, however, a wife and family at Florissant, to whom his visits would seem to have been "few and far between." He was garrulous to excess, in spite of an impediment in his speech, in the form of a barrier, which it was necessary to break down by an effort, after which the words composing the meditated sentence, came tumbling out headlong. He was a weaver of interminable stories, all about himself and his hunting exploits. We soon found out that he was a most determined and audacious braggart; but it was sometime before we all came to the unanimous conclusion, that, for lying effrontery, none of us had ever seen his equal. In fact, such was the ingenious and whimsical way in which he could bring a host of little lies to cover a big one, that it became a matter of amusement with us to watch his manoeuvres.[100]

What both Irving and Latrobe seem to have failed to grasp was that Tonish was an example of the frontiersman who, whatever his racial origin, reveled in the telling of the tall tale. It is a pity that, having associated closely with such a lively specimen, both writers were so complacently superior, so immersed in stale literary tradition, so without understanding of an unfamiliar type that they missed the finest opportunity the trip offered them of originality and genuine truth of creation.

It remains for us to see what Ellsworth had to say that would justify Irving's representation of Tonish. Although Ellsworth had occasion to mention Tonish at least a dozen

---

[100] *Ibid.*, 147–48. Examples of characteristic behavior Latrobe gave in recounting the difficulty of Tonish over the presents of buffalo meat that he had promised to Colonels Chouteau and Arbuckle, and over the skunk that he was fattening for the table (*ibid.*, 245–46, 247).

times, not once does he make a disparaging remark. "He is a good cook—a fine hunter—a stranger to fear, and as fleet as a deer . . ." the commissioner wrote to his wife. "Whenever we came to swift water courses, whose depth was uncertain, either Billet or Tonish would plunge in, with horse or on foot, and many, very many, short fords were secured, by their daring intrepidity."[101]

When Irving and Ellsworth discovered that they had brought with them neither plates nor knives and forks, they were glad to find knives and forks in Tonish's saddlebags. When Ellsworth complained that he could not stand coffee or India tea, Tonish introduced tea made from goldenrod, which Mr. Irving was "so much pleased with" that he ordered (from whom?) a quantity for New York. When Irving's saddle girths broke and he was thrown from his horse, it was Tonish who repaired the girths. "Tonish was a wonderful fellow for strings; every pocket was full of something to mend with," Ellsworth remarked, "and we always called upon him for help of this kind and were never disappointed in getting aid." When holes were knocked in the coffeepot, Tonish could fix that, too. As a hunter, also, Ellsworth allowed Tonish some honor: he did not record repeated failures but he did report that the Creole shot buffalo and deer and noted his success in catching a wild horse. In the *Narrative* of Ellsworth there is nothing to sustain the concept of Tonish as he appears in the *Tour*.

And what did Tonish think of Irving? It is not often that a figure in a book can "talk back" to his originator, but, amusingly, we have a report of Tonish's opinion of Irving. I think it only fair to let him speak his mind. If the report is second-hand, so is Irving's account of the frontiersman.

[101] *Narrative*, 32. The quotations and comments in the following paragraph are from Ellsworth's *Narrative*, 12, 17, 35, 37, 104–105, 118, 110, 128.

St. Louis Missouri:[102]

My Dear Jones—   July 12. 1837

I must give you an early account of our yesterday's visit to the humorous little old town of Florissant situated in the midst of the flowers of the Prairie & celebrated enough as you shall see before I have concluded. Well then we were off before six o'clock to deliver a letter of introduction to a gentleman residing some twelve or thirteen miles from the city in the neighborhood of Florissant. A heavy mist accompanied us part of the way through the skirts of the city & the old French chateaus that are not altogether driven out by Yankee bustle & enterprize. We stopped on the rough edge of the Prairie which lies around the city where the scrub oak and marshy weeds ill set off by the thick fog gave us no impression of the beautiful flowers & plants that lay beyond us in the fields to give so pretty a name to little Florissant. Here we breakfasted with exceeding relish on bread and milk & were away again in the field. The mist gradually rolled away taking parting leave of the earth in a dim shadowy rainbow & I had my first view of the Prairie rolling away & broken into innumerable landscape with its unfenced fields of flowers and trees. A smooth level road lays through the Prairie which is rarely enclosed by fences and as B remarked it was a ride through a garden or the private lane on a gentleman's estate. We had spare seats in the barouche & I heartily wished you could occupy one of them. Jerry [?] the botanist should have had the other. What a fine lecture he would have delivered in the afternoon as we rode back over the same meadow on the rare bouquet of these wild flowers which was soon collected in a short stroll along the way. But I intend—all things well—you shall hear enough of Prairies hereafter so I will not trespass on them now.

We reached the gentlemans farm & found him absent when what next? Drive on Frank to Florissant. There must be some humors in that old French town of Florissant. We will drive there at any rate when I remembered that this was the home of that notorious scamp [?] & braggart of the woods, the celebrated *Tonish* of the "Tour to the Prairies." Here was the scent of an adventure & in good

---

[102] Evert A. Duyckinck to William A. Jones. I am indebted to the New York Public Library for a photostat of this letter.

spirits we alighted at the low roofed village inn where a good square
fat hostess whose Scoto-Irish I mistook for Frenchified English made
us sure of the best possible dinner. After a stroll through the village
which had a quiet well shaded appearance & just such a relief of repose
& pleasure as the cits sigh after from the hot city we returned to the
inn and enquired for Tonish—rather doubtingly as of a man of that
name who lived about the village, when she pointed to a house opposite[103]—one of the best in the street where she said Tonish lived & he
was now at home! We soon stepped down to the house & unlatching
his gate knocked at the door which stood open with a cross and saviour
piously hanging on the opposite wall. The feet of one of his daughters
—a pretty brunette—made their appearance on the stairs. Mr Antoine
was in the fields working at his farm but she would tell him two gentlemen had called upon him who were at the inn. In a little while we
observed from our stoop the gate opening over at Tonish's and a
thin [?] sized rather oldish man coming up towards us. He evidently
took us for youngsters in search for the Rocky mountains & in want of
a guide. At any rate I had shaken hands with him & we were all three
seated together in a trice. We told him we had heard of his fame &
being accidentally in the village thought we would call upon him. He
said yes Washington Irving had "made books" about him but he was
a bad man—told a great many things that were not so. Indeed I soon
saw that the Buffalo hunt & the more grievous scandal of the Indian
wife among the Osages were not palatable. Our hostess told us that
Tonish had threatened to make his own book of the journey. He did
cross the Arkansas in the Buffalo skin but he might have found a ford in
sight. Beatte the hunter & family had been swept off by cholera. He
liked Latrobe and Portales but there was no pleasing Irving. *Let me
meet Irving on one of the Prairies and one or other of us shall lose his
scalp!* And by way of reply to the Indian wife story he cautiously cast
his eye around on the stoop & whispered something very dark concerning Wash. Irving and a "yellow woman" at Fort Gibson.[104]
Tonish is a lithe active fellow—say five feet eight—about 45 yrs of

[103] At the time of his death (1854), Tonish was living in his house on
St. François Street; the lot, a 150-foot front, ran back 300 feet to Ste Catherine
Street.

[104] There was probably no more truth in this story than in many of the
statements Irving made about Tonish in the *Tour.*

age—is thin, has a dark sunken eye that looks mischief, stammers broken English and is celebrated in the village for the number of his family. Indeed I hardly looked out on the street but one of Tonish's wild Indian looking boys was in the field pulling at the legs of the goats that his eldest son brought from Santa Fe—racing with one another & some way or other on the alert. Tonish is evidently the great man of the village. He has seen a great deal of the world & is in repute for his friendship with the Indians. When these come to town they quarter upon Tonish. I would give a trifle to see his two piazzas crowded with the red men, smoking their pipes, to his delight & the admiration of all Florissant. This little place has its humors & one could spend a week there drawing out the trappers of the wilderness, wild blades of the desert & the other vagrant population at this skirt of the great Prairie. A trapper has just come home who has been six years in the Rocky Mountains. Tonish a year or more ago had a great wedding of one of his daughters & our hostess seemed to consider it very [?] for she remarked he was a most excellent cook.

But to our noon dinner. This was served up to us—muffins delicious—coffee good—fowl moderate, the chickens she said were too *supple* to be caught at this time of day, & salad superlative. We dined heartily—& I amused myself for the afternoon with watching the main street and Tonish's peaked roof extending over the piazzas—his father's plastered log house and corn mill—the old fellow[105] grinds all of the corn of the village by horse power—and the goats from Santa Fe not forgetting Tonish's outlandish dog that he had brought home from one of his expeditions—that had no [?] in him but by way of fierceness around the neck & at the tip of the tail.

So with a glorious ride through the Prairie homeward ended the day at Florissant—May we meet with many such together!

Let Mathers look out for a letter on the "Mounds." [?] too may enquire at the Post Office. To-morrow I shall go to Alton on the Mississippi & thence across Ilinois & Indiana by land to Louisville on our way to Virginia which after our late magnificent distances will be quite homeward—

Yours as Ever

Evert A. Duyckinck

[105] Hyacinthe Deshetres. See n. 89 above.

III

Often the spontaneous and unpremeditated account of a traveler's experiences is more effective from many points of view than the most carefully constructed artifice. Certainly we find this to be true whᴗᴗ we compare the Journals with the *Tour on the Prairies.* Tʰᵉ day-by-day jottings[106] which Irving made upon this memorable trip form a very interesting and valuable set of documents.[107] In them the passages in which the writer's romantic bias dictated a scene or a character are so few that they are negligible. The Journals are remarkably factual and reliable. Here Irving did not bother with fancies; he wanted facts, scenes, actions. We find a rich variety of detailed observation unhampered by literary ideas, uncolored by literary style.

Furthermore, the Journals give much more western material than the *Tour* gives. Of the first two Journals, part of the third, and the entire last one, Irving made no use in his book published in 1835. His notes of travel from Cincinnati to Fort Gibson, and from Fort Gibson down the Arkansas River, which add so greatly to the value of his account, he left in their original state, for they did not serve any literary purpose.[108]

[106] Ellsworth gives us several interesting glimpses of Irving writing up his Journals: "I reached the shore safely, and was greeted by my friend Mʳ Irving, who was busily filling his little sketch book, with the interesting events of the day;" "Before he sits down to write his sketches or other works, he always washes himself up nice, and with everything clean on him and around him, he says his ideas flow properly—but when he is dirty, the power of association dries up every literary pore;" "Several pages of Mʳ Irving's book is filled with the incidents of these 2½ hours" (*Narrative,* 42, 70, 111).

[107] The five extant Journals cover Irving's trip from Cincinnati (September 3) until he was on the Mississippi River, possibly two hundred miles below the Arkansas (November 17), with two exceptions: There is no journal for the trip from St. Louis to Independence (September 15–25) nor for the prairie excursion between October 18–30. At the end of each Journal there is a quantity of undated notations, gathered at odd times during the trip.

[108] "I have, as it were, plucked a few leaves out of my memorandum book, containing a month's foray beyond the outposts of human habitation, into the wilderness of the Far West. It forms, indeed, but a small portion of an extensive tour; but it is an episode, complete as far as it goes" (*Tour,* vi).

The scenes on the Ohio and the Mississippi rivers, the glimpses of Louisville, Ste Genevieve, St. Louis, and Independence, the road to Fort Gibson, the Indian missions, the trading establishments, the fort, steamboat travel on the Arkansas River, views of Little Rock and Arkansas Post, the many persons of all classes and occupations whom he watched and talked with—all these and more we find only in the Journals.

Irving was intensely interested in people. Ellsworth told his wife that the famous writer at this time desired most "to ramble among the natural actions of men" and to look "with microscopic eye into the hidden wheels that move men along, on the common walks of life."[109] In the Journals we find simple, quick sketches which do catch both the significance of the individual and the relation of the individual to his background. The farmer from Pennsylvania who was lonely for his neighbors and unhappy about the education of his children was not consoled by Indiana corn that grew fifteen feet tall. A little Frenchman and his wife, induced by a fellow countryman to come out to a crossroads paradise in Kentucky, were making their way cheerfully down river once more with their bedding, equipment for a café, and other worldly possessions. An Irishman in Paducah boasted of his wealth and of his great neighbor, Lord Castlereagh. Traders, Indian agents, army officers, rangers, missionaries, Indians, hunters, lawyers, politicians, farmers—there is scarcely a western type which is not here presented with some sharp, lifelike detail.

Irving missed no opportunity to observe ways of life in these regions new to him. The solitary cabin with its cornfields surrounded by forest, the great richness of soil that could produce fine crops for thirty-eight successive years, the abundance of game impressed him repeatedly. The showboat tied up at the bank of the river, the wooding stations, the travelers trying

[109] Ellsworth, *Narrative*, 71.

BUILDINGS IN CINCINNATI
from a pencil sketch by Washington Irving
on the first page of Journal I

Reproduced from a microfilm
of the original Journals

to thumb a ride on the steamboat, the shot towers at Her-culaneum, the arrangement of the common fields at Ste Gene-vieve—few activities that could be seen from the deck of a steamboat or at occasional landings escaped Irving's Journals. On the frontier he was equally interested in the affairs of the missionaries and the conduct of their Indian schools, and in the conditions of life among the Indians—their burial customs, their humor, their folklore. The bee hunt, the deer hunt, the buffalo hunt, the character of frontier towns, the appearance of the country through which he rode, the difficulties of travel through the Cross Timbers and the pleasantness of travel over the prairies—all these are recorded day by day as Irving ex-perienced them.

The importance of the Irving Journals lies not merely in the fact that the writer made note of these people and places and activities, but that he had an excellent eye for detail. In a few broken sentences he would catch effectively the spirit of his subject. Here, for instance, is an evening scene on the Ohio:

Steam boat aground with 2 flats each side of her—we take part of cargo on board—moonlight—light of fires—chant & chorus of negro boatmen—men strolling about docks with cigars—negroes dancing before furnaces—glassy surface of river—undulations made by boat—wavering light of moon & stars—silent, primeval forest sleeping in sunshine [moonlight?]—on each side still forest—forest—forest.

However, Irving sketched not merely the landscape pic-ture in his Journals; he recorded sweeping action as well:

A few miles further we see another Prarie wolf beside a ravine near the road—all set off in chase—Mr. Choteau & the doctor head him—come to a bare, burnt patch of prarie—the greyhound gets sight of him—fine race—hound turns him—manoeuvers & fight between wolf & hound—horsemen come up with [them] & try to trample on him—fighting retreat of wolf—Pourtales fires one barrel of his gun —breaks wolf's leg—we surround & kill him.

Beautiful sight of hunt. Horsemen galloping over green prarie—

golden sunshine—Antoine towards conclusion of chase leaves his waggon, mounts his stallion, & comes thundering along bringing up a corps de secours of bull-dog, cur, & c.

In addition to these excellent qualities, the Journals are historically valuable. Captain Bean was supposed to keep a journal of the expedition on the prairies; if he did so, it is not now to be found. Irving's Journals and Ellsworth's *Narrative* are the only firsthand, day-by-day accounts extant. The mere report of a minor military expedition is not particularly important, but the picture given of the conduct of such a party and of the casual and unmilitary behavior of such a detachment of irregulars is of definite historical interest.

From these records the student of western history receives a valuable report upon the topography of the region covered. The countryside along the road from Independence to Fort Gibson is described in detail unusual in most travel accounts; and the route over the Oklahoma prairies and through the Cross Timbers was one for the most part not hitherto reported.

These Journals are filled with glimpses of persons who have won some place in American history. General William Clark, Judge Stephen Ormsby, Black Hawk of the Sauk and Fox Indians, Clermont of the Osage, Colonel A. P. Chouteau, General Matthew Arbuckle, General Nicks, Nathaniel B. Dodge, William C. Requa, William F. Vaill, Henry L. Ellsworth, John Rogers the Cherokee, General William Montgomery of Arkansas, and others are described, briefly or at length, in such a way as to add to our understanding of them.

In his Journals, then, Washington Irving adds greatly to our knowledge of the actual West and Southwest of the 1830's, and he has also caught the spirit of the time and the region. The little books that he filled with daily notations prove to be vivid and stimulating documents, giving us vital insight into a most important, but inadequately known, period in the development of the United States.

The Western Journals of
WASHINGTON IRVING

JOURNAL I

Cincinnati, September 3—St. Louis, September 14,
1832

MONDAY *Sept. 3.* Left Cincinnati[1] at 5 oclock in the steam boat Messenger,[2] for Louisville— thunder showers—after which a remarkably clear tract in the west—moonlight night—mist on riv[er]—passenger on board wounded with slash in the face.

At Cincinnati saw Mr. Wood, with whom I once travelled in Rhode Is[an]d. [words illegible]

Tuesday Sept 4. Grey morning—in the night steam boat stops here & there where lights gleam on the wooded shore.

Stop at Madison in Indiana. Neat little place built of brick.[3]

Old negro steward—very black, with bright madras handkerchief on head—large feet, gold earrings—shirt collar up

---

[1] Cincinnati in 1832 had a population of 30,000.

[2] Flint listed a steamboat (130 tons) of this name as built at Pittsburgh in 1825 (*Geography and History of the Mississippi Valley*, II, 518).

[3] "*Madison*, . . . it has a population of about 1,500. The society here is pleasant, intelligent and moral. It is a place of much business, and is destined to be an important place," said Bache in his *Valley of the Mississippi*. Cumings, in *The Western Pilot*, said, "It has a fertile and flourishing back country, and is one of the most pleasant and thriving towns in the state. It was commenced in 1811, and is well built. The public buildings are a court house, bank, and two or three houses of public worship. A newspaper is also printed here."

to his ears—white jacket & trousers, chequered apron to his armpits.

Clearings on the banks of riv[er]—solitary log hut with corn fields among the forests—canoe by the shore.

Arrive at Louisville[4] ½ past 12—dine at Throgmorton.[5] Quay of city presents a motley scene—huts—steam boats— carriages—heaps of Iron—of lead—leather & c.

Take places on board the steamer Illinois from Louis- ville—after going on board we run ag[ain]st post—break some of the machinery and have to remain all night. Called in ev[enin]g on the mayor, Mr. Burkland, who once boarded with me at Mrs. Ryckman's[6]—Mr. Smith, & c, & c & c— Take warm bath.

Sept 5. All day detained by arrang[ing] of machinery— after dinner drove out in comp[an]y with fellow travellers & Capt Chambers to Judge Ormsbys.[7] Poplar 13 feet diameter —ruin of tree 45 feet round root—entrance, straggling road thro butternuts—grape vines—a wild stream running across the land—old negro & dogs—gate way built in stone—Swiss barn.

Wooden house among trees flanked by negro houses— negroes of all ages—[words illegible]—on our approach a little negro head seen at one of the windows of hut opposite —[phrase illegible]—few chairs—brass andirons—broken hole in ceiling over fire place & old litter of all kinds.

[4] In 1832 Louisville had a population of 15,000.

[5] Irving perhaps referred to Aris Throckmorton, veteran of the war of 1812, landlord of the Lower Blue Lick Springs Hotel and, from 1835–65, of the Galt House in Louisville.

[6] At 16 Broadway, New York City, where Irving and Henry Brevoort took rooms together in 1811. John C. Bucklin (not Burkland) was mayor of Louis- ville, 1828–33; in 1832 he was living on Jefferson Street, between Fourth and Fifth Streets according to Johnston in *Memorial History of Louisville* (I, 645, 86).

[7] Chambers was apparently captain of the *Illinois;* Stephen Ormsby was born in Ireland, went to Louisville and was admitted to the bar in 1786, served in Congress from 1810 to 1817, and later in the judiciary, and died in Louisville in 1846.

Bugle sounded to call Mr Ormsby—shy figure of negress
& white children stealing about house.

Little, well dressed negro girl brings in salver of peaches
—fat negro wenches, drying apples & peaches on board under
trees—wild gorse, flowers, & c, about house.

In neighbouring field negro boys exercising race horses—
flower garden—iron gate on cotton wood —stanchions—
flowers & fruits of various kinds.

Mr. Ormsby the younger comes home. Son of Judge by
an Irish [word illegible] woman. The latter is crazy &
lives [?] in a log hut on the farm—young Ormsby normal—
pretty wife—walk with him to see Elks [three words illegible]
wild geese.

Sept 6. Start at 9 o'clock—get to canal—machinery de-
ranged[8]—get there about 3.

Ev[enin]g scene on Ohio—steam boat aground with 2
flats each side of her. We take part of cargo on board—moonlight—light of fires—chant & chorus of negro boat men—
men strolling about docks with cigars—negroes dancing before
furnaces—glassy surface of river.—undulations made by boat
—wavering light of moon & stars—silent, primeval forest
sleeping in sunshine [moonlight?]—on each side still forest
—forest—forest.

Old negro steward scolding young negro for lying—He
aims at a monopoly.

Friday Sept 7. At 5 oclock morn[in]g stop to take on
wood and wait till fog rises—neat log hut—woman & 6 children—the latter half civilized and ignorant—abundance

[8] That is, the machinery of the canal. Latrobe wrote that they passed
through "the newly-constructed canal, which, by the aid of three noble locks at
the lower end, secures the uninterrupted navigation of the entire river. . . . All
obstacles overcome, we found ourselves once more fairly afloat on the bosom of
the river again. . . . At the lower extremity of the canal, and before the small
towns in the immediate vicinity, we left thirty or forty of the most splendid
steamers of the first class, waiting for a rise in the water." (*Rambler*, I, 101–102).

round the house—cattle, hogs, poultry, corn, forest, & c.—see patch of cotton plant in blossom.

9 oclock—river glassy—golden sunshine on forests—rude ark rowed by one man—roofed—with chimney, & c.

Ducks in couples on the river—cloudless sky—mellow weather—passengers on board. Black Hawk[9]—a young river dandy—green merino short coat—domestic cloth trousers— low crowned broad brimmed white hat—plays cards with a kindred genius.

All serenity—a Quakeress—the Princess Hullabulloo.

Saturday Sept 8. Detained from ten last night till 7 this morn'g by fog—an intelligent man comes on board—gives us ac[count] of his farming & c.

9 oclock—serene, sunny morn'g—clear reflection of objects—small flock of wild ducks doubled on the stream— bland atmosphere.

Pass Diamond Island[10]—well wooded.

Near Wabash—Horses ranging along sandy shore—long glassy reach of river—smoke rising on sunny shore. Stop for wood near Wabash on Virginia [Kentucky] side—negro woman in log hut—who cooks for the men who get wood—a cheerful, contented being—plenty to eat and drink—good whistling—no one to worry or trouble her—does not think she'll marry again. Mr. Ellsworth[11] asked about her children, but the tears started into her eyes—she got up—crossed the hut—["]I am not allowed to live with them—they are up at the plantation.["]

Pourtales[12] killed a racoon in the woods adjacent.

½ past 1 pass mouth of the Wabash—farm on left bank opposite the mouth on a wooded island—Wabash Island.

---

[9] Whoever this Black Hawk was, he is not to be confused with the Sauk chief.
[10] Cumings (*Western Pilot*, 61) located Diamond Island thirty-one miles above the mouth of the Wabash River.
[11] See Introduction, page 5, n. 4.
[12] See Introduction, page 11, n. 11.

Wabash enters peacefully into the peaceful riv[er]—water clear, greenish blue—Ohio yellow. Men on sand bar with a seine sack.

Aground near natives house—show boat on the Illinois shore with flag—groups assembled there—rifle shooting—horse race along shore—negro laugh—sunset—party breaks up—some in boat across glassy river singing ballad—others on horseback through the woods—some on foot—some loiter on the shore—beautiful, clear ev[enin]g sky—moon nearly full —rising over the Virginia [Kentucky] shore above tufted forests—night hawks.

Gross plenty that prevails throughout the country—in hotels, steam boats, &c.—meats, poultry, vegetables, excellent bread, pies, puddings—food seems to be wasted—as if of no value.

Passengers in steam boat from every part of Union—merch[an]t from N York—smug, dapper, calculating Yankee —reckless, boastful Virginian—Black Hawk from Kentucky —a Swiss count.[13]

Sunday 9th Sept. Still aground[14]—go to shore—log house

[13] The Swiss Count was obviously Pourtalès; Black Hawk was mentioned by Irving in the entry for September 7. Otherwise it is not possible to identify the passengers on the *Illinois*; of course, Irving would also have in mind the Englishman Latrobe and the Yankee Ellsworth, but Ellsworth is not the Yankee described.

[14] "The 'Illinois' was certainly not a fortunate boat, in spite of the horseshoe nailed to the capstan. After many scrapings and bumps upon the sand-bars and shoals with which at low water the Ohio is becoming more and more impeded from the vast quantity of alluvion washed down into it since the partial clearing of the forests, it was our lot, somewhere above the remarkable cavern called the 'Cave in Rock,' to share the fortune of two other steamers, and get so irreparably shoaled about sunset, that, after many hours spent in attempting to extricate ourselves, by carrying out anchor after anchor, the use of the lever, and furious press of steam, it was decided, that whether the prospect were agreeable or not, the vessel must be partially unloaded, and for this purpose lighters were procured from the nearest settlement. After a glorious moonlight night, finding that many hours must elapse before there was any possibility of moving, we went ashore, and passed the morning in the forests of Illinois; and it was not till after a detention of twenty-four hours, that we got in motion again" (Latrobe, *Rambler*, I, 113–14).

with cornfield in wood—man & his wife from Philadelphia County—good looking man, & woman & children decently clad—been here 15 years—if it were to be done over would not come here—no means of educating his children—wants neighbours—people in neighbourhood rough & rude—some live by hunting, poaching, &c.—says he finds a great difference in himself since he has been here—his sons prefer hunting to learning—pays 1½ doll[a]rs an acre for land—Indiana corn 15 feet high.

Stop at log house on the shore—pretty, delicate woman from near Nashville Tennessee—wishes herself back—no church in neighbourhood—people rude. If there comes a Quaker the rude fellows pelt him, & cut his horse loose, & play all kinds of tricks. Her husband a good looking young man. Has lease for 4 years, after which will return to Tennessee.

The fete yesterday was shooting for merchandise and a pedlars bout—a quarrel occurred & fighting.

Enormous sycamore—cotton-wood trees &c.—vines— white cranes.

Get off at 3 oclock—to see land at Rock Cave[15]—a limestone cavern—9 o'clock ev[enin]g arrive at mouth of Cumberland river[16]—land passengers—get aground & remain aground all night.

Monday Sept 10th. Eight oclock still aground—shower of rain—procure keel boat from Smithland[17] to take part of cargo and at ½ past 12 get off—fat old fellow in flat [?] rowed by negroes—with cargo of flour to sell. After dinner stop at

[15] Better known as Cave-in-Rock. This was on the right (Illinois) bank of the Ohio River, about thirty miles below the Wabash. Four years later Edmund Flagg described the cave graphically in his *Far West* (I, 72–74).

[16] The *Illinois* was now about forty miles below Cave-in-Rock. Apparently the captain did not heed sufficiently the warnings of such a manual as that of Cumings: "If you wish to stop at the mouth of the Cumberland, guard against a low bar, on the left, below the foot of Dog Island, and then keep close in to the left shore" (*Western Pilot*, 67).

Paduca,[18] a small village or town & quite new—court holding in piazza of post office—judge in linsey corduroy coat & trousers—deer skin sandals with hat on—seated in chair lolling back—farmers discussing their cause with hats on. Meet with an Irishman who has been out 6 years—56 years of age— lets me know immediately that he is a rich emigrant—talks of his neighbour Lord Castlereagh,[19] who was the greatest statesman in Europe.

Take on board here a little Frenchman and his wife who are rolling a big box through the country like a pair of tumblers. He is a blacksmith—she kept a caffé in Touraine— natives of Tours—beguiled out here by Frenchman, the same Lucas[20] who had bought land in Kentucky & represented it as a paradise—from turnpike could meet diligence every day— the very place to set up blacksmith shop & caffé—tells her to bring all the linen she c[oul]d. The little French[man] & his wife packed up all their worldly effects in three small boxes, bundled up their bed & embarked—landed at New Orleans— good opportunity presented to fix themselves, but rec[eive]d letter from their friend pressing them to come on—embarked in steam boat—arrived at the promised land & found it a wilderness covered with trees—the fine roads were 4 tracks thro' forest—the diligence a stage waggon that plied 2 months in year when there was no steam boat. They re-embark to return to New Orleans.

[17] Smithland, county seat of Livingston County, Kentucky, is immediately below the mouth of the Cumberland River. Maximilian, in *Travels in North America* (I, 203), described it in 1833 as "a small village . . . which reminded me of a little Brazilian villa, the houses, mostly one story high, lying in a row by the waterside."

[18] Paducah, laid out in 1827, the county seat of McCracken County, Kentucky, lies just below the mouth of the Tennessee River. Maximilian noted in 1833 that "the little village, Paduca, on the left bank of the Ohio, appeared to have much traffic, and a number of new shops had been built" (*Travels*, I, 203).

[19] Robert Stewart, Viscount Castlereagh, second Marquis of Londonderry (1769–1822). The Irishman whom Irving met was possibly from County Down.

[20] Frederick Lucas, one of Napoleon's soldiers, who came to America after Waterloo, finally settling in the West, according to Trent and Hellman in *The Journals of Washington Irving.*

A little Canadian who had been passenger on our boat hitherto was making arrang[emen]t with captain for them & wanted to know if no one on board spoke French. I offered my services.

8 at night—arrive at Caledonia[21]—at the point of confluence of Mississippi and Ohio[22]—land part of cargo.

Little Frenchman & wife go ashore—I speak to the landlord for them & put them under care of a passenger—rolled their big box up bank—carried bedding up to inn—little Frenchman remained on bank—put all his boxes together— lit fire—mounted guard by moonlight—left him humming tune & watching.

At 1 o'clock at night get under way—enter Mississippi by moonlight—

(Mem: This ev[enin]g a splendid sunset on Ohio—full moon rose from behind forest, attended by a virgin star).

Tuesday Sept 11. On the Mississippi—broad, turbid stream—sand bars—low, alluvial shores with forests— chemin de forge [raft] of snags—streaming files of ducks & geese. ½ past 8 land for wood on Missouri side—corn field, where crops of corn have been raised for 38 years successively, without manure—rich covering—sandy soil—level—sound, rich corn 20 rows on a cob—country still lonely—travellers— some adventurers embark without money—are put ashore at wood piles—remain there till next boat comes along—hoist a handkerchief on pole—taken on board—boat under way—too late to set them ashore—carry them to next pile—so they work their way from wood pile to wood pile.[23]

Woman with family of children appeals to capt—occa-

[21] Cumings, on his map No. 20, located Caledonia on the right, or Illinois, shore, about twenty miles above the mouth of the Ohio River; he did not mention the place in his text *(Western Pilot, 68–70)*.

[22] The town nearest the confluence at this time was Trinity, Illinois, about five or six miles above the Mississippi.

[23] Cf. Audubon's description of this country twenty years earlier (McDermott [ed.], "Audubon's Journey up the Mississippi," 150–65).

sionally get passage for nothing—a subscription among passengers.

Illinois merch[an]t on board—says he trusts for a year—then 25 per cent.

If a man won't pay, he hangs about him like fever & ague, whispering to him until he pays—does not lose above 5 per cent.

Go to farmhouse—woman spinning—young lad sitting idle—their beds in room—full of negro children—fat little round shaped one cries—the lad tells another child to amuse it by rolling ball on floor—have lived here 33 years—man says he never struck a negro since he was a boy—would not sell one unless the negro wished to go away.

House open to the weather—pigs, fowls, corn, vegetables, fruit—fine well of water—neighbouring cypress swamp—deer, bears, panthers, wild cats—turkeys in abundance—no snakes.

Wind now—pure soft air.

Frenchman the same Lucas who came to Touraine in grand way one winter & has not a negress.

Pass limestone cliffs looking like old castle towers—light foliage below—wild ducks—sand bars—after sunset stop at apple orchard—Mr. Kemmels new store & house—thriving place—children ill with fever—wife "first rate woman" educated in convent about 18 miles off—where there is also a seminary. She is from Kentucky.

Saw at the landing a negro merchant 36 years old—going to New Orleans with 40 doz. fowls—had canoe or boat with corn to feed them—goes down in steam boat—gets passage for nothing from some—buys 1$ doz. sells 3$—has followed the business 12 years—brings back nothing but money—pays his master 50$ a year—lays up money to buy himself free—buries it—cannot buy himself till next year—has wife & children but cannot buy them—means to go far where he can make most money—means to go [word illegible] where he can make most money but means to see his wife & children occasionally & take care of them.

The lady of the house says that there are different meetings here—Catholic, Presbyterian, Methodist & c.

Beautiful moonrise on Illinois—fire of woodman at front of island—red-yellow moon—silver star—calm, cobalt-green sky reflected in river—here & there at distances a solitary light twinkles down from some big house among the trees.

Moon regent of lakes & woods.

Wednesday Sept 12. Fog comes in about ½ past 4—stop at wood yard a few miles above Kaskaskia River—

visit log house—people from Louisiana—discouraged at the coldness of climate here—soil abundant—game plenty—hunt turkeys by moonlight—the settlers northern—anxious to return to Louisiana.

Ste. Geneviève[24] fine level with range of hills behind it to the north—one of the oldest French settlements—people live in the village where the houses are private property—20,000 acres in front in common—each one has a right to cultivate a portion for his own use—strangers apt to marry the Ste. Genevieve girls to get the right—college on hill back of the town—above the settlement pretty openings and views as through side scenes of a theatre—low banks of cotton trees—willows, & c.[25]

[24] Ste Genevieve, the oldest town in Missouri, was described by many travelers. In 1833 Maximilian noted: "St. Geneviève, an old French settlement, now a large village, with 600 or 800 inhabitants, is about twenty minutes' walk from the landing-place, and appears to be in a state of decline. . . . The houses, which are of one story, are separate from each other, and have, in general, a verandah in front. The church is built of red brick" (*Travels*, I, 211). Cumings estimated the population at about 2,000 and declared that it was "a place of considerable business" (*Western Pilot*, 76).

[25] "One fence encloses the whole village field, and this is kept up at the common expense. The river side is left open, the steepness of the bank rendering any enclosure unnecessary. This field is divided into a number of small lots, of an equal size; a certain number of arpents in front, and a certain number in depth.

Ste. Genevieve. Tall man comes on board with saddle bags, steel traps, bundle—conducted by man in blanket coat & moccasins—turns out to be Col. Menard, who accompanied Atwater on the Indian expedition.[26]

Herculaneum—store—shot tower on brink of limestone precipice—beautiful precipice of limestone like towers of ruined castles, with many-tinted Virginia creeper hanging about the cold grey.[27] Land on island—immense cotton-wood

The more wealthy possess and cultivate several of these lots, while some of the poorer class do not own one entire. But nearly all the inhabitants have a share in them; they were ceded by the Spanish government, as an appendage to the possession of every resident in the village" (Brackenridge, *Views of Louisiana*, 227–28). The French and Spanish grants were commonly one arpent front by forty arpents deep (the arpent being .8449 English acres). Houck, in his *History of Missouri* (II, 234), gave the size of the "Big Field" at Ste Genevieve as about three thousand acres, and declared that in 1907 it was still being cultivated as a common field under a common fence.

"Beyond the first bottom rises a second steppe, and behind this yet a third, attaining an elevation of more than one hundred feet from the water's edge. Upon this elevated site was erected, some twenty years since, a handsome structure . . . intended for a literary institution; but, owing to the unfavorable reports with regard to the health of its situation, the design was abandoned, and the edifice was never completed. It is now in a state of 'ruinous perfection,' and enjoys the reputation, moreover, of being *haunted*. In very sooth, its aspect, viewed from the river at twilight, with its broken windows outlined against the western sky, is wild enough to warrant such an idea or any other" (Flagg, *Far West*, I, 96). Flagg's eyesight obviously was splendid, for the town was a mile from the river! The Ste Genevieve Academy was granted a charter in 1808 and occupied, in 1810, its still existing building.

[26] Pierre Menard (1766–1844) was born in Canada and, after some years at Vincennes, settled at Kaskaskia in 1790. He served as an officer in the Illinois militia, as a member of the Territorial legislature (1812–18), and as lieutenant governor (1818–22); he was also an important figure in the fur trade. He was twice married, first to Thérèse Godin, then to Angelique Saucier.

In 1829 Caleb Atwater (1778–1867) was appointed a commissioner to serve with Pierre Menard and General John McNeil of the United States Army in making treaties with the Indians at Prairie du Chien. An account of his trip ("Remarks Made on a Tour to Prairie du Chien; thence to Washington City, in 1829") will be found in his *Writings*, 167–392.

[27] Herculaneum, about thirty miles below St. Louis, was founded by Moses Austin in 1808. Maximilian, in 1833, said that it contained about thirty houses. Bryant, in "Illinois Fifty Years Ago," said: "Near a place called Selma I saw where one of these precipices was made into a tower, for the purpose of converting the lead of the neighboring mines into shot. A small wooden building projects over the verge of a very high perpendicular cliff, and the melted lead falls from the floor of this building into a vat at the foot of the precipice filled with water" (page 12).

trees—Uncle Sam's land, with poachers cutting & selling wood.

Ev[enin]g, 9 oclock—crash! A steam boat, the Yellow Stone,[28] coming down the stream at the rate of 15 miles an hour runs on us & staves in the upper works of our side—the wheel box—general alarm—some think the boat sinking— Kentucky lady threw herself into her husband's arms—alarm subsides—make for land to repair damages & mend wheel— speech of black fireman: ["]They have torn the d—— b—— all to sallad.["]

Arrive at S[t]. Louis[29] about 11—sleep on board.

Thursday Sept 13. S[t]. Louis—mixture of French & American character—French billiard room—market-place where some are speaking French, some English—put up at Union Hotel[30]—see Mr. Chouteau père et fils—Dr. O'Dwyer —Judge Peck—Mr. Bates.[31]

[28] The steamer *Yellowstone* was built at Louisville in the winter of 1830–31. In the spring of 1831, on its maiden voyage, it went as far up the Missouri River as Fort Tecumseh. See Introduction, page 14.

[29] The city of St. Louis in 1832 had a population of 6,918, of whom 5,227 were white, 296 were free colored, and 1,395 were slaves; the population of St. Louis County (which then included the city) was 16,796 (*Niles' Register*, XLIII [November 24, 1832], 196).

[30] In 1836 the Union Hotel, kept by H. Farrish, was located at Prune and First Streets *(The St. Louis Directory for 1836–7).*

[31] Chouteau *père* was, of course, Pierre Chouteau (1758–1849), who moved to the new town of St. Louis in 1764 and became one of the chief figures in the fur trade, as well as a person of great influence with the Indians. Chouteau *fils* might possibly be Auguste Pierre (1786–1838), the oldest son, with whom the Irving party traveled down to Fort Gibson, or it might be Pierre Chouteau *fils*, the second son (1789–1865), who was the resident manager of the Chouteau fur interests.

Dr. Thomas O'Dwyer in 1833 was an assistant surgeon stationed at Fort Smith. He traveled with Ellsworth from St. Louis to Independence. See the entries for September 27 and 28, and October 3.

James Hawkins Peck (*ca.* 1790–1836) was born in Jefferson County, Tennessee, settled in St. Louis in 1818, and four years later was appointed first judge of the United States District Court of Missouri. He died in St. Charles, Missouri.

Edward Bates (1793–1869) came to St. Louis in 1814, at the suggestion of his brother, Frederick. He was admitted to the bar in 1816, was elected to Congress in 1826, and served in the state senate from 1830 to 1834. About 1828 he

Drive out to Gov. Clark's[32]—cross prairie—flowering & fragrant shrubs—the Gov[ernor's] farm—small cottage— orchard bending & breaking with loads of fruit—negroes with tables under trees preparing meal—fine sitting room in open air—little negroes whispering & laughing—civil negro major domo who asks to take horses out—invites us to walk in the orchard & spreads table with additional covers—sitting-room —rifle & game bag &c. in corners—Indian calumet over fireplace—remains of fire on hearth, showing that morng has been cool—lovely day—golden sunshine—transparent atmosphere—pure breeze.[33]

Fine nut trees, peach trees, grape vines, catalpas &c. &c. about the house—look out over rich, level plain or prairie— green near at hand—blue line at the horizon—universal chirp and spinning of insects—fertility of country—grove of walnuts in the rear of the house—beehives—dove cote—canoe— Genl arrives on horseback with dogs—guns. His grandson on a calico poney hallowing & laughing—Genl on horseback— gun on his shoulder—cur—house dog—bullying setter.

Gov. Clark fine healthy robust man—tall—about 50— perhaps more—his hair, originally light, now grey—falling on his shoulders—frank—intelligent—his son a cadet of W. P. now in the army—aid de camp to Genl Atkinson.[34]

moved to Dardenne Prairie, St. Charles County, Missouri; he returned to practice law in St. Louis in 1842. His most notable public office was that of attorney general in Lincoln's cabinet.

[32] An excellent description appears in Flagg, *Far West*, 258–59.

[33] For another account of Governor Clark's home, see Flagg, *Far West*, 259.

[34] William Clark (1770–1838) was named brigadier general of militia for Louisiana Territory in 1807, and was governor of Missouri Territory from 1813 to 1821. In 1832 he was sixty-two, had no grandsons at this time. This must have been his son by his second marriage, Jefferson Kearny Clark, born 1824.

Meriwether Lewis Clark was a cadet at West Point from July 1, 1825 to July 1, 1830. He served first at Jefferson Barracks, St. Louis, and from July 22, 1831 until his resignation May 31, 1833, he was aide-de-camp to Brevet Major General Gaines. A document in the Clark Papers (Missouri Historical Society) informs us that the governor of Illinois named him aide-de-camp with rank of colonel in the Volunteers, June 10, 1832.

Brigadier General Henry Atkinson (1782–1842) was in command of

Dinner plentiful—good—hut rustic—fried chicken, bacon and grouse, roast beef, roasted potatoes, tomatoes, excellent cakes, bread, butter, & c.

Gov. C. gives much excellent information concerning Indians.

His slaves—set them free—one he placed at a ferry—another on a farm, giving him land, horses, & c.—a third he gave a large waggon & team of 6 horses to ply between Nashville and Richmond. They all repented & wanted to come back.

The waggoner was York,[35] the hero of the Missouri expedition & adviser of the Indians. He could not get up early enough in the morng—his horses were ill kept—two died—the others grew poor. He sold them, was cheated—entered into service—fared ill. ["]Damn this freedom,["] said York, ["]I have never had a happy day since I got it.["] He determined to go back to his old master—set off for S^t. Louis, but was taken with the cholera in Tennessee & died. Some of the traders think they have met traces of York's crowd, on the Missouri.

Returned by another route escorted by young Clark[36]—ride thro prarie—flowers—waggon—huts, etc.—pass by a noble farm—every thing in abundance—pass by a circle of Indian mounds—on one of them Genl Ashley has built his house so as to have the summit of it as a terrace in the rear.[37]

---

the *Yellowstone* expeditions of 1819 and 1825, and of the United States troops in the Black Hawk War. He established Jefferson Barracks in 1826 and commanded there until his death.

[35] For York, consult index to Thwaites (ed.), *Original Journals of Lewis and Clark.*

[36] Either Jeff Clark or, possibly, his brother G. R. Clark (born 1816).

[37] William Henry Ashley (1778–1838) was a fur trader, general of militia, lieutenant governor of Missouri, and representative in Congress for Missouri. According to Frederic Billon, Ashley in 1826–27 built (near Broadway and Biddle Street) "a very fine house, on one of the lower Indian mounds, which he occupied for a number of years. The grounds [eight acres] were beautifully laid out and improved, with a fine fountain in front, the first thing of its kind we had in St. Louis" (quoted in Scharf, *History of Saint Louis*, I, 196–97).

St. Louis—old rackety gambling house—noise of the cue & and the billiard ball from morning till night[38]—old French women accosting each other in the street.

Friday Sept 14. Drive out with Judge Peck, Judge's uncle,[39] & our party to Fort Jefferson[40] to see Black Hawk— ride thro open country—formerly forest—drive to Genl Atkinson's quarters.

Black Hawk.[41] old man upwards of 70 with aquiline nose —finely formed head—organs of benevolence[42]—his two sons —oldest a fine-looking young man—his brother in law the prophet[43]—the little Indian stables.

They are all chained arms & ankles with cannon, but are allowed to walk about escorted by soldier.

[38] The first billiard tables in St. Louis were set up in 1767, according to Billon in *Annals of St. Louis, 1764–1806* (86).

[39] Trent and Hellman read this word as *uncle;* it is possible that Irving wrote *Easton.* Rufus Easton (1774–1834) came to St. Louis in 1804, was one of the first judges of the territory of Louisiana, and served in other public offices. In 1822 he moved to St. Charles, where he lived until his death. It is not unlikely that he was in St. Louis when Irving was there.

[40] Jefferson Barracks, established in 1826, is about one mile below the present boundary of St. Louis; the St. Louis of Irving's day was about ten miles from the Barracks.

[41] The Black Hawk party arrived in St. Louis a few days before the Irving party: "The Steam Boat Winnebago, Capt. Hunt, from Galena, stopped for a few minutes yesterday at the wharf, on her way to Jefferson Barracks (ten miles below the City). The boat left Galena having on board BLACK HAWK, the Prophet and eleven other head men of the Sacs and Foxes, together with about fifty Warriors of less distinguished fame. The latter were landed on this side of the Lower Rapids, on their pledge of remaining quiet and inoffensive. Black Hawk, the Prophet and the other eleven have been taken to Jefferson Barracks, there to remain as hostages for the peaceable conduct of their tribes until the final settlement of all difficulties shall be made. . . ." (*St. Louis Times,* as quoted in the *Missouri Republican* [St. Louis], September 11, 1832). Maximilian saw Black Hawk in the spring of 1833, just before he started on his first Eastern tour, and described him then as "a little old man, perhaps seventy years of age, with grey hair, and a light yellow complexion; a slightly curved nose, and Chinese features, to which the shaven head, with the usual tuft behind, not a little contributed."

[42] Apparently the opinion of Dr. O'Dwyer, whom the travelers had met in St. Louis the day before, and who was to travel with them to Fort Gibson. See Introduction, page 16, n. 18.

[43] The elder son, Nah-se-us-kuk (Whirling Thunder), according to Catlin (in *Letters and Notes on the North American Indians*), was "a very handsome

83

Old French town nicknamed Vuide Poche[44]—old French settlers retain their dress, manners &c.—cared little for money or lands, but avaricious [?] about their negroes. Met two or three times a week to dance—very sober and temperate tho gay—kept aloof from Americans but begin to intermarry with them.

Black Hawk—had a skin of a black hawk in his hand & fanned himself with the tail.[45]

[*The following undated notes are found when this Journal is reversed.*][46]

Cumberland Mount[ains]—sunny, enchanted mounts.

On some spurs of the Cumberland Mounts, called the Enchanted Mounts, are marked in the solid limestone footsteps of men, horses, and other animals, as fresh as though recently made, and as distinct as tho impressed upon clay mortar. The tracks often indicate that the feet which made them had slidden, as would be the case in descending declivities in soft clay. They are precisely of the same class with the impress of two human feet found in a block of solid limestone, quarried

---

young warrior, and one of the finest-looking Indians I ever saw." The younger son was Wa-saw-me-saw (Roaring Thunder), according to Catlin. Hodge gives their names as Nasheakusk (Loud Thunder) and Nasomsee or Gamesett.

Wabokieshiek, or White Cloud, also known as the Prophet and the Winnebago Prophet (1794–1841), was half Winnebago and half Sauk; Irving seems to be the only authority for the statement that the Prophet was the brother-in-law of Black Hawk.

[44] Carondelet, nicknamed "Vide Poche," was first settled in 1767, and was later named for the Baron de Carondelet, governor of Louisiana; in 1876 it was incorporated into St. Louis.

[45] It was in this characteristic pose that Catlin painted Black Hawk: "When I painted this chief, he was dressed in a plain suit of buckskin, with strings of wampum in his ears and on his neck, and held in his hand, his medicine-bag, which was the skin of a black hawk, from which he had taken his name, and the tail of which made him a fan, which he was almost constantly using" (Catlin, *Letters and Notes on the North American Indians*, II, 211). For portraits of Black Hawk, his two sons, the Prophet, and others, see *ibid.*, plates 283–89. For the individuals concerned, see Donaldson, *George Catlin Indian Gallery* (1885), 22–36.

[46] First appear a few almost completely illegible notes, among which one can pick out "Gen¹ Ashley," "Judge Wash," "mosquito bar," and "shoes." Several other items seem to be notes concerning purchases.

on the margin of the Mississippi.[47] The manner in which they were produced is utterly inexplicable.

Flint Essay, Vol II, "Tennessee."[48]

Screaming of the jay in the solitudes of the woods and mountains. Pine woods—solemn sound of the wind thro them—no whispering among leaves. Few evergreens in the west—objected by Mrs. Trollope—a sign of futility.[49]

The cypress grows in deep & sickly swamps—the haunts of fevers mosquitoes moccasin snakes alligators & all loathsome and poisonous animals, & c.

It loves the deepest, most gloomy & inaccessible and inundated swamps, and south of 33° is generally found covered with the sable festoons of long moss, hanging as it seems a shrowd of mourning wreaths almost to the ground. It flourishes best where water covers its roots for half the year.

Flint, V. 1 P 62[50]

Hunter's ac[count] of himself—his father's log hut solitary on margin of river, surrounded by forest—mode of living, careless—plenty—shot deer, wild turkey—children half wild—without education—two or three books which they could not read.

Big rivers—all peaceful & gentle—[word illegible] Ohio

Little rivers noisy & unruly

[47] Consult H. R. Schoolcraft, "Remarks on the Prints of Human Feet, Observed in the Secondary Limestone of the Mississippi Valley," *American Journal of Science*, V (1822), 223–31. Rapp moved this stone from St. Louis to (New) Harmony, Indiana, where it now may be seen.

[48] Flint, *Mississippi Valley*, II, 12–13.

[49] ". . . in Tennessee, Indiana, and Ohio, I never found the slightest beauty in the forest scenery. . . . The beautiful variety of foliage afforded by evergreens never occurs; and in Tennessee, and that part of Ohio that surrounds Cincinnati, even the sterile beauty of rocks is wanting" (Trollope, *Domestic Manners*, 32).

[50] Flint, *Mississippi Valley*, I, 62. The quotation, in which Irving has not been strictly accurate, begins with the sentence following the reference to Mrs. Trollope.

Invincible strength of big, giant rivers.

Two Kentuckians quarrelling—one says, ["]Put down that rock & I'll fight you.["] The rock was a stone as big as an apple.

Double-barreld gun—mighty little giving about the lock. [six words illegible]

Moon—handmaid, a virgin star.

Missouri—50 miles above confluence of Ohio and Mississippi.[51]

Indian corn—38 years successive crops—ground rich—20 rows.

Negro driving team of 6 oxen in Louisville exclaims—["]Get along, you fat money making rascals.["]

Negroes—some prefer hoeing—others ploughing—others driving wagons—some dislike wagoning because they have to take care of the cattle at night & on Sunday. Merriest people in these parts—if you hear a broad, merry laugh, be sure it is a negro—politest people—fine gentlemen.

Evil of negroes—they may be parted from their children —but are not white people so, by schooling, marriage, business, &c?

Observation of French trader in West Indies on shutting up country house: ["]If I could go home & not think till morning, I should be a happy man, but this thinking will kill me.["]

Ice spring between Niagara & Hamilton—frozen in summer—thawed in winter.[52]

[51] What Irving meant by this note is not at all clear. According to Cumings, the Missouri River was 191 miles above the Ohio River (*Western Pilot,* 71–83). Perhaps Irving was recording the location of the corn crops mentioned in his next note.

[52] Irving was at Niagara late in August. Latrobe described the Falls at length but did not mention this spring.

Illinois—famous for children & dogs—in house with 19 children and 37 dogs.

Chèrokees & Kickapoos used to say will fight, fight, fight, until we are all dead & then our bones will fight together— but they are now neighbours and friends thro necessity.[53]

The various western tribes call the Delaware their grand-father & mediator. If one kills another, a friend, relative of the murderer, hastens to the Delaware who interposes & prescribes a certain quantity of wampum to cover the deceased.

Indians never quarrel & fight when sober—only when in liquor—& then lay it all to whisky. When one kills another he considers himself doomed—sometimes mounts his horse & proclaims it—but says ["]Come and take me who can.["]

[53] These notes concerning Indians were quite likely derived from William Clark in St. Louis. At this time Irving had not come in contact with the Cherokee or the Delaware. He did not visit the Kickapoo Reservation in Kansas.

JOURNAL II

Independence, September 26—Cabin Creek

October 6, 1832[1]

INDEPENDENCE. *Wednesday Sept 26*[th].[2] Arrived at the Globe Hotel—M[r] Dodge a former missionary among the Osages, comes in a covered waggon with his son & c.[3] —disagreed with the Indians—is settled near the White Hairs —among the Osages—keeps school—feathers his nest. The Southern Indians more shrewd and intelligent than the Northern.

[1] No notebook exists for the trip from St. Louis to Independence; for an account of this part of the travels see Introduction, pages 17–20.

[2] Independence, county seat of Jackson County, Missouri, was laid out in 1827. "Our last halting-place before entering the Indian Territory," John T. Irving wrote in 1833, "was at Independence, a small town on the Missouri River, containing about twenty or thirty houses, a court-house, and a non-descript population of trappers, Indian traders, and frontiersmen. It seemed to be the starting-place for all kinds of adventurers . . ." (*Indian Sketches*, 11–12). "The site of the town is beautiful, and very well selected, standing on a high point of land, and overlooking the surrounding country, but the town itself is very indifferent; the houses, (about fifty,) are very much scattered, composed of logs and clay, and are low and inconvenient. There are six or eight stores here, two taverns, and a few tipling houses" (Townsend, *Narrative of a Journey Across the Rocky Mountains to the Columbia River* [1834], 135).
Latrobe stated that he, Irving, and Pourtalès arrived at Independence on the afternoon of September 24 (*Rambler*, I, 126).

[3] Nathaniel B. Dodge (1781–1884) was born in Washington County, Vermont, married Sally Gale (1784–1866) in 1803, came out to Harmony Mission in 1821, and was superintendent of Harmony until 1829. In that year he may have had some trouble, because he moved from the Mission to Independence.

The Western Journals of Washington Irving

Mr. McCoy—son of missionary—employed as surveyor.[4]

Thursday Sept 27. This morn'g M[r]. Ellsworth & D[r]. O'Dwyer arrive in old, flimsy carriage with two horses driven by a tall negro. Had left the steam boat aground & come by land.[5]

Preparation—packing of waggons—Genl Clark—thinks the clergymen the only class of people on earth that he hates—thinks we ought not to set our faces ag[ain]st Indians stealing horses—must not shut up only road left them to honour & promotion.

Waggons set off at ½ past 2 oclock.—M[r] Ellsworth & M[r] Latrobe set off about 3 with Genl Clark for Mr. McCoys.[6] I set off at three with Mr. Choteau,[7] Pourtales, & the Dr.

The next year, however, he established Boudinot Mission on the Neosho River (see page 99, n. 31 below) and remained there until 1835. He then moved to Vernon County, Missouri, and settled on the Little Osage River in Metz township. His children were (Dr.) Leonard, Philena, Sally, Nathaniel B. Jr., Jonathan Edwards, Samuel N., Thomas S., and Harriet. Some of his descendants live in Vernon County today. On September 17, 1832, he had left Boudinot with "some of our young men to procure a place & means for their education" (Nathaniel B. Dodge to David Green, December 1, 1832, A.B.C.F.M. MSS, Harvard-Andover Theological Library). No doubt he was headed east on this trip when Irving met him.

[4] The surveyor employed by the government was Isaac McCoy, who, on occasion, hired his sons to assist him. The one referred to by Irving must have been John Calvin McCoy, who a year later laid out the town of Westport; for Dr. Rice McCoy, who had assisted on a number of surveys, died in June, 1832.

[5] Latrobe wrote that Ellsworth and the doctor "finally had been obliged to leave the boat aground, about one hundred miles below Independence, and get forward through the woods as best they might. Judging from the querulous tone which pervaded their remarks, we concluded that the journey had been far from agreeable" (*Rambler*, I, 127).

"The Doctor was, I am happy to say, quite an unnecessary appendage, and I believe he would have felt no disappointment, had his lot been cast otherwise, as this kind of adventurous life was not consonant with his tastes. He had not made up his mind to all those petty troubles which are unavoidable beyond the pale of civilization . . ." (*Ibid.*, 146). Ellsworth, however, gives a different impression of him: "My late travelling companion, Doct O Dwyer says, Eden was here [on the western prairies], and not on the Euphrates—'Adams paradise was in these praries'!!" (*Narrative*, 61).

[6] Marston G. Clark, Kansa Indian agent.

"In the evening of the 27th I accompanied the Commissioner alone to the Shawanese Agency on the frontier" (Latrobe, *Rambler*, I, 143). Apparently they

Lose our way in the Praries—after a while get to where the waggons are stationed—by Mr. Yates[8]—scene at Mr. Yates—log hut—large fire—tell stories to children.

Camp—fire—meat roasted on sticks—savory—our salon of trees lighted up by fire—sky & stars in centre—bat flitting across—faces of men & black boy roasting meat—greyhound with spectral face[9]—we sit on bear skins & the meat put on spits before us—cut it off with knife & eat—coffee—Mr. Yates comes & sits with us—tall, strong, pleasant faced fellow—stretch a tent on cords—spread our mats and sleep—Mr. Choteau sleeps at foot of tree.—Dr. O'Dwyer in waggon—men on blankets with feet to fire.

Friday, 28. At peep of day fire made in the camp—preparations for cooking—water bro[ught] from neighbouring brook—dogs prying about for food—showers of rain—mats & c. spread over waggons—day breaks—find ourselves in a light grove on the edge of a prarie.

Horses led in strings to water—man riding one, leading other—whooping to hounds who follow.

Breakfast like supper—spits placed before us as we sit on mats & cut off strips—

Leave at quarter to 8—ride along ridge & over grassy prarie—meet people going to camp meeting—encamp at 12

must have gone both to the Shawnee Agency, where Ellsworth talked with Major R. C. Cummins, the agent, and to Isaac McCoy's house—see Ellsworth's letter of October 9, page 24 above. McCoy had just returned home on September 24. About this time McCoy acquired a farm in what is now Kansas City—55th Street to 64th Street, Belleview Avenue to the State line. It is possible, however, that he was living at the Shawnee Mission (which he had established a year earlier) just west of the Missouri state line and about seven miles from the junction of the Kansas and Missouri rivers.

[7] A. P. Chouteau, according to Latrobe, had come overland from St. Louis but separately from the Irving–Pourtalès–Latrobe party, and had arrived at Independence on the evening of September 24.

[8] This name may be Gates. Apparently he lived in Jackson County, Missouri, six or eight miles south of Independence.

[9] William, a black boy belonging to Colonel Chouteau; the greyhound, called Henry Clay, also belonged to Chouteau.

beside a brook to wait for Ellsworth & Latrobe who are to come in by McCoy's trail. A couple of Bee Hunters arrive at the brook, with waggon driven [drawn?] by 4 oxen—with barrels & c. to contain Honey—going to Grand river about 2 days journey from Independence[10]—all the country down here being hunted out—Bee hunter—23 years of age—plaid upper coat—tan cloth trousers with deer skin tied over them —his companion lying in waggon with rifle—Prarie hen that they had shot.

Midday camp—men dispersed cutting wood—one making fire—blowing up spark among dry leaves—horses turned loose—some hobbled, others free—rolling on grass—saddles put round foot of tree—dogs scattered about nosing & prying —Dr. O'Dwyer dragging dry branches—wind rustling thro tree tops but passing over the hollow in which we are placed.

Dogs lying down watching with hungry eye all the cook operations.

At dinner—stories, jokes, & c.

After dinner another gang of bee hunters—waggon—4 oxen—2 saddle horses—long fellow with rifle—two younger ones with rifles—says they get 37 cents gallon for honey— collect 100 or 150 gals—go for amusement as much as anything else, being a time of year they have little to do—shoot deer elk & c. for their food.

In the ev[enin]g Mr Ellsworth, Mr Latrobe, and young Mr. McCoy arrive with another dearborn waggon[11]—encamp for the night.

10 The Grand River enters the Missouri River from the north, between Carroll and Chariton counties, about one hundred miles below Independence. Irving describes a bee-hunt on October 13.

11 "The following day [September 28] we struck across the wide prairies to overtake our companions, who had meanwhile left Independence, cutting the Santa Fe traders' trail, and, finally bending more to the southward, hit upon that of our own party, which we followed till we found them encamped in the twilight in a low skirting of wood under the edge of the prairie" (Latrobe, *Rambler*, I, 143).

Saturday 29. Start after breakfast—Mr. Younger who was to have driven our new dearborn deserts—Mr Ellsworth drives—road winds along a ridge—with prarie sloping down into beautiful copses.[12]

Stop at log house, pretty young married woman with pretty sister & fine child. Encamp at midday after 18 miles—in pine grove—repast under tree—preparations of guns—Latrobe arranging plants[13]—dogs lying about—plan for Antoine[14] to go deer hunting while we journey this afternoon—yelping of young hounds—wind rushing thro trees—fire at our kitchen at foot of gigantic old tree, threatening to undermine and bring it down—autumnal tint of trees.

Ev[enin]g encampt about 5 oclock on a beautiful plat of land made by the winding of a sluggish brook—fine oak & walnuts—herbage full of flowers[15]—opposite banks of brook fine woods—Mr. Latrobe saw two stags—Antoine returns without game.

Barking of dogs at wolves prowling round the camp— hooting of owl—pond nuts like fresh almonds—dined buffalo meat—rich.

Sunday, 30. Morning, rise before daybreak—breakfast by light of fire—day breaks thro forest.

After breakfast set off with Pourtales on horseback ahead of the rest to look for prarie hens—Mr. Latrobe precedes us on foot.

[12] Their road was south from Independence to Harmony Mission, cf. Tixier's description of the countryside eight years later (McDermott and Salvan, *Tixier's Travels*, 105–10).

[13] Latrobe was an amateur botanist, among other things; see *Rambler*, I, 125–26; Ellsworth, *Narrative*, 69.

[14] Irving's first reference to Tonish—Antoine Deshetres—for whom see Introduction, pages 16, 49–62, and n. 89.

[15] "You may have some idea of this class of open country, by recollecting the general outline of our higher and more extensive moorlands—allowing your fancy to clothe them with a deep rich soil, instead of dark peat, and with a carpet of the brightest flowers and grass from six inches to six feet in height, according to circumstances, instead of monotonous purple heather" (Latrobe, *Rambler*, I, 154).

93

Scale a hill—limestone rock & stones full of shells and miniature basalt like Giant's Causeway—boundless view of silent Praries—distant hill like Paté de Strasbourg. Overtake Latrobe 12 miles off by a brook—waggons do not arrive—wait for them—scene on knoll—lying among prarie grass with guns —dogs—game—horses grazing by us—one & the other go alternately as scouts to edge of distant hill to look out for waggons—

give up hopes of being rejoined and resume our route— Mr. Latrobe on foot—Pourtales & myself on horseback— fatiguing ride—wide, bare praries—small strips of woodland —12 miles further on come on a clearing in wood—log house —M[r] Fuller of East Hadham[16]—his wife daughter of Dr. ———, of Philadelphia—hospitable reception—good wife busy baking cakes—gets dinner for us—countryman arrives who brings tidings from the camp—horses had strayed. While at dinner Mr. Ellsworth arrives—then Col Choteau and dr. Take leave of Mr. Fuller, who refuses compensation—ride with Mr. Latrobe by moonlight to Harmony Mission—arrive at Mr. Bright's—kind reception—blazing fire—half breed Indian girl who waits on us—Mr. Requa a missionary.[17]

Quartered at night with M[r] Jones,[18] missionary who teaches girls—several Indian girls in the house—one about 11

[16] Fuller must have been living in Bates County, south of the present town of Butler, for the party was now within a "moonlight ride" of Harmony Mission.

[17] Harmony Mission was founded in 1821 by the United Foreign Missionary Society (Presbyterian) among the Great Osage; in the following year White Hair moved his village to the Neosho River in Kansas, but the Mission flourished until about 1836. It was located on the Marais des Cygnes (Osage) River, about six miles above its junction with the Little Osage. Samuel B. Bright was the farmer at Harmony Mission. For accounts of the mission see *History of Vernon County, Missouri*, 144–51, and Atkeson, *History of Bates County, Missouri*, 50–73, 309–14.

For William C. Requa, see page 107, n. 3 below. Apparently, Irving met Requa at Harmony, not at Hopefield.

[18] Amasa Jones (1796–1870), missionary and teacher at Harmony, was born in New Hampshire and died at Deepwater, Henry County, Missouri. He married Roxana Stearns and was ordained at Harmony Mission in 1830.

—very pretty—ev[enin]g prayer—examination of children in chapter of Bible—neat log house well furnished—
40 children at Harmony—
School kept by Mr. Jones—Indian children good at writing, ciphering, and geography.

Monday October 1. Dinner at Mr. Austin's[19]—boys at table on one side—girls the other—comp[an]y in centre—rich beef—beautiful honey—cakes—vegetables.

Osage River—clear stream—willow banks—navigable in part of year for steam boats[20]—Harmony about 500 miles from mouth.

Leave Harmony at 3 oclock—cavalcade—4 waggons—horsemen led horses—we hire a half breed called Broken Hoof—Mr. Choteau hires another—crossing of the Osage River—group of Indians on a knoll looking on.[21]

Camp after sunset in a beautiful grove at the foot of immense trees—by a brook opposite a prarie—moonlight—owl hoots—prarie wolf howls—barking of dogs—bells of our horses among the trees—supper—beef, roast ducks & prarie hens—others boiled. Fine effect of half moon among lofty trees—fire of camp with guides Indians & others round it—dogs lying on grass—waggons—tents by fire light—groups of attendants lying at foot of trees & round fires.

Farm in neighbourhood—Mr Summer[22]—river—Little

[19] There were two Austins at Harmony: Daniel H., mechanic and steward; and John, teacher. After the closing-down of the mission, Daniel Austin built a mill on the Osage River at the site of Balltown, Vernon County, Missouri, in 1836; he sold it to Cecil D. Ball and moved to a farm about one and one-half miles east of Balltown. Balltown, which no longer exists, was in the northeastern part of the county.

[20] According to one authority, steamboat navigation did not begin on the Osage River until 1837 (Schultz, "Steamboat Navigation on the Osage River," *Missouri Historical Review*, XXIX, 176). It is not clear whether Irving means actual navigation or potential.

[21] These were probably the Piankishaw Indians mentioned by Latrobe (*Rambler*, I, 155–56).

[22] Jesse, Moses, and Allen Summers, brothers, originally from Wayne County, Kentucky, removed to Warren County, Missouri, in 1820, then to Arkansas, and finally to the Osage River country in 1829. Allen Summers settled

Osage—*Ugatagakuge monsahn*—meaning "*where there is much dogwood.*"[23]

Tuesday Oct 2. Cold but beautiful morn'g—revive the fires—dogs creeping round fire & into tent—whipped off with many a yelp—sun breaks among pine trees—winding stream near by. Yesterday passed place of old Osage camp near branch of Osage River—wild plum trees—beautiful prarie—river where they fought the ———— into the stream, & killed them with knives—the place deserted—over-grown with sumach, hazel-nut, wild plum—prarie silent & lifeless.

In the course of the morning we see a Prarie wolf in the distance—half breed Indians instantly on the qui vive—mount my pony (I being in the waggon)—general gallop across the Prarie—Henry Clay the greyhound in full chase—Mr. Choteau sends half breed boy mounted to turn the wolf, but Pourtales dashes straight forw[ar]d & makes the wolf keep ahead so as to escape—returning we start a deer, which after a run couches in a hollow & we lose him.

A few miles further we see another Prarie wolf beside a ravine near the road—all set off in chase—Mr. Choteau & the doctor head him—come to a bare, burnt patch of prarie—the greyhound gets sight of him—fine race—hound turns him —manoeuvers & fight between wolf & hound—horsemen come up with [them] & try to trample on him—fighting retreat of wolf—Pourtales fires one barrel of his gun—breaks wolf's leg—we surround & kill him.

Beautiful sight of hunt. Horsemen galloping over green prairie—golden sunshine—Antoine towards the conclusion of

south of the Osage. He married Elizabeth Wright (1808–56), and died in 1849 in his fifty-first year. It must have been near Allen Summers' farm that the travelers stopped on October 1; the brook mentioned was probably either Hogle Creek or Pryor's Creek, which enter the Little Osage some twelve and fifteen miles west of its junction with the Osage River. The camp was in the northwest corner of Vernon County, close to, but north of, the Little Osage.

23 Of the first of these words I can make nothing; the second apparently should be mon-ca hi: *dogwood* (La Flesche, *Osage Dictionary*, 95).

chase leaves his waggon, mounts his stallion, & comes thundering along bringing up a corps de secours of bull-dog, cur & c.

A few miles further on we pass a run of water[24]—here Broken Hoof visits cabin of his mother & determines to return —pay him off—just then a half breed (Joseph),[25] whom Mr. Choteau had left word to follow us, arrives & takes his place. He is accomp[anie]d by an old Indian—tuer du village— from having, with a party he commanded, surprised and massacred a whole village—Indian with his bald head & single tuft of hair—strings of beads hanging from the upper part of his ears—his shoulders & bust bare—blanket swathed round his body—leather leggings & moccasins—mounted on strong black horse—carries his rifle athwart.[26]

Encamp & dine in a thicket of trees[27]—then perform journey of 17 miles across wide naked prarie—extensive prospect from a hill—ridge beyond ridge in smoky distance—Indian points it out—pass Pawnee Hill where 5 Pawnees defended themselves ag[ain]st large party of Osages—see two Prarie wolves which escape—white cloud of smoke from burning prairie—sun enters into smoke—spur on to light fires—limestone country. Wind by moonlight down into wood—pass thro it to bank of brook where we make fire and where joined by carriages—encamp.

[24] Perhaps the Marmaton River.

[25] Possibly the Joseph Suisse who is mentioned in *Tixier's Travels*, 153. See n. 29 below.

[26] "An old Osage warrior of the Grey Hairs' Band, whose name was 'the Destroyer of cities;' alias, 'the Burner of Wigwams,' then attached to our party, and acting as our guide, was riding at the head of our small column. When he arrived at the brink of the ascent, he paused, reined in his poney, and turning half round as he beckoned us forward, spread his arms, signifying to us the wide expanse that burst upon his sight; and that this broad extent of country, dimly descried in the deep red haze, was the present domain of his tribe" (Latrobe, *Rambler*, I, 158).

[27] They must now have been at the Missouri–Kansas line; from now on, therefore, they would be in Indian territory.

Story of Antoine and the two kegs of powder behind him on horse with which he dashed thro prarie on fire. Encampt at Pawnee Creek—branch of Osage.[28]

Old Osage Indian—killer of village—great warrior—chief—at present ambassador to procure a bag of nails.

Wednesday Oct 3. Beautiful morng—breakfast scene—men round pans and kettles—groups of little hounds looking on—growling & snapping of large dogs—now & then yelping from a scourged cur.

At daybreak Indian gets up—mounts his horse & away—Osages never eat early in morning when travelling—stop about 10 or 11 for that purpose.

In the course of the morning we meet various parties of Osages, men & women, on hunting expeditions—women leading horses—with packages—skins for beds, meat corn or pappooses & puppy dogs on the packages—lads with bows & rifles walking—fine, erect port of Osage warriors—noble attitudes—meet Osage interpreter—with wife & daughters—the former a daughter of Choteau.[29] Squaws riding with umbrellas—warm day—wide, treeless prarie— trembling with heat—columns of smoke hanging lazily in various directions of horizon—kindled by Indians to drive the game to the Praries.

[28] Pawnee Creek flows north to join the South Fork of Marmaton River about one mile above its junction with the Marmaton. The Irving party was now in present-day Bourbon County, Kansas, southwest of Fort Scott.

[29] The Osage interpreter was probably Baptiste Mongrain, son of Noel Mongrain, a Canadian, and a daughter of the first White Hair. Tixier, who described him in 1840 as about fifty years of age, said that he was both an interpreter for the Fur Company and chief of a village and that he then had "two legitimate Indian wives." I have not been able to identify the wife mentioned by Irving. One of the Osage interpreter's daughters, Julia Mongrain, was married to Joseph Lasweese [*sic*] by Nathaniel Dodge at the Osage Agency, on February 6, 1834; the husband had been educated at Union Mission (*Missionary Herald*, XXX [1834], 259).

[30] Probably Walnut Creek, which enters the Neosho River below St. Paul, Kansas; they were now on the Arkansas watershed. Cf. Latrobe, *Rambler*, I, 158–59.

Encamp about 11 at clear brook[30]—party of Indians, squaws & children encamp by us—squaws cutting wood & dragging great branches of trees.

Our dinner, surrounded by Indians—groups of squaws & children who keep somewhat aloof.

Ride 12 miles after dinner to Rev. N. Dodge's house[31]— near Osage Village—put up at the house—comfortable—tea furnished by Mrs. Dodge.

Young Osage couple in the neighborhood, the girl well educated at Harmony Mission—the young man but slightly educated—recently married—undertaking farming—their relatives come to see them, camp before the door & eat them out of house & home—young man cannot help giving away provisions &c. to his tribe. When we visited them we found two Indians (man & wife) lying at a fire kindled before the house.

Indian we met to-day in mourning—dirt on his face— does not eat till sunset.[32] The dead are painted white & other colours when buried—

A chief lately deceased was buried sitting up under a mound.

We spread our skin beds on the floor of room in house. Antoine, &c. light a fire—cook their supper & sleep under trees. ["]Every one has his caprice,["] said Antoine, ["]for my part I think it much better to camp here.["]

Intense curiosity with which an Indian watches D^r ODwyer while he shaves.

[31] Neosho Mission had been maintained in this vicinity from 1824 to 1829. In 1830 Nathaniel B. Dodge, formerly superintendent at Harmony Mission, was "authorized to remove his family and form a new station near one of the large Osage villages" *(Missionary Herald,* XXVII [1831], 46). When Irving stopped there, the staff consisted of Dodge and his wife. Boudinot Mission was on the left (east or north) bank of the Neosho River, just below Four Mile Creek, and near present-day St. Paul, Neosho County, Kansas. Dodge was away from the station on mission business. For the Dodges see page 89, n. 3 above.

[32] Cf. *Tixier's Travels,* 137.

Beautiful, clear river by Mr. Dodges.[33]

Thursday Oct 4. Leave Mr. Dodges at ¾ past 7 provided with large family loaf of bread—we have a journey of 30 miles to make over open Prarie before we can find a camping place, there being water in the interim but no wood—pass thro the village of the White Hair (Osages)—monument of chief who died lately[34]—mound on a hill surrounded by railing—three poles with flags—trophies—a scalp, scalping knife &c. He had killed 4 Pawnees. While looking at it an Indian approached and stood by the tomb—a relation of the deceased. After we had rode on we saw him standing like a statue by the tomb. Passed over vast prarie—here not a tree or shrub was to be seen—a view like that of the ocean. Col Choteau[35] & Pourtales (who had left us yesterday at the dining place to go to the Agency) rejoined us, with three spare horses. About 3 oclock arrived at a grove on the banks of stream & encamp—place called La Bête—wood entangled with rich underwood —grape vines—pea vines, &c. Fine trees—flights of Perroquets—called la Bête, or the Beast, because the Indians saw a great & terrible animal there, the like of which they never saw before or since.[36]

Story told by Col. Choteau lying at the foot of a tree.

[33] The Neosho River.

[34] White Hair's Town must have been then located on the right (west) side of the Neosho River, a few miles below the present town of Erie, Neosho County, Kansas. This chief had died between April and mid-June, 1832. For the White Hair family see *Tixier's Travels*, 127, n. 29.

[35] Presumably Chouteau was going to see his younger brother, Paul Liguest Chouteau, United States agent for the Osage. The Agency was on the right (west) bank of the Neosho, about six miles west of Boudinot Mission.

[36] Labette Creek rises in the southwestern part of Neosho County, Kansas, and flows south-southeast to enter the Neosho River from the west in the southeast corner of Labette County, near the Kansas–Oklahoma line. Tixier called it "the river A-la-bête." If Irving's party had traveled thirty miles from Boudinot, the camp must have been on the Labette, not more than half a dozen miles above the Neosho River.

These paroquets were then a common sight throughout the West. "Near the village [Franklin, Missouri] we met with innumerable flocks of paroquets . . . whose beautiful plumage of green and gold flashed above us like an atmosphere of gems" (Ferris, *Rocky Mountains*, 4).

Wagrushka e abbe[37]—creek—next to this creek is Nick-anansa.[38] A tribe of Indians hunting on that creek struck their tents to come on this—a young man who had been to St Louis returned to the creek and came to the encampment—found it deserted—a young girl alone there—to whom he was engaged to be married—["]Where is the camp?["] ["]It is struck. They are gone to such a place.["] ["] & what are you doing here?["] ["]Waiting for you.["] He gave her his bundle and walked ahead according to Indian custom—approaching the camp the girl sat down at foot of a tree & said, ["]I will wait here. It is not proper for us to return together.["] He entered the town—told his sister to go after the girl—["]she is dead —died a few days since.["] His relatives surrounded him weeping & confirmed the story. He returned with them to the tree. The girl was gone—the bundle lay there—the young man fell *dead*.[39]

A little girl at White Hair had died—they buried with her her playthings—she had a favourite little horse—they killed & buried her with it.[40]

An old squaw left alone when her party had gone hunting prayed the Great Spirit to make something to amuse her—he made the mosquito.

[37] Labette Creek. According to La Flesche, it should have been spelled *Wa-gthu-shka i-a bi*: "where a strange animal was seen at a tributary of the Neosho on the west, near where the town of Parsons, Kans., now stands. According to the legend, a party of Osage warriors was crossing this creek on what seemed to be a log. When all but two had crossed, the monster turned its head downstream and went away. In an unpublished manuscript Father Shomaker [*sic*] refers to the creek as 'Labeth.' " (*Osage Dictionary*, 190).

[38] It is not possible to identify this creek. As a guess I suggest Bachelor Creek, which enters Labette Creek from the west about five miles below Parsons, Kansas. The Osage word nearest *Nickanansa* seems to be *ni-ka no^n thi-shto^n*, one who has reached manhood.

[39] Irving used this story in the *Tour*, 205–207. McCoy recorded another version of this Osage story in *Indian Missions*, 361–62.

[40] Used in the *Tour*, 205. The child is there declared to be the only child of one of the chief warriors, "a beautiful girl of a very tender age."

Pawnee Boy. At Mr. Choteau's agency there is a Pawnee boy 12 years of age who is anxious to run away & return to his own people. They fear if he did he would reveal where the horses were kept &c. & all the secrets of this land. He has a sister with whom he is always plotting in Pawnee language. Once, when 7 years old, he ran away with horses, but was re-taken. He was told, ["]If you run away again we will send 12 Osage boys with bows and arrows to shoot you.["] ["]Give me,["] he said, ["]twelve arrows and let your boys come & we'll see who has the worst of it.["]

Chattering & laughing of the Frenchmen & half breeds at their meat—Mr. Choteau lying at foot of tree and joining in —screaming of flights of parrots—snapping & quarrelling of dogs—

Moonlight vista thro the forest—distant dewy tint of trees—Hooting of screech-owl—Col. Choteau remarks super-stition of Indians when an owl is heard several nights. They think it follows the encampment & forebodes the death of one of the party.[41]

These creeks empty into the Neosho.

Friday 5. Towards morning rain and thunder—holds up about daybreak. An Indian visits us—encamped about a mile distant—attracted by the tinkling of our horse bells—had been hunting yesterday & killed two small deer.

After a while he departed to his camp—from whence three Indians came and brought pieces of fresh venison. Col. Choteau made them presents of tobacco.

Leave enc[a]mp[men]t at 10—ride all day over wide, monotonous praries—cry given of a wolf at a distance—saw something seated on a hill—all hands on the alert—flankers sent out—turned out to be a solitary Indian who begged for

[41] "To the Osage and the Omaha the screech owl is a bird of ill omen. When the cries of a screech owl are heard near a house the occupants hurry out to scare the bird away" (La Flesche, *Osage Dictionary*, 61).

food—gave him biscuit—gave us the disagreeable intelligence that all the Osages had departed some time since from Fort Gibson, on their buffalo hunt. Showers in the distance—lowering sky—ride after dark across gloomy plain—descend into thick grove and encamp for the night.[42]

Saturday, 6. Soft morning—misty—beautiful forest— large trees intertwined with grape vines & clambering vines —rich verdure—yesterday saw prickly pears—sent Joseph the half breed on foraging party among the groves—brought rich store of pawpaws. This night horses had excellent range—pea vines and cane.

[*With the Journal reversed Irving made the following undated notes.*]

Race of dogs in the Rocky Mount[ain]s supposed to be a cross breed of the buffalo and wolf.

Old Father Vail[43] addressed the Indians on the necessity of industry, & c., to happiness. An Indian replied, ["]Father, I don't understand this kind of happiness you talk of. You tell me to cut down tree—to lop it—to make fence—to plough— this you call being happy—I no like such happiness. When I go to S^t. Louis I go to see Choteau or Clark—he says hello— and negro comes in with great plate with cake, wine, & c.—he say 'eat, drink.' If he want anything else he say 'hello'—three —four five six negro come in and do what he want—that I call happy—he no plough—he no work—he no cut wood.["]

["]Ah, but he has negroes to do all that.["]

["]Well, father, you go to our Great Father—tell him to find me one, two, three negroes to cut wood & plough for me and I'll be willing to be happy like white man—but for a man 50 years old to have to plough, & c.—him too old.["]

---

[42] The last entry for October 5 is almost completely undecipherable; it seems to refer to their camping place on the (west?) branch of the Cabin de Planch (Plank Cabin) Creek, and is followed by another of Irving's Osage transcriptions: *Shong e te shinga* (?).

[43] William F. Vaill of Union Mission. See page 110, n. 10.

An agent newly arrived was preaching up as usual about their being civilised & happy—one old Indian affected to sleep, then waking up—["]What, father, still about that old happiness?—don't talk of that any more. I'll tell you what I call happy—to have my gun—a wide range—to hunt—to kill buffalo—to have plenty to eat—to eat and drink till full—to smoke—to lie down on our backs—beat our bosoms & sing.["]

Juror declines to be empanelled in a trial of an Indian for murder—he pointed to a scar on his head—["]This scar I rec[eive]d when two brothers were murdered by Indians—I cannot be an unprejudiced arbiter of them.["]

Place of old Osage camp on branch of Osage River—overgrown with bushes, wild plums, etc.

Backwoodsmen go ahead to tread down the nettles.

Mr. McCoy—missionary, appointed to treat with Cherokee Indians. A Cherokee was at Washington when he was there. Mʳ McCoy applied for his son to be appointed doctor—another, surveyor—another agent. The Cherokee returned and told his friends this man is not for God, not for us, but for himself—he wants to grasp everything. They would not make a treaty with him.[44]

Farmers beyond Independence the frontier town seldom come to the village—they are content to raise food enough for themselves—get wild honey to sell for clothes, &c.—lead a lazy life in this easily cultivated & prolific country.

[Four lines illegible]

Prarie dogs live in villages—owls & rattlesnakes live with them—some say the latter inhabit only such holes as the dogs have deserted in consequence of the death of some relation.

---

[44] What prospective treaty is referred to here is not known. McCoy had now been very active about western Indian affairs for some four years.

Story of prarie dog, owl, and rattlesnake who kept house together.[45]

Indians at Mr. Dodge's Mission—had eighty acres & ploughed & sown with corn for them—each sent his horse, hobbled, into his part of the patch—but as there were no divisions the whole was nearly eaten up.[46]

Indians had near 200 head of cattle—oxen, cows, calves, & c. When the warriors went to the Buffalo hunt they left old men to guard them—after several days the old men called a council. ["]Our brothers,]"[said he, ["]are by this time in the midst of the buffaloes and have meat a plenty. It is great pity that while they revel we should want. Suppose we have a chase of our own.["] So said, so done—they killed four oxen and all ate till they could scarcely crawl. A few days after another council. ["]Our friends must be still among the buffaloes —suppose we have another chase.["] So said, so done, and the 200 head of cattle melted away before these domestic hunters.

[45] Obviously a folk-story Irving picked up. The statement may be partly explained by a sentence in the *Tour*, 243: "Other fanciful speculators represent the owl as a kind of housekeeper to the prairie-dog; and, from having a note very similar, insinuate that it acts, in a manner, as family preceptor, and teaches the young litter to bark."

[46] Latrobe told the same story but made it twenty acres of ripe corn, and attributed the action to the agent rather than the missionary (*Rambler*, I, 161).

JOURNAL III

Cabin Creek, October 6—On the Red Fork

October 17, 1832[1]

OCT 6. Left encampt[2] this morning and rode through mist which gradually cleared up & showed wide prarie—with distant line of green wood and hills that looked like cultivated country. It seemed as if we could distinguish fields of grain, leaves, partridges, glades, &c.

Our sportsmen shot two turkeys near our last night's encampt—about ½ past eleven arrived at Mr. Requa's establish[men]t[3]—on the bank of the Neosho, which is here a broad, fine stream, clear and with a gentle current.

Mrs. Requa from Connecticut (Fairfield)—fine looking

[1] On the inside of the front cover and first leaf of this Journal there are illegible notations about postage, purchases, and possibly other matters.

[2] Since they were not many miles above Hopefield Mission, it is likely that this camp was at the crossing of Cabin Creek. See page 103, n. 42.

[3] Hopefield Mission was on the west side of the Neosho River, just below Cabin or Plank Cabin Creek. It was sometimes called New Hopefield to distinguish it from the first establishment of that name, founded in 1823 about four miles from Union. In 1832 the Hopefield Mission family consisted of William C. Requa, farmer and catechist; George Requa, farmer; Mrs. W. C. Requa; Mrs. G. Requa. William C. Requa (1795–1886) was born in Westchester County, New York, and came out to Union Mission in 1821. Eventually he settled northwest of Harmony Mission in Lone Oak township, Bates County, Missouri. He was married four times. His first wife, whom Irving met, was Susan Comstock of the Harmony Mission. See Introduction, page 23, n. 34.

woman—says when she first came here they had no house—slept under trees—was in fine health, never better—

Indian farms—old Indian guard left at home to take care of house.

Our dinner, four steaks of venison cut from venison ham.

Leave Requa's at 2—ride over Praries twelve miles until we come in sight of the river—pleasant country—looks like park land—well where Pawnees used to hide their effects when going hunting or to war—holes still to be seen—old Osages told Colonel of it—covey of prarie hens—pigeons—come in sight of Col's house—white log house with Piazza, surrounded by trees. Come to beautiful, clear river, group of Indian nymphs half naked on banks—with horses near—arrival at house—old negro runs to open gate—mouth from ear to ear—group of Indians round tree in court yard—roasting venison—horses tethered near—negroes run to shake hand and take horses—some have handkerchief across head—half breeds—squaws—negro girls running & giggling—dogs of all kinds—hens flying & cackling—wild turkeys, tamed geese—Piazza with Buffalo skin thrown over railing—room with guns—rifles.[4]

Supper, venison stakes, roast beef, bread, cakes, coffee—waited on by half breed—sister of Mr. Choteau's concubine[5]—adjourn to another room—pass thro open hall in which Indians are seated on floor. They come into the room—two bring in chairs—the other seats himself on the floor with his knees to his chin—another Indian glares in at the window. House formed of logs—a room at each end—an open hall with staircase in the centre—other rooms above—in the two rooms on

---

[4] This was the Saline or the Grand Saline; it was A. P. Chouteau's principal establishment in the Indian country. Although Irving does not mention it, they must have crossed the Neosho River, for the road came down the west bank and Chouteau's trading house was on the east. Salina, Mayes County, Oklahoma, occupies this site.

[5] Rosalie, a halfblood Osage, who later married a Cherokee. Foreman (*Pioneer Days*, 92) gives the sister's name as Masina.

ground floor two beds in each room with curtains—white washed log walls—tables of various kinds—Indian ornaments, & c.

Half breeds loitering about the house—dogs & cats of all kinds strolling about the hall or sleeping among harness at one end of the piazza.

In these establishments the world is turned upside down— the slave the master, the master the slave. The [word illegible] has the idea of property—the latter of reality; the former owns—the latter enjoyes it;[6] the former has to plan & scheme and guard & economize—the latter thinks only of living, enjoying—cares nothing how it comes or how it goes.

Sunday Octr 7. Breakfast, coffee & cream, roast ribs of beef, venison steaks, wild turkey fricasseed. Indians send in roast venison & beef—milk that looks like cocoa nut milk.

After breakfast Mr. Smith,[7] who keeps school for Col. Choteau, calls at house—wears calico surcoat after the Indian cut—has lived many years with the Cherokees.

Ride to the Saline[8]—Major Rogers house—he & his wife Cherokee half breeds—he absent at Cherokee council—which has been in session four weeks, being discordant.

Mrs. Rogers fine looking woman—her son a tall, fine looking young man, married to a handsome, tall half breed.

Log house with Piazza—locust trees—Saline in valley— bubbling springs.

[6] Two lines in the manuscript are here scratched out and illegible.

[7] B. H. Smith, according to Foreman, *Pioneer Days*, 92.

[8] This was the actual salt spring for which the locality was named; it was about a mile from Chouteau's establishment. From about 1831 to 1843 John Rogers worked the springs. Rogers had come to the West with the first of the Cherokee in 1817; he died in Washington in 1846.

"The Grand Saline, about fifty miles above Fort Gibson, near the Neosho River, was considered a curiosity of its kind, before its natural beauties were effaced by 'improvements.' In the border of a little valley, a number of small salt springs break out, around the orifice of each of which was formed, in the shape of a pot, a kind of calcareous saline concretion. None of the springs are very bold, but the water is strong, and sufficiently abundant for extensive works" (Gregg, *Commerce of the Prairies*, II, 186).

Ride to hill above, where Pawnee village formerly stood —holes in the hill where the Pawnees used to hide their effects when they went hunting.

In crossing the river we see the same nymphs whom we saw yesterday—they were wading across—one returned and played about in the water.

A quarter mile from the Col's house is his race course on a beautiful little level Prarie. He has a great number of horses which the blacks drive by the house in a drove.

Leave the Saline at 2 oclock with Mr Ellsworth in dearborn for Fort Gibson.[9] Antoine drives the dearborn—William, the black boy, follows in smaller Dearborn—cross Prarie— Prarie hens—heavy thunder storm on prarie—put down the oil skin sides of waggon—cross swollen brooks—drive thro woods—pass river where a negro servant and horse belonging to Mr. Choteau were drowned by swelling of the river—

Sun sets in clear streak—but clouds overhead—arrive about seven at Union mission—Mr. Vail[10]—his wife a Connecticut woman—comfortable house—at ring of bell repair to refectory in another building—50 scholars—Cherokees Delawares. & c. These tribes shew great anxiety for the education of their children.[11]

Monday 8. Leave the mission after breakfast—9 oclock— towards noon see an Indian on a mound who mounts his horse and comes to inquire news of the Cherokees.

[9] Latrobe and Pourtalès remained for a day or two at the Saline.

[10] William Fowler Vaill was born at Hadlyme, Connecticut, June 7, 1783, and died at Wethersfield, Illinois, February 24, 1865. He graduated from Yale College in 1806, studied for the ministry, and married Asenath Selden December 28, 1808; he went out to Union Mission in 1820 where he served until 1834.

[11] Union Mission, founded in 1820, was on the west (right) bank of the Neosho River, opposite to and about one mile above Spring Creek, in Mayes County, Oklahoma. The mission family consisted of William F. Vaill, missionary; Abraham Redfield, farmer and mechanic; Mrs. Vaill; Mrs. Redfield. In the report on the school, made June 1, 1832, it was announced that eight white and fifty-four Indian and mixed blood children were being taught reading, grammar, arithmetic, geography.

Arrive at Genl Campbells[12]—banks of the Verdigris— leave luggage there for Pourtales & Latrobe—ride thro woods & cane breaks to the Arkansas—Indian on horse back with Indian girl behind him & strapping squaw before. Arrive on banks of Arkansas—tolerably clear stream—neat look of white fortifications—blockhouses. &c. of Fort Gibson opposite.[13] Cross in scow and arrive at gate of garrison—guard cleanly dressed round the gate—sergeant with Irish brogue— culprits in pillory & riding the wooden horse—arrive at Col. Arbuckle's[14] quarters—log house.

Tuesday 9. Leave Fort Gibson escorted by fourteen rangers[15]—Lt. Penticost.

Wednesday Oct 10th. Ride with Col. Arbuckle, Genl Houston,[16] to Col. Choteau's—picturesque scene crossing river —Creek with turban, one end hanging down—blue hunting shirt—horn—rifle—looked like Arab.

Scene at Col. Choteau's on the banks of the Neosho[17]—

[12] John Campbell, agent for the Western Creeks, 1830–34. At this time the Agency was on the east bank of the Verdigris River about three miles above its mouth. It was housed in buildings bought from A. P. Chouteau in 1827.

[13] The post was located on the east (left) bank of the Neosho River about two miles above the Arkansas. Ellsworth was not much impressed by the buildings there.

[14] Colonel Matthew Arbuckle (1776–1851) was commanding officer at Fort Gibson from its founding. At the time of his death he was a brigadier general, commanding the Seventh Military Department.

[15] Bean and the main body of his rangers had left Fort Gibson on October 6 (see Introduction, pages 28–34). The fourteen were among the sick who had been left behind. According to Ellsworth, it was on the morning of the tenth, soon after breakfast, that Pentecost appeared with the escort and they set out for the Verdigris River; the ninth had been given over to making preparations.

Joseph Pentecost, first lieutenant of Bean's company. Ellsworth thought that Pentecost and Robert King, the second lieutenant, did not possess "energy enough for the station . . . [they] were pleased to take the execution as gentlemen, but rarely appeared as soldiers on duty and under pay" *(Narrative, 24).* But then Ellsworth was pretty generally annoyed by the air of "republican equality" among the rangers.

[16] Sam Houston apparently had arrived from Nashville, Tennessee, on the evening of October 8.

[17] Unless this is a flash back to October 6–7, Irving wrote *Neosho* where he should have written *Verdigris.* This must not be confused with Chouteau's Saline

group of Osages—blankets, leather leggings, & moccasins—hair cropped except bunch at top—bust bare or wrapped in blanket.

Creeks—calico hunting shirts—scarlet & blue handkerchief round head—leather & scarlet leggings—

groups of riflemen [two words illegible] with horses—green blanket coats—half breeds—horses and dogs—hunters in leather shirts—log cabbins—stately trees about river, with Virginia creeper.

Bustle at blacksmiths—shoeing horses—breaking spoons to melt lead for bullets—

old trapper is there—half breed boy in moccasins—light straw col[ore]d hunting shirt—rifleman in calico shirt, leggins, &c.—

negro shoeing horse—

tall half breed in rifle shirt, blue trousers, moccasins—with pack saddles—

little dog looking on at shoeing horse as if studying the art or waiting for his turn.

Rifle in corner—old rifle against work bench.

Leave Col. Choteau's at 2 oclock—ride thro rich, entangled bottom by hamlets of Indians, negroes, &c. to ———

Encampt of rangers in circular grove—rich bottom—high trees—horses tied round, feeding on corn—brook near—trees tinted with autumn—tinkling of bells—men making messes at fires—some shooting at mark with rifles—parrots flying chattering through trees.

———

establishment. Apparently Chouteau had come down to the Verdigris post with Pourtalès and Latrobe, who wanted to accompany the other party as far as the Osage trail.

"We left the Garrison about 9 o clock, and crossed the Grand River and proceeded to the ford, over the Verdigris about 6 miles from the fort, and having crossed the river, we passed down the stream to Col. Chouteaus store at the Creek agency so called" (Ellsworth, *Narrative*, 10).

18 Ellsworth spoke of Berryhill as a half-breed. In the *Tour*, Irving described him only as a "settler . . . named Berryhill" (page 18). Ellsworth noted that they traveled ten miles before camping.

CARONDELET OR VIDE POCHE
from a drawing by Henry Lewis, 1846–47

Reproduced from Henry Lewis,
Das Illustrirte Mississippithal, *1857*

We pitch our tent in the farmyard of Mr Berryhill[18]—
family suffering with bloody flux—log houses of various sizes
—skin of bullock stretched & drying—dogs—full moon—
pale—damp air—distant fires of rangers in grove below.

Robin Hood life & characters.

Mr. E.—in half Osage, half chasseur dress—embroidered
leather Indian pouch—powder horn with red worsted band.

Thursday 11. Up before day—half breed pointing out the
north star & positions of 7 stars as indicating daylight.

Our landlord large man with squeaking, broken voice—
Mr. Portales boots lost on the road—one was found—a Creek
Indian was seen with the lost boot on, looking for the other.
"That's really a funny tale," said our huge host, with a small
voice.[19]

Set off at ½ past 7—ride through deep, rich bottom, by a
village of Creeks extending along a rising ground[20]—pass several Creeks—one with scarlet turban and plume of black
feathers like a cock's tail—one with white turban and red
feathers—Oriental look—like Sultans on the stage—some
have racquet with which they have been playing ball—some
with jacket and shirts but legs and thighs bare—middle sized,
well made and vigorous. Yesterday one had brilliant bunch of
sumach. They look like fine birds on the Prarie. Pass house of
a tall, red-haired, lank, leather faced settler with one eye
habitually closed when he winks—says some of the Osages are
near. They had stolen one of his horses—says they will steal
horses and then bring them home, pretending to have found
them and claiming a reward.

Pass on to house of the last settler[21]—the last trace of

---

[19] Cf. Latrobe, *Rambler*, I, 177; Ellsworth, *Narrative*, 12.

[20] They were now in Creek country. In 1834 there were more than 2,000
Creeks living in the triangle between the lower Verdigris and the Arkansas rivers.

[21] Ellsworth identified this last settler, whose house they passed about ten
o'clock in the morning, as Mr. Hardriger, a Creek. This man, whose name was
really Hardage, lived in the Arkansas bottom near Choska, Wagoner County,
Oklahoma, between twenty and twenty-five miles from Fort Gibson.

civilization informs Portales & Latrobe of a camp of Osages in a swamp. They determine to go there & seek guides to conduct them to the Osage hunting party. We find ourselves off the track of Capt. Dean's[22] party of rangers, which set off several days since, and set off to find it—said to be 2 miles off —part with Latrobe & Pourtales—lose our way in a swamp— tramp for some time through brake & briars and mud—after extricating ourselves we are overtaken by Latrobe & Pourtales with the old frontiersman who is guiding them to the Osage camp.

Just then we meet old lanthern jawd man who had lost his horse—had just met with Osage leading him back, who said he had wandered to their camp.

Lanthern jawd man was for tying him up & giving him a swing of rushes, but we interfered.[23]

Find that frontiersman advised Latrobe & Pourtales not to go on to Osages—they were too far to be overtaken— Pawnees were out—Osages were prepared for war & c. Pourtales was not to be dissuaded. He & Latrobe procured an Indian guide & set off on their quest[24]—but a young man clerk of Mr. Choteau, who had set off with them from his house,

[22] The name here is certainly *Dean*, as it is in one or two other instances. However, after meeting the Captain, apparently Irving got his name straight and later appearances show the name corrected from *Dean* to *Bean*, or show it written correctly at the first try.

[23] Neither Ellsworth nor Latrobe mentioned the lantern-jawed man. Ellsworth said that "some Cherokees" saw the Osage with the horse, declared he had stolen it, and wanted to flog him.

[24] According to Ellsworth, it was not a frontiersman, but the Osage leading the stray horse who told Latrobe and Pourtalès of the Osage camp. The Europeans left the others about eleven o'clock in the morning.

[25] "Mr Brailey although starting with them for their jaunt, became alarmed, and refused to go with them & while they turned off, he kept along with us, much to our surprise—He conversed freely with me, and told me his fixed determination not to go with them; for he doubted whether they could overtake the Osages, and even if they could, there would be much danger, and the Osage hunt might be protracted untill winter, and it would be hazardous to return alone. . . . Mr Brailey was then without provisions, thrown upon us—he was Col Chouteaus clerk. Mr Chouteau had treated us with great hospitality, and we invited him to share with us our limited portion of provisions" (Ellsworth, *Narrative*, 13–14).

abandoned their enterprise & joined us.[25] Stopped about noon in rich bottom, tall trees, fine *range* of Pea vines, for the horses to repose and feed for an hour—flock of paroquets—beautiful transparency of the varied autumnal leaves with the sun shining through them—horses cropping the pea vine—men lying about on the deep bed of foliage.

Resume our route—come in sight of the Arkansas river and pass frequently thro rich bottom in sight of it—view beyond of beautiful country—looks as if cultivated—groves—blades—woody upland—willowed shores—sandy beaches—sunny look of the groves.

Pass thro Osage war camp recently deserted—cabins formed of twigs [word illegible] & rushes—fire in centre—council wigwam—dancing place—arrive about 3 at fine grove in rich pea vine bottom, with clear stream of water—traces of recent encampt of Capt. Dean—one fire still smoking—encamp here for the night—hobble the horses and turn them loose to graze. Latrobe & Pourtales arrive, finding it impossible to get on with their slender attendance—determine to continue with us. Their Indian agrees to accompany them for a blanket & [waist?] cloak.[26]

Firing at mark with rifles.

[26] Cf. Ellsworth, *Narrative*, 15–16. And they had to return after the commissioner was congratulating himself and Irving on being separated from that scandalous young man, Pourtalès! This Indian deserted them the next night, but they had another servant, a halfblood named Antoine. In his character, Latrobe wrote, "indolence seemed to be the prevailing feature. It was depicted in his heavy, sleepy, dark eye; and the Indian blood evidently predominated over the French. He was willing and active enough when excited, but it was no common occasion that would incite him to action. For an hour together he would stand at the camp-fire, with his cloak tightly twisted round his body, his arms motionless within, and gaze upon nothing but a fixed gaze, in which was neither life nor speculation. In form, he was an object of admiration to us all, and I suspect to himself no less. His body and limbs were most symmetrically moulded. His bust was that of Antinoüs. Indeed, I may here observe, that the finest living models of the human figure I ever saw, were among the Indian half-breeds" (*Rambler*, I, 177–78). Ellsworth identified him as "Antoine Lumbard, the Servant of Mr Latrobe & Co." Irving described this "Adonis of the frontier" in similar terms; he spoke of Antoine as "one of the worthless brood engendered and brought up among the missions." In the report of the Union Mission school,

This day in the woods we encounter a wandering dog. ["]He is mad,["] cried one—["]He is blind,["] cried another. He came rambling along with inflamed eye, taking notice of no one, but bewildered by the noises—the poor animal was following the traces of his master. ["]I'll shoot him,["] said a ranger. ["]By no means,["] cried I, ["]let the poor animal go on.["] He rambled among the horses and pursued his course.

Two Creeks arrive at the camp to accompany us.[27]

Friday 12. This morning the two Creeks return who had carried message to Capt. Dean's camp—had letter to Col. Arb[uc]kle which Mr. E. opens—said they are encamped in fine place on the Arkansas—about 50 [miles] distant, where there is plenty of game & are waiting for us.[28]

Breakfast, delicious ribs of pork—after breakfast go and wash ourselves in beautiful stream.[29]

Gaiety in camp—shots of riflemen—songs of Antoine & c.

Osage Indian & his wild horse—attempts to put blanket of ours on him—fine scene—figure of Indian—naked bust—blanket—with piebald horse—wild eyes—collar with red tuft of horsehair.

Set off at half an hour after sunrise—ride through fine forest—cross a narrow, deep stream upon an old beaver dam—see streaming line of wild geese squalling as they fly high overhead—pass an old Osage war camp—at half past ten stop

---

September 21, 1824, his age was given as fourteen. He had entered school a year earlier and could now read in the Testament and write. Entered with him was a Robert M. Lombard and an Ellen Lombard, aged six and four years. Ellen possibly was the sister whom Irving, in 1832, said was "concubine to an opulent white trader." In the several printed narratives Antoine Lombard is called Antoine, whereas Antoine Deshetres is Tonish.

[27] This day, Ellsworth noted, they had traveled "along the north side of the Arkansas . . . at least 20 miles in a north west direction *(Narrative,* 15).

[28] Ellsworth placed this a day earlier *(Narrative,* 15).

[29] Probably Coweta Creek, which enters the Arkansas River from the north in Wagoner County, Oklahoma.

in forest where there is plenty of the pea vine—let the horses feed—fires made—one man runs to spring for water—coffee prepared—groups—some lying down with head on saddle—others seated at foot of tree by fire—smoke rising among the trees—some pulling up pea vines—some rolling in the vine—rangers practising at mark with their rifles.

Old Osage Indian arrives at our camp—had been out to hunt but lost his horse & was looking for it—says the rangers' camp is but 10 miles off.[30]

Half breed[31] says we will see no buffalo until past the Osage hunters—they frighten everything off like a prarie on fire. Leave the encampt about 12, pass thro bottoms, across praries—by a lovely pool covered with water lilies—see distant smokes of Indians come down to banks of Arkansas—tracks of horses down to the river side (afterward understood to be made by hunters who had crossed to go buffalo hunting). Let our horses drink & continue along bank & across prarie—see smokes—fancy one to be the rangers' camp—follow track—find horses grazing (Osage horses)—arrive at Osage village[32] on banks of the river. Old man comes & shakes hands—women and children stare & laugh—Mr. Ellsworth makes speech—retrace our steps—find rangers' trail—meet Indian & squaw—misunderstood them that the rangers' camp is 3 miles off. Push on until dark & then encamp on the borders of ravine—drops of rain—pitch tent. Three Osages visit us and sit by our fire—give them coffee

Scene of rangers' fire—Indians—rangers—men cooking, eating, drinking.

This day we made about 35 miles.

After we retire to our tents the Indians lie by the fire before

---

[30] Ellsworth reported that he said twelve miles (*Narrative*, 17).

[31] Identified as Beatte in the *Tour*.

[32] Not a village but an encampment of about 500 Osage, which Ellsworth described at some length. It was on the Arkansas River. They were probably now near the site of Tulsa, Oklahoma.

it and sing a nasal, low song in chorus, drumming on their breasts[33]

rain towards morning

young Osage leaves us clandestinely in the night.

Saturday 13. Breakfast in tent—weather promises to hold up—give breakfast to Indians.

Mr. Brailey tells of his having nearly been over taken last year by fire on the Praries—saw it approaching and was so confused that he was hardly able to make free and set the prarie on fire before him.

After breakfast prepare for march—Pourtales sets off, guided by the half breed, to go back to the Indian village & [two words illegible][34]

Set off about 7—after riding some distance pass a bee tree in the forest, recently cut down—empty flakes of honeycomb, remaining. Travelling a mile or two further on, we come to a bottom of woodland—see horses among the trees, recognised by the men as horses belonging to their troop. Coming to the edge of a ridge the camp lies below us in beautiful open wood by a stream of water—undergrowth of low shrubs—blanket tents—venison hanging on stick to smoke over fire—buckskins spread—cooking at fires—horses—stacks of saddles & rifles —congratulation of men with their companions.

Capt. Bean,[35] about forty years of age, in leather hunting dress and leather stock[in]gs—Dr Holt—grey jacket, linsy woollen jacket & trousers, cloth hunting cap—old huntsman

---

[33] See Introduction, page 34.

[34] It was Pourtalès's intention to get himself an Osage wife. He was unsuccessful because Ellsworth had instructed Billet (Beatte) to lead the young man to a small encampment, rather than the big one they had passed. "Disappointed in his main object, he exchanged some of his goods, for articles highly valuable to our mess, and for which we often thanked him" (*Narrative,* 21).

[35] "Capt Beans is a very worthy, good natured, easy sort of man—personally brave, and possessing the qualities of a good woods man—He is worthy of confidence, and actuated by correct motives—But he is greatly deficient in energy and more so in discipline" (Ellsworth, *Narrative,* 24).

in rifle shirt of leather asks permission to go hunting[36]—granted—men of all kinds of dress—some lying under trees—rifles leaning ag[ain]st trees—powder horns, etc.

Bee hunt—led by a young fellow in a straw hat not unlike a beehive—one without a hat following him with rifle on shoulder—Capt. Bean, Dr. Holt, Mr. Latrobe, Mr. Brailey with rifles & guns—come to see first a honeycomb on bush— watch which way the bees who are at it fly—pursue the track— come to high, dry oak tree—see the bees about a hole high up —men go to work at foot with axes—by and by down comes the tree with great crash and breaks to shivers—one man runs up with whisp of lighted hay to smoke off the bees. The poor victims are pacific and suffer us to assemble round the ruin of

---

[36] Dr. D. Holt was assigned in September to attend Captain Bean's rangers. On July 8, 1832, Dr. Zina Pitcher, assistant surgeon at Fort Gibson, had informed the Surgeon General that Dr. D. Holt had been employed from June 5, at $82 a month, to attend the troops near Fort Gibson. One month later Arbuckle, in a letter to the Surgeon General, enclosed a certificate relating to a contract with Dr. David Holt. On September 29, Arbuckle informed the Surgeon General that Dr. Holt had been assigned to attend Captain Bean's rangers. Dr. Daniel Holt, writing from Fort Smith on April 12, 1833, applied for a post as assistant surgeon and enclosed a letter from H. L. Ellsworth, and on May 26, 1833, Irving wrote from New York to the Secretary of War recommending Dr. Holt for a permanent appointment. Holt was still at Fort Smith on August 7 and on December 19, 1833, but in the latter part of that year he was incapacitated by illness (Surgeon General's Office, Letters Received, Vol. II, 1831–34; War Office, Letters Received, Vol. XXXIII, Nos. 19, 20). Unfortunately these letters exist only in abstracts.

Ellsworth referred to Holt as "an experienced practitioner, and well calculated to his station—He does not belong to the Army, but is hired, at assistant surgeons pay, by the Commander of the Post. . . . [he] had a compas and was Capt Beans adviser and scribe" *(Narrative*, 24). Latrobe also spoke well of him: ". . . [he was] a medical man,—the very reverse of our scientific querulous companion in the former part of our tour,—being a man of a thousand; of sound mind and body; moreover an excellent marksman and fully accustomed to the life of hap-hazard and adventure we were prosecuting" *Rambler*, I, 181). Dr. Holt presently became a citizen of Little Rock (Pope, *Early Days in Arkansas*, 152).

The hunter was called Ryan in the *Tour*, 49. "Ryan, a fine old man, who, out of love to the hunter's life, had joined the expedition and the messes of those far younger and less experienced than himself. He was a fine specimen of that race for which the frontier has been celebrated ever since Daniel Boone led the way across the mountains. . . . The Captain, the Doctor, and Ryan, were, perhaps, the best shots of our party" (Latrobe, *Rambler*, 196–97).

their habitation—trunk spread open discovers stores of honey —cut open the other part above—combs much broken— some white, clean & new, others old—take out flakes in a pail —every one with spoon & knife helps himself to the rich honey. Bees returning to their hive from abroad find the tree levelled and collect on the point of a withered branch of a neighbouring tree, contemplating the ruin & buzzing about the downfall of their republic.[37]

Some strange bees arrive and begin to banquet on the honey of their ruined neighbours—men know them by their greediness and their clean jackets.

Since being at this encampt they have taken 6 or 7 bee trees and killed 9 deer—camp abounds with honey and venison —15 turkeys.[38]

Bees have spread into this country within a few years.

Leave much honey in the ruin of the tree. ["]It will be all eaten by varmint,["] said one of the men. ["]What varmint?["] ["]Raccoons, opossums, skunks, bears &c.["] The latter will remain for days at a bee kill. They make a hole and get in their paws and haul out honey, bees and all. When queen bee is killed the hive goes to ruin.

Shooting—leaping—wrestling—in the camp— dinner, venison—roasted, fried, &c.—bread baked before fire—Prarie tea.[39] Capt. Bean & Latrobe go off to look after a beaver tree—to hunt &c.

Seated with D[r] Holt—man brings kettle of honey & sets

[37] Ellsworth described this at greater length than Irving; he said that the hive broke in the middle and the bees poured out on them, but that they stood still and the bees did not bother them.

[38] Ellsworth gave the score as "10 deer—20 turkeys, and 15 bee trees."

[39] See Introduction, page 59. Pourtalès collected some for Switzerland, and Ellsworth preserved some seed and wondered if it could be reproduced at home. It was "*sudorific, gently stimulating,* and an active diuretic—in large quantities it is laxative" (Ellsworth, *Narrative,* 17). Latrobe identified the plant as *solidago odora* (*Rambler,* I, 240). In everyday language, this is goldenrod.

before us—from a tree just taken—the 15th tree—swarm round it like bees—getting out the rich, white flakes.

Pourtales arrives at the camp and Billet—each with a turkey strung each side of his saddle—the Indian camp had moved across the river—found another camp—bought old wooden bowls and a buffalo skin & c.

A hunter returns to the camp on horseback with a wild turkey. He had put his leggins on the horse to protect him from the briars.

Lay on the grass talking with Capt, Lieut, Doctor, & others about route—looking at map—to-morrow will get to the Red Fork—will cross there & then in two days will crack buffalo bones.[40]

Hunter comes in with flakes of honey—another tree found —18 trees.

Shot heard—there's a buck killed—more honey brought in —20 trees—100 men in camp feasting on honey—towards ev[enin]g sentinels posted—fires lit up in advanced posts— horses dashing thro the camp—over fires—Capt & Doctor dine with us—roast leg of venison—roast turkey—Prarie tea, coffee. Owl hoots over the camp—has visited the camp several nights—men mock him and bring him down—is called Charlie's owl because sentinel coming in this morning fired gun contrary to orders and said he fired at owl because he was told it made good soup.

Pourtales fires at owl—kills it, and it falls on our tent.

Charlie is called in to eat it but declines as he did not kill it.

Mess at one of the tents singing psalms[41]—others whistling —sit by Captains fire and hear old hunters tales—various

---

40 Cf. Ellsworth, *Narrative*, 33. Probably it was at this time that they decided to shorten the itinerary included in Arbuckle's orders to Bean (Introduction, pages 31–33).

41 "While this boisterous merriment prevailed at some of the fires, there suddenly rose a strain of nasal melody from another, at which a choir of 'vocalists'

groups round camp fires—bells of horses—neighing of others
—stories of Pawnee fights—ruddy light in the west above the
trees. ["]That's a prarie on fire by the Osage hunters.["]

["]That's at the Red Fork,["] said Billet.

["]It seems but three miles distant—it is perhaps twenty.["]

About half past 8 a beautiful, pale light begins to spring
up in the east—forerunner to the moon.

Sleep at foot of a tree by fire—towards morning lie looking at moon and stars—horses straying about the camp.

Sunday 14th. Bugle sounds at daybreak—bustle in camp
—catching horses—driving them in—["]Have you seen
my horse? ["] cries one. ["]What horse is that broke loose
over the brook? ["] Night guard comes in—dismissed—fires
made—breakfast preparing—some packing—blankets that
have formed tents dismantled—singing—laughing—joking,
whooping—saddling horses. In a little while the forest so
suddenly & temporarily alive and animated soon relapses into
its primeval silence and solitude.

1 Ranger: ["]Whose wallet is this? ["]

2   "   ["]Why, I guess its mine.["]

1   "   ["]What kind of a wallet is it? ["]

2   "   ["]Why, it's a borrowed wallet. I borrowed it
before I started, but you easily know it by a bit of lead in it.["]

Bugle sounded to saddle & prepare to march.

Capt ["]Which way lies the Red Fork? Have none of you
hunters hunted out here? ["]

---

were uniting their voices in a most lugubrious psalm-tune. This was led by one of
the lieutenants, a tall, spare man, who we were informed had officiated as schoolmaster, singingmaster, and occasionally as Methodist preacher, in one of the villages of the frontier. The chant rose solemnly and sadly in the night air, and
reminded me of the description of similar canticles in the camps of the Covenant-
ers; and, indeed, the strange medley of figures and faces and uncouth garbs con-
gregated together in our troop would not have disgraced the banners of Praise-
God Barebone" (Irving, *Tour*, 62).

Billet ["]You go three miles. I have only went along yonder by the edge of the prarie. You will find a bald hill, with stones on it.["]⁴²

Capt ["]Yes, I have seen cliffs.["]

Billet ["]Stones which the Osages put up—from that hill you will see the Red Fork.["]

Leave encampt at 8 oclock, ride through tangled bottoms and up and down rough, broken, rocky hills—picturesque look of troop winding thro thickets and up heights. In climbing a rocky hill the girths of my horse give way and I have a fall, but am not hurt. Road winds by deep brook—a link of clear pools—fine views from height of distant praries, and of hills beyond the Arkansas—golden day—pure, delightful air. After much tortuous march & climbing hills, threading narrow but romantic valleys, we come upon the Arkansas—broad sandy shore—forests—elk—deer—buffalo—opossum—turkeys—banks of cotton tree & willow. Picturesque look of troops straggling along the shore—some in groups among the willows—turn in through thick bushes tangled with grape and pea vines—come to open woodland—herds of deer in all directions. The leaders of the troop start a deer—shots of rifles —we come to a small oak tree with marks of a bear's having tapped it—about ¼ before three the troop encamp in a beautiful basin under oak trees—we take our station on a rising ground overlooking the camp—hunters start in different directions to kill game—horses hobbled & turned loose—fires made—men silent—no whooping as in the morning—all busy or reposing—this day we made about 14 miles.

Huntsman brings in buck hanging across his horse—shots heard from time to time—concert of bells of all tones among the horses—

---

⁴² Their route on October 14 was "much to the north of west;" they passed half a mile to the left of Bald Hill according to Latrobe.

mode of roasting bread by twisting dough round a stick and standing it endways before a fire.

Beverage of corn just ripe but not quite fit for grinding—parched before slow fire—pounded—sifted a couple of spoonfuls to half pint of water—sweetened with sugar.[43]

Captain Bean returns from hunt—unsuccessful—had seen track of buffalo on the bottom since the last rain and of an elk that had walked out on the bar and then re-entered the woods above. If he had shot him we should have all feasted this evening. Had seen traces of a bear—lad comes in with doe round his shoulders—companion follows him—a laugh raised at him for shooting in partnership.

Clamour in camp—a young fellow, McLellan, has shot an elk for the first time and brought home some ribs as a specimen. He is hoisted on the shoulders of his companions—groups round fire examining the sport.[44]

Bee hunters on the track of a tree—this day after leaving the Arkansas we came thro a bottom where there was a great quantity of persimmons.

Monday 15th. Before daybreak howling of wolves—at daybreak imitations of cocks crowing, hens cackling, among the youngsters of the camp—horses driven in—breakfast—whistling—singing—dancing—hallooing after horses—joking, laughing, scampering after horses—

troop detained for party which went out at daybreak in quest of the elk which was killed—to bring in the meat. They are said to have got on the trail of the other elk.

Story of Uncle Sam's gun.[45]

[43] This "most agreeable beverage" was made from corn "taken before quite ripe and boiled—it is then dried and hung up untill wanted—it is finally pounded or ground & sifted." It was "good in water without sweetning, but mixed with a little sugar it possesses a peculiar zest." Ellsworth resolved not to travel again on the prairies without it, ordered half a bushel for his own supply, and ventured to think that it would be "palitable even in Hartford" (*Narrative*, 36).

[44] Ellsworth said the celebration was for the first elk killed by anyone in the camp.

Bugle sounds to march—Capt leaves guard to await return of hunters—after mile or two come upon Indian or buffalo trail—view of Red Fork from high hill[46]—rolling of bear by stream—grove & intervals of various trees—rocky ridges—lines of heights—then down through rich bottom of land—affair of Billet with a skunk[47]—traces of deer—of a bear—marks of bears on the oak trees—come to a halt—Capt & Billet looking out for a ford of the Arkansas. We are about one quarter of mile above the fork—river narrower than below & deeper—current strong—banks crumbling and abrupt—no crossing—Billet is sent to look above at a sand bar.

Resume our route—about a mile distant come to ford pointed out by Billet who strips and wades nearly across[48]—council—Capt determines to make rafts & cross—troops return to bottom of pea vines. Our Frenchmen lead our horses to bank & prepare to make a raft of buffalo hide.

Pile luggage in centre of hide drawn up the sides by the loopholes & tie the strings across.

Launch it on river and the Frenchmen and half breeds conduct it across, yelping like Indians. Some of the troop headed by Lieut. Penticost cross 1½ miles up the river—fording a long, oblique distance—others seeing this abandon the con-

---

[45] A double-barreled gun Ellsworth had obtained from McCoy. It was called "Uncle Sam," Latrobe wrote, because of the initials "U. S." stamped on it. "It was a piece of respectably ancient mould and fabric, about four inches across the breech, and two at the muzzle." On one occasion the Englishman, asked to determine why this fully loaded gun would not go off, "found three buckshot under the powder in one barrel, and a roll of dog-wood shavings and tow in the chamber of the other" (*Rambler*, I, 206–208, 220, 245). It was put in shape and, eventually, at least a duck and a skunk fell victims to it.

[46] The Cimarron River. "The Red Fork appeared worthy of its name, pouring down into the main river at our feet, a turbid bright red stream, broken by wide level sand bars and mud banks" (Latrobe, *Rambler*, I, 184).

[47] Billet (Beatte) killed a skunk, but when he was absent Irving threw it in the river. The amusing part of the story is that Irving later ate fritters fried in skunk grease as well as roast skunk—and liked both. See Latrobe, *Rambler*, I, 184–85; Ellsworth, *Narrative*, 47, 109; Irving, *Tour*, 72–74, 77.

[48] According to Ellsworth, the water was soon up to Billet's shoulders and he had to swim to the opposite shore. (*Narrative*, 39).

struction of their rafts and set off to follow their trail.[49] I cross in the buffalo skin—seated on a quantity of luggage, with a double barrel'd gun and rifle—saluted by Lt. Penticost & two rangers who had crossed—return their salute by discharge of carabine—land safely & dryly at 2 oclock.[50] [FOOTNOTE: Billet who went before had a towing line and when he came to where he had to swim he held the cord between his teeth—Antoine followed the boat—]

Arkansas at this place beautifully diversified by high bluffs of wood rock—long, willowed reaches—rich bottoms and embowered promontories on the west bank where I landed, tracks of elk, deer, bears, raccoons, waterfowls—woods tinted with autumn—this morning in rich bottom passed a stately pecan tree.

Capt & Dr Holt form raft of logs & cross—long line of troops crossing at distance from point to point.

Break our way through thick underwood to the camp which is in a small wild rocky dell in the narrow and which is like a cul de sac—encampt in green, grassy bottom of the dell—ridges of limestone rocks above—lofty tree.[51]

[49] See Tonish's opinion, Introduction, page 61. Latrobe and Pourtalès (and Brailey with them) watched the adventure of the bull-boat and then followed the rangers to this ford.

[50] "Mr Irving was going also [to the ford]—I proposed to him, to try the Buffaloe skin—our servants were almost exhausted but we cheered their spirits by giving them a dollar each for the ferriage—I offered to go first, but Irving desired the opportunity and I consented—his boat was filled nearly full and launched regularly into the river—He was then taken in the arms of Billet & Tonish and placed with great care in the centre of the tottering craft, and requested to sit *perfectly still*—The swimmers plunged in with their hideous yells, and Mr Irving sat *motionless*, proud enough to be borne across the deep in a Buffaloe skin!!—when the swimmers had passed more than half the distance, and become able to touch the bottom, Mr Irving . . . [seized] one of the guns which lay beside him, [and] he fired a salute to those who were behind him" (Ellsworth, *Narrative*, 41). In the *Tour*, Irving said that he fired the gun "to please the vanity of little Tonish." The servants, as Ellsworth and Irving persisted in calling their hired men, had some little reason to be disgruntled: Latrobe said that they made six or seven trips across the river.

Irving was busily writing in his notebook when Ellsworth was delivered on the next trip of the bull-boat.

[51] Latrobe called this camp the Bear's Glen; Ellsworth the Bear's Den.

My horse & pony missing—fearful that they have not crossed—Mr. Ellsworth & Billet set off in quest of them.

Fires lit in dell—looks like a robbers' retreat—groups of men round fires—rifles—powder horns &c. leaning ag[ain]st trees beside them—horses grazing around with bells tinkling —baggage, blankets &c. hanging on horizontal poles to dry— no account of my horse—

Walk with the Doctor to the head of the hill—splendid view of the Arkansas, with picturesque bluffs of tinted wood-lands—bottom of fresh green—long reaches of distant hills— blue lines of untrodden country—gleam of the red fork among hills—beautiful sunset.

See smoke from the low dell of our encampment—see two laggards of the troop rafting over—shots among the forests on the other side—distant smoke of praries on the horizon.

Return to camp—a deer and five turkeys brought in—sup on excellent venison steak & coffee—repair to Captain's fire— after dark see glow of fires in western heavens. Capt ["]If they are on this side the Arkansas, they must be Pawnee fires. No Osages dare hunt here.["] Antoine thinks them Osage fires on the other side of the Arkansas.

Capt ["]We must now look out. I must issue written orders—no man hunts without leave or fires off a gun on pain of riding a wooden horse with a sharp back.["]

It will be difficult to teach our young fellows caution— they are in the land of a silent, watchful, crafty people.

One man says, ["]Where I go my gun goes—I never like to leave it behind—there's no one will take such care of it as me—and there is nothing that will take such care of me.["]

Capt & others determine our position.

["]Do you see that blazing star? That's the evening star.["] Another, ["]That's the planet Venus that looks down into our camp.["]

A band of hunters are still out on the other side of the river.

Capt ["]I should send to look after them but old Ryans with them, and he knows how to take care of himself & them. If it were not for him I would not give much for the rest. He's quite at home—never lost in the woods—It will be four to keep watch and one to tend the fire. ["]⁵²

Story of the Sergeant⁵³

["]I was once belated in passing thro a forest near the Tombigbee—heard wolves howl—my horse came crowding near me—drove him off but he returned & stood looking at me & the fire & dozing & nodding & loitering on his fore feet for he was powerful tired. By and by I heard a Panther cry —thought at first it might be an owl—felt awkward—had no weapon but double blade pen knife—prepared to defend myself. [FOOTNOTE: I prepared for defence—piled up small branch of fire to pepper him with.] The company of my horse seemed a comfort. He laid down then beside me and fell asleep, being so tired. In the morning I found the tracks of a Panther within sixty paces—they were large as my two fists. He had evidently been walking backward and forward trying to make up his mind to attack me—["]

Wild look of dell with fires glaring here and there among the rocks & trees—

fine spring of water at the head of it. This day we made about 4 miles besides crossing the river.

Tuesday 16ᵗʰ Oct. Awake before day—fine night—moon shining feebly down into the camp—fires nearly extinguished —men lying about their fires—light clouds drifting across the

---

⁵² Apparently some who could not swim. The next morning they were discovered making a raft by which to cross. These various bits of dialogue were worked into the *Tour*, 84–87.

⁵³ Identified in entry for October 17 as a brother of Captain Bean.

LE SOLDAT DU CHENE

a typical Osage chief

Reproduced from McKenney and Hall,
History of the Indian Tribes of North America, *1838*

moon—at daybreak Billet sets off to cross the river in search of my horses.

Returns about 8 oclock with all three. Bustle of preparation —some men sent back over the river in quest of guns left behind—demand for tall horses to stem the current—intend to make a raft and return.

Yellow leaves showering around us—signs of autumn.

At meal times great borrowing of frying pans, kettles &c when about to set off, loud demands—["]Who has a frying pan from the mess?["]—["]Who has seen my horse?["] &c &c &c

Capt resolves to start & leave a rear guard to bring up stragglers—bugle sounds—troop files off—we remain, as our packing is not complete. Antoine who accomp[anie]d Billet to look after the horses, the other side of the river, got on false trail and has not yet returned.[54]

Rear guard in groups—some seated round their fires— others lying on ground lazily talking—their horses unsaddled stand dozing by—one takes the occasion to shave—some distant mounted—among the trees—with guns over shoulders— quiet of the grove except low talk of lazy groups, or a pensive whistle of some solitary laggard.

We leave the encampt at ½ past 9—our route lies over a rolling country of oak openings—grand distant prospects like cultivated country—our route at first is by mistake about N W, but we alter it to W. Crossing a beautiful range of open hills— four deer are descried grazing on side of a hill. One of the rangers gets permission of Capt and started off for an intervening wood. The troop halted & watched—bang went the gun —one deer fell—the rangers are starting forth, but Capt with-

---

[54] This was Antoine Lombard, not Tonish Deshetres. He returned later loaded with bear meat, according to Latrobe and Ellsworth.

On this day, "Mr. Irving complains much of a swelling of the eyelids and an eruption around the wrists—Doc Holt gave him a wash of the sugar of lead but salt water was his greatest relief" (Ellsworth, *Narrative*, 43).

held them—let the man have another shot (the surviving deer having stopped)—the deer started & ran—the whole line broke—horsemen galloping in every direction—Antoine, who had been skirting the forest, on white horse, came in sight but had no chance—the deer got off.

Found an old Indian camp—some thought Pawnee, but Dr said it is some bold Delawares who have hunted here—old skull of a stag by the encampt—fine stream close by—immediately after we come on an old well beaten trail of either Indians or buffalo.

After leaving the place where we had the first affair with deer, we came in sight of others on a hill—hunters sent forward—shoot but miss. A fine buck starts up from side of stream & escapes—several other deer seen.

We proceed—passing side of a hill we see two horsemen on the bald ridge of a distant hill who appear to be reconnoitering us—["]Pawnees,["] cry some—Capt and others regard them —Portales brings his opera glass. They prove to be two of our men who had remained behind and had lost their way.

Antoine starts up a fine buck—shoots but misses him— cross the dividing ridge of Red Fork and Arkansas—the former making a great bend—push on and encamp about ½ past 3 on a beautiful peninsula made by a deep, clear, but almost motionless brook. The huntsmen start off immediately—our man Billet among the first.

This day we made about 15 miles—we are about 102 miles from Fort Gibson.

Delightful mode of life—exercise on horseback all the fore part of the day—diversified by hunting incidents—then about 3 oclock encamping in some beautiful place with full appetite for repose, lying on the grass under green trees—in genial weather with a blue, cloudless sky—then so sweet sleeping at night in the open air, & when awake seeing the moon and stars through the tree tops—such zest for the hardy, simple, but savory meats, the product of the chase—venison roasted on spits or broiled on the coals—turkeys just from the thicket— honey from the tree—coffee—or delightful prarie tea. The weather is in its perfection—golden sunshine—not oppressive but animating—skies without a cloud—or if there be clouds, of feathery texture and lovely tints—air pure, bland, exhilarating—an atmosphere of perfect transparency—and the whole country having the mellow tint of autumn. How exciting to think that we are breaking thro a country hitherto untrodden by white man, except perchance the solitary trapper— a glorious world spread around us without an inhabitant.

Young man comes into camp who has killed a deer—has made a sack of the hide—filled it with meat and slung it on his shoulder.

Capt returns—has seen a gang of 60 elk—followed and refrained from shooting in hopes of getting shot at a large buck—at length wounded one but lost it.

Billet returns with a fat doe on his horse—skinned. In a little while some ribs are roasted & furnish a delicious treat— such is hunter's life—feasting and fasting—we had just before made a meal of remnants of turkey and salt pork.

Wind changes—driving clouds—threatens rain, but moon breaks out about midnight.

Wednesday 17^(th) Oct. Cloudy morng—threat[enin]g rain —halted for the day[55]—preparations for hunting—hunters summoned—charged to go to river and below but not to go up the brook—to bring all their spoil into camp & lay it down by the Capt's fire that it may be portioned out.

Hearty breakfast of ribs of venison and coffee with cakes baked in pan before the fire.

---

[55] They were to remain in camp because several men were sick with the measles, and several others had not yet caught up with the company since crossing the Arkansas River (Ellsworth, *Narrative*, 46).

Set off with Capt. Bean, his brother, Sergeant Bean, & Lieut. Penticost and accomp[anie]d by two men on foot who are to bring home a doe killed by the Sergeant last ev[enin]g. Soon come to the doe lying on hillside disembowelled & leave the footmen to cut it up and carry it to camp—Come upon elk trail—deep prints like a cow—elk beds where they laid the night before last—go quietly, Indian file—come to where Capt shot the elk last night—see blood on shrubs & grass—on the trail for some time when it ceases—see a deer or two scampering in the forest. Capt looks for separate trail of wounded elk—thinks it must be somewhere about the neighbourhood as some buzzards hovering in the air—regain the trail of the elks—carries us thro open oak forested hills until we come to a bend of the Red River where the elk had forded. It is probable they did not stop for ten miles last night—give up the pursuit and turn our course to creek on which is the encamp[men]t. Sergeant & Lieut take one side of the creek— Captain and myself the other—pass old Buffalo trail on road —come up with two hunters on foot who had wounded an elk but lost him & had found the elk killed by Capt last night. They conduct us to it, about 1½ miles from where it was shot. It had abandoned the trail of its sound, unhurt companions and had turned off to die alone [FOOTNOTE: The elk when mortally wounded always leaves the trail & turns aside to die.] to-day in open oak wood on side of a slope—already begun to spoil. Capt & men go to work to cut it up—flesh tainted inside— Capt & men skin it and cut collops off of the ribs & the outside generally—Buzzard soaring in the air waiting to banquet on the spoil—Capt forms sack of the hides gathered up through holes in the edges by thongs cut from the same—puts it on his horse and sets off for camp—footmen pursue their sport.

Return to camp. Antoine the half breed returned with a bear which he killed near our old camp. Old Ryan & his party

[56] See n. 54, above.

had met with Antoine & hearing of the ford had crossed the river with him.[56]

Picturesque scene of the camp—some roasting bear's meat and venison—others stretching & dressing skins—some lying on skins in the shade—horses feeding—hunters coming in with game—turkeys, & c.—groups relating the morning's exploits —clothes hanging to dry[57]—tent pitched—fine luncheon.

Latrobe has caught mess of small fish in the brook.[58]

One hunter brings in an otter—the rest return without success—game frightened from the neighbourhood.

Dinner, bears meat roasted—excellent—the rest of bear's meat and venison is roasted to take with us—venison and bears meat cooked at Capt's fire.

Camp nearly surrounded by deep glens with quiet, clear pools at the bottom, in which the autumnal glory and mellow ev[enin]g skies are beautifully reflected.

[*With the Journal turned around, Irving made the following undated notes.*]

Carandolet or *Vuide Poche* few miles below St. Louis.

A traveller from New Orleans nearly out of provisions, stopped his canoe there and asked for food—no beef—no mutton—no bread—old—all sick with fever and ague—turned upon him and asked what he had—nothing but a few fragments of biscuit in pouch—begged them—shook them out and gave him the empty bag to travel on with—thence the place took the name of Vide Poche, or empty pouch.

Capt. Courtois[59]—old, round, dried fellow—looked like

[57] "Mr Irving & myself went to the Creek and washed our linnen & wollens —it was a *new employment* to *both*—I soaked mine sometime in the water but it was extreemly difficult, to get out the dirt, especially from my wollens—I plied soap liberally and made my clothes tolerably decent & that is all—ironing was of course dispensed with" (Ellsworth, *Narrative*, 46).

[58] "Roache or sun fish", according to Ellsworth.

[59] The only Courtois associated with Carondelet seems to have been Louis Courtois, who was listed in the statistical census for 1791; Houck identified him as the son of Joseph Courtois and Marguerite Perthuis, and said that he

Don Quixote—could not read or write, but study French, afternoons—was [two words illegible] made Duke under Spanish govt—and had title of commandant with small pay— when asked when was Carandolet founded, replied, "De tout des temps." When the province was transferred he was recommended to gov[60] and was made Capt of Militia, with which he was well pleased. Having no silk sash, he made one of red silk handkerchief—invited Gov. Lewis,[61] Genl Clark, & others to dine with him at Vuide Poche—militia drawn out— ordered to fire at each toast—then asked permission for them to come and drink to health of the party. Shouldered their arms, entered, drank and returned to their stations like statues. After transfer of govt he remained here living in the village—old people looked up to him—settled all disputes— his word was law. He was a good farmer—kept a small shop and was well to do in the world.

Capt. Coutrois wore old-fashioned cocked hat when on militia duty.

He was once put on a jury which was a new institution in the country and quite strange to him—when asked he observed —["]My mind is made up on the subject.["]—["]And what is it, Capt. Courtois? ["]—["]Why, if the man is guilty he should be punished, and if he is innocent he should be set at liberty and no harm done him.["]—["]Aye, but, Capt. Courtois, that is not the thing—you must say guilty or not guilty.["] ["]I tell you my mind is made up—if he is

---

married Genevieve Hunaud at Ste Genevieve in 1770; he died, at the age of seventy-one, in 1815 *(Spanish Régime in Missouri*, II, 378, 385). Between 1811 and 1814, a J. M. Courtois was lieutenant in the military company of which Hyacinthe Deshetres was captain; Louis Courtois was captain of another company, and his son Louis was a lieutenant in that same company (Bates, *Life and Papers*, II, 193, 233, 284). The first-mentioned Courtois is the more likely one, but at the time of the transfer of Louisiana, Treget was commandant.

60 This word is either *Gen*l or *gov*t; since no name follows, the latter seems the more satisfactory reading.

61 Meriwether Lewis.

guilty,["] & c. There was no getting any other answer from old Capt. Courtois & the jury had to be dismissed.

Chief cook of Osage villages—a great dignitary—combining grand chamberlain, minister of state, master of ceremonies and town crier—has under-cooks. He tastes broth & c. When strangers arrive he goes about the village and makes proclamation—great white man, great chief arrived—warriors turn out and prepare to receive him properly. Chief lodge prepared for reception—mats placed, etc.[62]

In the course of our journey from Independence we met with camp of Osage hunters—the cook a tall man painted—head decorated with feathers—had an old greatcoat, with a wolf's tail dangling below.

In the Chilhowee Mountains of N. Carolina is a rock called the garden rock—Indian superstition so strong concerning it that no one dared to approach it—supernatural being inhabited it—gigantic—one eye—not seen by men but the wandering hunters now and then had a gleam of his eye.

Near the mountain lived an old woman and daughter. He fell in love with and gained her—mother & no one ever saw him—mother watched—surprised her in the lodge with him. He disappeared and has never been seen since then. Hunters say he still inhabits the mountain, which is in the reservation in N. Carolina.

Col. Choteau's comparison of two half breeds—this one has been twice as long at the Mission as the other and therefore is twice as good for nothing.

The Choctaws, Col. Arbuckle says, are very good, honest fellows.

The Choctaws are sly, bargaining, avaricious. They have become civilized enough to know the value of property. They

[62] Cf. E. James, *Long's Expedition*, I, 289–93; McDermott and Salvan, *Tixier's Travels*, 119 and note 10, 172, 187, 199, 216.

are factious, electioneering—chiefs try to get adherents and make parties.

Old trapper at Blacksmith's.[63]

Capt[ain]—["]What are you doing up here?—Trapping bear?["]

["]There's none to trap only now and then.["]

["]What's become of your party?["]

["]Scattered—some gone to California—some down Columbia River.["]

This flour is bad enough to kill a snake—there's lumps in it as big as terrapins.[64]

The Osages are brave Indians—hunters full of ceremonies and superstitions. We are poor people, say they—we cannot farm and our hunting is falling off. The pride of the Osages is broken.

They steal horses—give you a grand ceremony and then perhaps follow you and steal your horse.

Wild horses—tell you by the smell if the wind sets from you, and run off—otherwise come near and gaze at you. Stallions prance round and snuff at mares.

Horses, if they smell mares, make off

wild horses in droves of one colour—some black—some brown

one gang will be good—another bad.

Best horses cannot be taken.

Buffaloes—when the cows have calves the bulls keep scattered round the prarie, keeping guard ag[ain]st wolves—charge furiously at anything that approaches.

[63] This scene took place at the Verdigris River on October 10. Irving evidently liked the remarks for their casual tone.

[64] This Irving overheard at the camping place on the night of October 10. Ellsworth also heard it, but he reported the soldier as saying that the flour "contained terrapins" *(Narrative,* 12).

Saline near the Wachile which used to be and still is a fighting ground of the Osages and Pawnees—their skulls and bones may be seen bleaching there.[65]

A grey horse has been noted for six or seven years on the praries and the hunters have in vain tried to catch him—he perceives our tracks and outstrips the fastest horse.

Six men, a detach[men]t from a large force, came upon what they thought were wild horses—they approached them and found they were tame—thought to take them—but perceived Indians near in lodge—supposed them Osages—and came near them when they discovered they were Pawnees—they turned and fled. Pawnees sprang on their horses and pursued them—one badly wounded—fell behind—a Pawnee gained on him—one launched arrow—missed him—launched another arrow—the man dodged it—his stirrups gave way—he fell—turned and shot Pawnee between the shoulders with his rifle—the other Pawnees turned to cry over their friend—the man escaped. Pawnee's horse followed the white men to their camp—and was taken.

Story of young lady carried off by Indians:

Young man by name of Philips followed her with a band —came upon track of Indians on a prarie—saw they must come near a point of wood—made a circuit and got into wood —young lady saw them & fell behind Indians—Philips, seeing they would not come within a certain distance of wood, sallied forth—young lady ran toward him—Indian pursued her—gained on her—began to strike at her with his tomahawk. Philips says his horse seemed to stand still, tho at utmost speed—within——yards young lady stumbled over log and

---

[65] The Osage made regular expeditions to the Salt Plain and the Salt Rock. The first of these lay between the Salt Fork of the Arkansas and the Cimarron rivers, west of the ninety-eighth meridian, the other about seventy-five miles to the northwest of the first (McDermott and Salvan, *Tixier's Travels*, 240, n. 8, 249–51).

fell partly thro loss of blood—Indian was just going to tomahawk her when Philips shot him thro' head—narrator had the
story from Philips brother.

Indians when they have killed game and cannot bring it
home, leave a blanket or some other garment by it, the smell
of which keeps off wolves.

A rag with powder rubbed on it is said to do the same.

Billet ["]I want to know what way to go anyhow.["]

Charley the hero of the owl camp a kind of butt in the
camp.[66]

Billet—half Frenchman—half Indian—talkative & forward at times—taciturn & sulky at others—brings in game—
throws it down & says nothing about it.

Antoine thorough Frenchman—vaunts, exults, sings,
boasts.

Ring fires—made by Indians on prairies to drive game to
a point—a few men will run from point to point and make a
range of fires for miles.

[66] See the entry for October 13.

JOURNAL IV

On the Little River, October 31—Fort Gibson

November 10, 1832[1]

WEDNESDAY *1832. Oct. 31.*[2] Encampt on the little river—Canadian.[3] For a day or two past, discontent in the camp as among the children of Israel in the wilderness—want of bread—for a week past the troops have been out of flour. A corporal last night was put under arrest for mutinous talk on the subject. Determined that we start from here, direct for the garrison. Capt & Dr's horses & the horse of a ranger had strayed yesterday & men had been sent back to the last camp in search of them. Capt & one man set off this morning on their trail. We made every preparation for starting—horses of troops all saddled—10

---

[1] On the page before the Journal begins appear these faint notations: "Chilowy Mont[s]   N Carolina & Tennessee   Nashville, Knoxville to the right."

[2] No Journal exists for the period of October 18–30, inclusive. A day-by-day summary from Ellsworth's *Narrative*, 49–128, gives some continuity to Irving's account. Cf. *Tour*, 111–246.

18 October. Sick left behind with a guard—Irving's horse lame—Bean told story much like that of Hugh Glass. *19 October.* Made only about 10 miles headway—hard rain. *20 October.* Course west by south—passed rocks called by Holt Irving's Castle and by Irving Cliff Castle—increasing signs of buffalo—camped after making 13 miles—Ellsworth summed up long conversations with Irving about his life, writings, and earnings and gave opinions of Latrobe and Pour-

oclock & Capt not returned. Mr. Ellsworth determined to start on ahead & let Capt & troops overtake us. We set off under escort of 14 men under Lieut. Penticost at 10 oclock— skirt the Prarie—see white wolves, deer &c. See Buffalo & wild horses—Billet [word illegible] & Antoine⁴ set off in pursuit of horses, but in vain—Portales shoots at Buffalo. Keep a S[outhern] course and then turn Southeast in old Osage war track Terrible brush wood⁵ thickets—deep ravine—see deer— fine bucks &c.—Buffalo—encamp 5 minutes before 3 in a

tales—Lieut. King and three others arrived in camp, announcing killing of three buffaloes—Ellsworth wrote in detail about buffaloes and wild horses. *21 October.* Ellsworth and Irving saw grey horse mentioned in Irving notes—passed through "terrible woods, called Cross Timbers"—Irving lost "the whole of one skirt of his coat" in making his way through the "cast iron stuff"—Irving generally in a bad temper—Billet leaped twenty-five foot precipice to capture a beautiful wild horse—made fifteen miles. *22 October.* Billet broke in his horse—party traveled 3 miles south southwest to cross Red Fork (Cimarron)—buffalo-hunting—fire in camp—false alarm of Pawnee and ludicrous scenes in camp. *23 October.* Stopped to examine beaver dam—more wild horses—Irving had exchanged his pony and $70 for Lieut. Caldwell's horse a few days earlier—now traded that horse and $35 for a sorrel belonging to Clements, a ranger—made about fifteen miles on their course—Ellsworth went into council with Bean, Holt, and Irving concerning remainder of tour—Ellsworth determined not to go beyond Canadian River. *24 October.* Buffalo hunt—Irving as a hunter—made 14 miles. *25 October.* Irving ate skunk stew—wild horses and buffaloes discovered at the same moment—Irving rode about, watching everything—crossed North Fork of Canadian—trouble with quicksand—made 15 miles. *26 October.* More hunting —met small war party of Osage—Billet and Tonish had adventure with bear— made 18 miles. *27 October.* Rained all night—remained in camp. *28 October.* Weather still bad—remained in camp—Billet reported open prairie not far off. *29 October.* Weather cleared—travel six miles—camp outside Cross Timbers— buffalo hunt—Pourtalès lost. *30 October.* Pourtalès found about ten miles from camp—Irving afflicted with breaking out on wrists and face—Ellsworth and Holt visited prairie dog "republic."

³ That is, on the morning of October 31 they left their camp on the Little River (which flows southeast to enter the Canadian River from the north in Hughes County, Oklahoma). They traveled southeastwardly, parallel to the Canadian, for some miles and then turned northeast. Latrobe said that the camp occupied on the nights of October 29 and 30 was three miles north of the Canadian. On these last days in October they were near the site of Norman, Cleveland County, Oklahoma.

⁴ The illegible word is quite possibly *Tonish*. Ellsworth wrote "Tonish Billet & Antoine" *(Narrative,* 133).

⁵ They had turned back into the Cross Timbers. For Irving's earlier experience with this patch of forest, see Ellsworth, *Narrative,* 87–88; see also n. 2, above.

small valley—near pools of water. Made this day 14 miles or thereabout. Form our little camp—set guard—make fires—sup on stewed buffalo, roast venison, pig nuts [?]—tea without sugar—Spread our skins under trees. Old Mr. Sawyer[6] sits at foot of my bed & gossips until I fall asleep. Large bear seen in neighbourhood of our camp—but excaped the huntsmen—Fine star-light night—shooting stars.

Thursday November 1. Beautiful daybreak—camp cheerful—in good spirits with prospect of soon being at home and getting bread—notes of quails—Billet singing Indian nasal song—prepare for marching but detained by the wandering of one of Latrobe's horses—at length (it being found) we set off at 8. Fatiguing march over hills through deep ravines of parched dwarf oaks with flesh tearing twigs, through tangled thickets &c.[7] Billet kills a fat doe—Latrobe a fine turkey—arrive at the valley of the Grand Bayou in little river—wander about in a labyrinth of swamps thickets, inundated lands—

[6] According to Latrobe, Sawyer was "a comical old fellow, the butt of the troop . . . one of those strange mixtures of simplicity and shrewdness. . . . Sawyer generally asked for a furlough three times a day when in camp, and was celebrated for losing himself, and spending the night nobody knew where. He was used as a 'cat's-paw' by the men, whenever they wished to pry into the plans and designs of the officers." Latrobe placed on the evening of October 27 one of these purposeful visits by Sawyer: "The Rangers, as was natural, began to look to their officers for a decided change of plan, as their own common sense showed the impracticability of our proceeding much deeper into the country in the present advanced state of the season; and Sawyer as usual pushed forward to sound the intentions of the Commissioner. Like most inordinately inquisitive people, he thought his best way was to be very open-hearted and communicative himself, and thereby to win us over to his own humour. He accordingly, without provocation, gave us the history of his whole life and former adventures:—how he had, after sowing his wild oats, been incited to turn a methodist, and remained such some time, till seeing, as he expressed it, 'the error of his way,' he had become a Shaking Quaker, and so forth. . . . all this expenditure of confidence elicited no sympathetic disclosures from our quiet friend the Commissioner, and Sawyer at length made a retreat to announce his discomfiture to his comrades" (*Rambler*, I, 195–96, 217–18).

[7] "The celebrated *Cross Timbers*, of which frequent mention has been made, extend from the Brazos, or perhaps from the Colorado of Texas, across the sources of Trinity, traversing Red River above the False Washita, and thence west of north, to the Red Fork of Arkansas if not further. It is a rough hilly range of country, and, though not mountainous, may perhaps be considered a

tangled with grape vines thorny vines which almost pull us off our horses—nearly mired in a deep creek—one of the pack horses falls on his side wets his lading[8]—tracks of bears, wolves, buffalo, wild horses, turkeys, ducks, &c. Try several times to find fording place of Bayou, which is deep and miry with steep [word illegible] banks—at length succeed—all get over girth deep and stop to rest the horses in a meadow about ½ past 11 having made about 10 miles Spread wet baggage to dry—hang up the two shirts which I washed yesterday.

Resume our march ¼ before 1—excessively fatiguing to men and horses—a broken, hilly country covered with Scrub oaks, with interlacing limbs as hard as iron, & intersected by deep ravines of red clay, down which the horses fairly slide, & then scramble up the other side like cats. The oaks are all brown & dried as if a simoom had passed across—a miserable, sterile, dreary country at this season of the year. Here & there is a bottom where there are cotton & elm trees which give a transient variety, and absolute thickets of persimmons laden with rich fruit. In a meadow of one of these bottoms we see a fine wild black horse. Billet approaches him, riding on a mare & whinnies to attract him. Horse prances round her at a distance. Billet dismounts, aims with his rifle over the back of his

---

prolongation of that chain of low mountains which pass to the northward of Bexar and Austin City in Texas.

"The Cross Timbers vary in width from five to thirty miles, and entirely cut off the communication betwixt the interior prairies and those of the great plains. They may be considered as the 'fringe' of the great prairies, being a continuous brushy strip, composed of various kinds of undergrowth; such as blackjacks, post-oaks, and in some places hickory, elm, etc. intermixed with a very diminutive dwarf oak, called by the hunters 'shin-oak.' Most of the timber appears to be kept small by the continual inroads of the 'burning prairies;' for, being killed almost annually, it is constantly replaced by scions of undergrowth; so that it becomes more and more dense every reproduction. In some places, however, the oaks are of considerable size, and able to withstand the conflagrations. The underwood is so matted in many places with grape-vines, green-briars, etc., as to form almost impenetrable 'roughs,' which serve as hiding-places for wild beasts, as well as wild Indians; and would, in savage warfare, prove almost as formidable as the hammocks of Florida" (Gregg, *Commerce of the Prairies*, II, 199–200).

[8] Latrobe's old horse Gumbo.

mare, and fires, hoping to criss the horse[9]—but he escapes. About ½ past 3 we resume our march [two words illegible] keeping easterly, approaching the North Fork obliquely—difficulty in finding a place to encamp where there is water—pass over a burnt prarie—at length about ½ after 4 encamp in a small bottom near the burnt Prarie & not far from the North Fork—good range for the horses.[10]

Make my bed under a big[11] tree on a hillock among long, dry, Prarie grass—a superb couch—sleep soundly sweetly warmly tho a heavy dew fell—Starlight—watch the stars on the prarie as at sea. Lightning in the East a sign of apparently bad weather—clouds about the horizon—flocks of wild ducks show cold weather at hand.

Camp short of provisions—improvidence of men who left piles of buffalo meat at their camp the day before yesterday.

Saturday Nov. 3.[12] Breakfasted early on coffee & the last of our Buffalo meat—march ¼ after 7—weather clouds up, low mumblings of thunder—wind veers to NE and it begins to rain—cross prarie & pass thro open oak forests—See deer, but

[9] "The mustang is sometimes taken by the cruel expedient of 'creasing,' which consists of shooting him through the upper *crease* of the neck, above the cervical vertebræ; when, the ball cutting a principal nerve, he falls as suddenly as if shot in the brain, and remains senseless for a few minutes, during which he is secured with a rope. He soon recovers. . . . But 'creasing' is so nice an operation that many are killed in the attempt" (Gregg, *Commerce of the Prairies,* II, 208–209).

[10] Possibly near the site of Tecumseh, Pottawatomie County, Oklahoma.

[11] The word may be *dry.*

[12] There is no entry for November 2. In the morning they came upon an old Creek hunting camp. "On the bark of the trees were rude delineations of hunters and squaws, scrawled with charcoal; together with various signs and hieroglyphics, which our half-breeds interpreted as indicating that from this encampment the hunters had returned home." At this midday halting place Bean and the main body of the rangers overtook them (*Tour,* 259–60). Of the art work Ellsworth said: "The Creeks have a *very indecent* manner of making pictures on the trees. The wood is first cut off, and with paints they represent the warrior in such attitudes of amorous feeling in going or returning as may be indicative of their true sensations, but very abhorrent to every principle of modesty or virtue—I forbear giving details" (*Narrative,* 136). Their course this day was northeast; their progress twenty-eight miles.

not within shot—several flocks of wild turkeys—men on the alert, eager for a dinner. A few days since, they despised such small game & I have seen dead turkeys left behind on marching.

Cross the North Fork[13] about ½ past 9—quite fordable —ride through rich, well timbered bottom—cross small branches, and 7 minutes before 1 encamp in an oak forest beside a creek—rain holds up until we make fires—pitch tent—dry our clothes. Hunters are gone out & Billet among the number on quest of food, for a great scarcity reigns in the camp—some of the men have not had anything since yesterday morn'g— Tonish is cooking flour fritters in Buffalo fat for us, to take with coffee, without milk or sugar.[14]

Billet returns with two turkeys—10 turkeys killed in this camp.

This part of country has good bottoms along the rivers— some good pasture land in the praries, & good mast in the forests—might make good land to raise stock on.

Billet had said the wind would be to the North—this morning a flight of brant flew from the north over our heads— ["]There comes the wind,["] said Billet—and in fact the wind soon veered—night cold, gusty with freaks of rain— large log fire before our tent.

In the night wild geese fly over, making cackling in the air.

Sunday Nov. 4. Raw, cloudy, gloomy morning—three men went out from each mess to hunt for the horses—very apprehensive that many of them have made for the fort, for horses have an instinctive knowledge of their approach to home and can make a straight course for it—as they graze, every step they take is towards home.

Set out on the march ¼ before 8—after marching an hour

---

[13] They probably crossed the North Fork of the Canadian River from Seminole County to enter the extreme southwestern corner of Okfuskee County.
[14] They made twenty miles on November 3.

ENCAMPMENT NEAR THE RED FORK

from a pencil sketch, presumably by Irving, in Journal III

Reproduced from a microfilm of the original Journals

or so we strike a Creek trail, leading directly on our course, which enables us to go on briskly though very irregularly, many of the horses being almost knocked up. Land improves— fine praries like park scenery, now mellowed by the sober tints of autumn. A young buck springs up on our right and dashes ahead, but Childers, a young ranger who had accidentally alighted from his horse, fires breaks his neck & the buck tumbled head over heels. Tonish flanked us on the left & killed a fat doe. Another ranger killed a buck. Mr. Latrobe kills a polecat which is treasured up by the men. Several turkeys killed—noble prospect from a hill over richly tinted woodlands, praries & c. and long lines of distant hills. About 3 we encamp in grove in a hollow, on the bank of a branch— after a march of about 25 miles.[15] The horses come straggling up, but many remain behind some it is feared will give out— our course this day a little to the northward of east.

Billet arrives late (we had to send a horse back for him). Poor Gumbo gave out nine miles off—& Billets bl[ac]k pony[16] mare not long after & had to be abandoned—

Supper, stewed venison ribs & turkey made into a rich soup.

Comes on to rain about 9—heavy rain in the night.

This afternoon we saw a round hill or mound 15 or 20 miles off—said to be within 8 miles of the garrison.[17] Still I fear some of the horses will give out before we reach there. "If we pass any house here and there are fat cattle or fowls, they will have to lock them up," said one of the hungry rangers.

Monday Nov 5. Cloudy dismal morng after a rainy night —camp before daylight—sounds with imitation of cock crowing—owls hooting—the poor fellows had supper last night and are cheerful again.

[15] Apparently this, as well as the camp of the third, was in Okfuskee County, Oklahoma.

[16] For *pony*, possibly read *fancy*.

[17] Even by crow flight they were at least fifty miles from Fort Gibson.

I had prepared my bed in the open air last night—when it began to rain, crept into the tent—sound of the axe in all quarters—men cutting poles to make booths of blankets & c.

Capt & troop start before us—Billet goes back for his mare and brings her to camp together with Portales' colt—has to leave his mare which is like to die. The wild mare lost her foal last night and had to be abandoned in the camp. We set off about 8—cold gloomy morng—overtake the Capt's troop— Capt misses the trail & makes a circuit towards the NW around a rocky hill. We leave the troop, & guided by Billet, strike NE —send word to Capt who has to follow us—wretched travelling among rocks & quicksand & c.—at length come out upon Prarie & after riding couple of miles we stop beside a brook to rest the horses—Capt & most of the troop go on. Two of our horses lie down with fatigue & sickness.

Some of the men set the praries on fire, but it is too damp to burn to any extent.

Resume our march after ¾ of an hour—traverse praries— a long, scattered line stretching 3 or 4 miles over hill and dale —encamp in a wood beside the deep fork[18] about 4 oclock, having made about 20 miles—cold windy night—wind sounding through the forest and whirling about the dry leaves. Long logs cut for firing—making long fires, before which men cook and gossip. Antoine arrives pretty late bringing up the tired horses—our party send all our horses across the stream, as it is rising.

Tuesday Nov 6. Cold windy morng—all the men have leave to go out hunting till 12, to supply the camp with food —great firing at turkeys with which the bottom abounds—

---

[18] The camp was on the south (right) bank of the Deep Fork of Canadian River (Ellsworth, *Narrative*, 139).

[19] "A temporary bridge [was] contrived by felling two tall gigantic trees on either side, in such a manner, that when they fell across the stream their top branches interlocked upon and below the surface" (Latrobe, *Rambler*, I, 239). Ellsworth said that Bean had more trouble than he had expected with his trees (*Narrative*, 139).

Billet brings home six. Preparations for crossing the stream—trees felled to serve for bridges[19]—but fall rather short—our men carry across the baggage on a felled tree, part of which is two feet under the water.

Capt & others pass afterward over trees felled from each side to meet each other.

Grove of peccan trees—

Latrobe kills two prarie hens—Mr. Ellsworth & I pass across felled tree, holding by a stretched cord & aided by Billet.[20]

Several of the horses too weak to cross stream—leave them with a guard of 12 men & leave two of our tired horses with them.[21]

Leave the camp ½ after 1—cross rough, stony, woody hills—have a fine prospect of woodlands & hills & Praries towards the Arkansas—flocks of prairie hens

Capt & Billet wound a buck on a small Prarie to our left, but it escapes.

Walk the whole way & lead or drive my horse—most of the rangers do the same—after marching about 6 or 7 miles encamp in a good bottom among lofty sycamores on the bank of a small stream—yesterday found out by examining maps that we were about fifty miles from the fort.[22]

[20] "Billet came to our camp, said the water was rising very fast and we had better cross on a log under water 3½ feet—we went to examine it—a part of the log was out of the water at one end and 3½ feet under in the middle and at the other end—the stream ran 5 knots an hour over it—I could not stand on it—I told Billet to stretch 2 Lariats over the creek—by the help of these to guide my hands, I would attempt it—I pulled off my clothes except shirt and stockings—I entered the water, oh! how cold! untill it came over my hips—I was forced to walk slow and circumspectly as my foundation was a *teetering log* 3½ feet under the water—a few inches mistep would inevitably throw me into the current—I will not detain you by telling how I felt—I got over safely—as did Mr Irving Latrobe & Pourteles the same way—I ought to say however that Billet went behind us on the log to steady us along—Our servants have been faithful and daring" (Ellsworth, *Narrative*, 139–40).

[21] Twenty men, said Ellsworth.

[22] Ellsworth had requested Bean to order the men to walk if their horses were in a bad way. The camp of November 6 was probably a little to the northeast

To-day in the course of the march Billet climbed a tree on a hill and saw the forest along the Arkansas. Towards the end of our march we saw smoke along a woody glen about 3 or 4 miles off, made, no doubt, by Indian hunters.

Some of the rangers met a Creek Indian who told them the fort was but about 15 miles off—(he must be mistaken.) Said he lived about 3 miles off & had meat & corn—rangers elated with the news.

This day weather cleared up sunny.

*Wednesday Nov*ʳ 7. Last night a fine moon light, but windy & cool—lay at the foot of a tree—This morning cloudy, but likelihood of clearing up—preparation for early start—our flour all out—pepper also—salt nearly gone—we live on soup & stewed game.

Two of the men (Lane, Penticost) lost their horses—have to remain to search [for] them.

Leave camp ½ past 7—cross rough hilly stony country—meet 5 Creeks—from brow of hill have a fine look over wide praries—Billet sees hill about 20 miles off and within 8 miles of fort²³—set off with fresh spirits—cold march across burnt praries where Indians had lately hunted—see smoke of Indian hunters at distance—straggling march of 20 men in clusters, or singly—deep, muddy ravine & brush. Stop about midday for an hour to rest horses & warm ourselves—sharp NW wind sweeping prarie—weather cloudy. resume our march just at dusk arrive at creek which empties into the Arkansas.²⁴ Encamp in grove where several trees have been prostrated by tornado—large fires soon blazing and sparkling—make sup-

of the site of Okmulgee, Oklahoma. At this time they were about forty miles from Fort Gibson.

²³ This is the hill they thought they had seen in the distance on the afternoon of November 4.

²⁴ Pecan Creek, which enters the Arkansas River about ten miles above the Verdigris River.

per of stew'd venison (Billet having killed a deer this morning). Fine moonlight night—sleep round camp fire.

This day we made from 20 to 25 miles NE by E.

Clear, moonlight, frosty night—a cup of water standing by the head of my bed froze ½ inch.

Thursday Nov 8. Cold, bright morning—make breakfast on the reliques of our provisions—remnant of venison—turkey—Polecat—some roasted—some stewed without salt—a little coffee with a remaining and long-treasured lump of sugar—rub each morsel of meat on the salt bag.

Set off at ½ past 7 in high spirits for the ford of the Arkansas which we were told by Billet was about 13 miles off[25] (some of the men this morng were seen to stew turkey bread and to rasp the bones for breakfast)—march briskly through thickets across branches over hills & praries—Portales horse Crop mires[26] in a branch & is extricated with difficulty. From a hill see mount[ain]s beyond the fort. We are told the ford is about 9 miles off—on we go—the miles stretch—the horses tire—we dismount, being fatigued ourselves—mount again—the horses stagger—lag behind—Crop [flings?]—Pourtales flogs him on—at length he gives out— & the wild colt likewise. Smoke of fires on Praries—get on tracks of Indians—at length to our joy come in sight of habitations of men—Creek Indians—log houses among trees[27]—push on, horses fagged—arrive at log house owned by white man with black, fat wife—delightful sight of hogs—poultry, crowing of cocks &c.—horse pricks his ears—

Stop at the door—Capt & officer eating at a table—huge iron pot with beef & turnips—put in for a share, fat negress

[25] According to Ellsworth's calculations, this proved to be about twenty miles, but I am inclined to think that Ellsworth, here as elsewhere, overestimated mileage.

[26] This was the racing horse Pourtalès had bought for $150 from Chouteau to be used in hunting wild horses. Most of these horses were brought in a few days later.

[27] These cabins were about four miles from the Arkansas River.

gives a plate heaping with beef & turnips, corn bread & but-ter—apologises for giving it in such poor style![28]

Capt determines to encamp there. I push on with Mr. Ellsworth to the ford where our companions were—corn crib on banks of river—give corn to horses—ravenous appetite for it. Scene with canoe crossing—baggage—cotton tree banks —stream swift—drive horses in—Mr. Latrobes & mine get entangled in dry trees and return—other horses swim in line —get to footing & land safely—canoe returns—we all get in[29] —lead two horses, who send large wave into boat—land safe —set off thro woods for Choteau Agency. Horse seems reno-vated by the idea of getting among corn—pricks ears, raises head, trots, &c. Arrive at Agency—supper at [word illeg-ible][30]—newspapers—moonlight on Verdigris River.

Friday Nov 9th. Leave my horse at the Agency & set off after breakfast for the garrison with Mr. Latrobe & Mr. Ellsworth, and resume our quarters at Col Arbuckles.

At night serenade of the widow by the quartermaster & one or two other old bachelors.

In the fort is the Widow Nix, a plump, buxom dame, whose husband was 50 years of age when he married her— amassed 20,000$ as Sutler to the Garrison, which functions he discharged from the first establishment of the fort.[31] The

---

28 "We determined now to stop at the first place where there was anything to eat for man or beast—And we found such a place—it was a negro house Madam *Bradleys*—her man, was a white one & absent at this time—Capt Beans & three others had got in before us and were seated at a table eating—if it is wicked to covet, I committed the sin—I asked for a plate and got some boiled turnips potatoes pork and Corn bread & butter—I never eat faster or more to my satisfaction—I cannot describe my pleasure at eating—for all, I paid 12½ cents—this was done most cheerfully—Mr Irving relished the meal quite as much as I did and will have a good story to tell in his sketch book about Madame Bradleys entertainment" (Ellsworth, *Narrative*, 143).

Antoine interrupted their meal to say that they must hurry to the river two miles away if they were to cross in time to get to Colonel Chouteau's that night. Apparently Latrobe and Pourtalès had not stopped at Mrs. Bradley's.

29 Eight men crossed at once in a pirógue.

30 Trent and Hellman read the illegible word as *Nanny's*.

widow came to the fort a short timé since & is the object of desires of all the men. The ghastly Q[uarte]r Master—Capt. Clark—the old Col himself—all aspire to her favor.[32] A lawyer with the militia title of Major Lewis has just made his appearance at the fortress as aspirant, & occasions some jealousy among the military men who all unite ag[ain]st the intrusion of the black coat. The serenade of the widow was a horrible drover's voice that broke the sleep of men women & dogs throughout the fortress.

Saturday Novr 10. Breakfasted at Dr Pitcher's.[33] Engage my passage in the steam boat Little Rock, which arrived last night & leave to-day for the mouth of the river.

Visited the theatre, a building erected for Indian council house. The soldiers get up plays—no negroes admitted.

Sail at almost 2 o'clock, Col & officers accompany me to the vessel. We go down Grand River & turn up the Verdigris to take in cargo of stores at the Agency. Take tea with Latrobe & Pourtales[34] at the Agency with Mr. ——— & Col. Lane[?]—picturesque groupes of Creek Indians crossing in canoe with horses—others lying about the banks—led horses & c

[31] John Nicks, born in North Carolina, was appointed captain in the Third Infantry, July 1, 1808, became lieutenant colonel in the Seventh Infantry in 1819, and was honorably discharged two years later. He was sutler at Fort Gibson from its foundation, and postmaster there from 1827. In partnership with John Rogers, the Cherokee, he maintained trading establishments at Fort Gibson and Fort Smith. He was appointed brigadier general of the militia of Arkansas Terrtiory in 1827. He died at Fort Gibson December 31, 1831.

About July 8, 1824 the Rev. William C. Vaill was called from Union Mission "to go down the river as far as Billingsley's settlement, 125 miles distant, to marry Col. Nicks to a lady of that settlement." Whether this was the widow Sally Nicks, appointed sutler January 1, 1832, to serve until she could dispose of the $10,000 worth of goods on hand, is not known. Sally married Robert S. Gibson, Nicks' successor as postmaster at Fort Gibson, December 5, 1835.

[32] Captain Isaac Clark, Jr., of Vermont. Why Irving called him "ghastly" is not known. Arbuckle was then fifty-six years old; he never married.

[33] Dr. Zina Pitcher (1797–1873) was post surgeon at Fort Gibson until his transfer to Fortress Monroe in May,.1834.

[34] Latrobe and Pourtalès remained at Chouteau's Verdigris post for a fortnight; the rangers went into winter camp about six or seven miles above Fort Gibson.

I am now writing on board the steam boat which lies about a mile below the Agency, close by one of the sandy banks of the Verdigris—beautiful embowered stream—gleam of sky along the water between the lines of trees which fringe each bank—moon rising among the groves.

[*The following undated notes are found when this Journal is reversed.*][35]

Mr. E.—spurs without rowel[1]s—when we met the 8 Osages charged them not to make war & then told Billet to tell them of skunk.[36]

Uncle Sam's gun three inches in breech, 1 in muzzle.

Corn diminishes as his warlike propensities increase.[37]

Pawnees always on horseback—their dwellings of mats & skins—here to-day, to-morrow 10[38] miles hence—sometimes dash upon you 40 or 50—look like a troop of wild horses—only a leg hanging over to hold on by—

Tonish says when he was about 15 years of age he was one day hunting in his neighbourhood & he saw a white deer. After a little while another white deer got up & so to the number of seven. He fired but missed—fired again and missed—could not hit the deer—went home and told the circumstance

[35] On the inside rear cover is a very faint, very rough, and not very accurate sketch showing the relative positions of the Arkansas River, the Red Fork of the Arkansas, the North Fork of the Canadian, and the Canadian River.

[36] They met the Osage on October 26. The skunk was one Ellsworth shot with "Uncle Sam." Writing to the Secretary of War from Fort Gibson on November 18, the commissioner said: "We . . . saw a few Osage warriors out on a 'stealing party.' They informed us the Pawnees were afraid to come in towards this, and through hunger had fed upon horses—The Osages are not entitled to full credit, and this story must be rec'd with some grains of allowance although they assured me they had visited the late Pawnee camp" (Office of Indian Affairs, Department of the Interior, National Archives).

[37] That is, the peacefulness of the Indian was to be measured by the extent of his farming.

[38] Possibly this should read "100".

to————, an old hunter or half breed—["]They're hard to hit,["] says he, ["] & can only be shot by a particular bullet.["] He cast balls but would not let Tonish see how he cast them—went out—shot—missed—but at length killed one—the rest ran off & were never seen again.[39]

This vast extent of country without human habitation—visited only by wandering hordes who make an irruption—pull out a few pieces of its rich game & then retreat to their homes.

["]My gun is so powerful dirty.["]

["]My horse goes quite peart.["]

Kentucky originally one of the finest hunting grounds in the west—the fertile soil, deep bottoms—praries & other ranges affording sustenance to the richest game. Salt licks. The Indians herd in it—some had their permanent villages in the south on the Tennessee waters—others north in Ohio—nearest town the———— Come into the country to hunt & then fight—called therefore the land of blood—traces of deep buffalo tracks, where the soil is worn away by the travel of ages—near Licking River & c.

Sewaculty the spirit of the mountain—gigantic—one eye perpendicularly opening in forehead—projected so that he could see in every direction—his mountain guarded by snakes. He stepped from mountain top to mountain top—where his steps had been all was clear and smooth—old Indian shewed a clear place to Rogers—["]Sewaculty has been here last night. If you throw firebrands & ashes here to-day you will find all clear to-morrow.["]

In the neighbourhood lived an old man & wife with one beautiful daughter sought by all young warriors & hunters. Her father said, ["]I will appoint a day for hunting—the

[39] In the Tour (211–12), this bit is credited to October 28.

best hunter on that day shall have my daughter.["] Day came—hunters assembled—went off at dawn—a young man made his appearance (describe him) sat down to breakfast tranquilly—on leaving, went forth—hunted—brought in load of game—laid it down—said nothing—smoked his pipe—went out again—brought in more—laid it down—other hunters had not come in—dined—went out again—brought in another load. When the other hunters came in and saw his great pile of game, they gave up to him & he rec[eive]d the bride. Lived with her a year—said he must go to his land to see his people—she might go with him if she pleased. She agreed—they went off—crossed a river at foot of mountain—their footsteps were seen on the sand on other side but no more seen or heard of them. Years rolled away—father of bride set out in quest of her—took the direction of footsteps—went to mountain—found snakes in abundance—proceeded—found his daughter in a wigwam—great rattlesnake lying beside her—["]How is this, my daughter?—Why do you not kill that snake?["]—["]It is my husband—gave me my choice—snake by day—man by night.["] Such are all the snakes of this mountain who are subjects of Sewaculty. Old man remains at night—finds his son-in-law a young man—remains in the mountain.—Every moon, whenever they want game, conjure & let it out from cave.

JOURNAL V

Fort Gibson, November 11—Stack Island

November 17, 1832

SUNDAY. *Nov. 11. 1832* On board of the steam boat Little Rock—River Verdigris—get under way about 6 oclock from ———— about a mile below the Osage Agency—Verdigris River—beautiful dawn—while yet twilight pass a fire on the shore—Indians around it—canoe fastened close by. Streaming flights of wild ducks—pigeons in clouds, some rising from the sand bars where they go to drink & pick gravel; others flying in successive clouds over the trees—Banks of river with growth of cotton wood—river of moderate breadth—finely wooded banks. Land Mr. Brown Creek Indian & trader at his place opposite the mouth of the Illinois[1]—cross the river & stop to get wood—go ashore and shoot pigeons.

As the day advances the temperature grows warm & genial. The forests very much stripped of leaves—young cotton-wood groves—grey branches—light tinge of green on tops—golden sunshine—loneliness & stillness of the scene—the Sabbath of the woods.

[1] Possibly Irving meant David Brown, Cherokee, and half brother of Walter Webber.

Persons in steam boat: Mr. Gregory, clerk—
Dr. Cunningham, editor sub rosa of
a paper[2] at Little Rock—originally of Philad[elphia][a]—then
N York—

Lieut. ——— educated at W Point.

One bank of the Arkansas settled by Cherokees, the other
by Choctaws—log houses along the river—

Touch at Fort Smith—right bank of river on rocky Bluff
—ruinous old wooden buildings & block house.[3] A number
of the inhabitants come down, among whom I was introduced
to Mr. Rogers, formerly of western part of State of N York,
who owns a great part of Fort Smith, and Mr. Cairns, merch[an][t].[4]

A daughter of Dr. Cunningham comes on board[5]—cross
the line and enter upon the Territory[6]—log houses occupied by
white men—groups of negroes in Sunday dress along the
shore—Songs and choruses of our negro firemen.

Pass Devil's Elbow, a great, sandy bend in the river.[7]

In the course of the day pass by a red boat bearing U. S.
troops on an expedition to destroy whisky stills.

Stop at Van Buren to take passengers—two men in fur

---

[2] Irving meant the *Arkansas Advocate*, of which Charles P. Bertrand, Cunningham's stepson, was editor. Dr. Matthew Cunningham (1782–1854) was one
of the first settlers of Little Rock. Born in Philadelphia, he studied medicine at
the University of Pennsylvania, married (about 1808) Eliza, the widow of
Pierre Bertrand, and lived in New York until 1817 when he moved to St. Louis
and later to Arkansas.

[3] Fort Smith was about 120 miles by water below Fort Gibson. Founded
in 1817, it was occupied until the building of Fort Gibson in 1824. From that
year until 1833 no troops were stationed there.

[4] ". . . a large new post was begun near the site of the abandoned Fort Smith
to bear the same name, on 306 acres of land sold to the Government June 17,
1836, by Capt. John Rogers, a merchant located there; he was formerly from
western New York and came to Fort Smith as a sutler to the troops stationed
there" (Foreman, *Advancing the Frontier*, 55). The other man was probably
Peter A. Carnes, of the firm of Duval and Carnes.

[5] Henrietta first married a man named Hill, and later a Dr. Savage. Matilda
married Peter Hauger.

[6] Arkansas.

[7] The big bend in the Arkansas River between Fort Smith and Van Buren.

caps with rifles bedding—Van B. as embrio town—at present 4 or 5 straggling log huts.[8]

About dusk stop to take on wood, having made about 100 miles since daybreak. This day (in boatmen's slang) we overtook the rise—*i.e.* we came to where the river was at the highest of its late temporary swelling—having commenced falling above.

Monday 12th—The fog which fell last night continued until late this morning so that we did not get under way until about 9 oclock.

Immence flock of pigeons on sand bar in the river.

Banks delicately wooded with cotton wood & willows—grey tints mingled with light green—now & then, at long intervals, come by settlement—log houses—cattle standing along shore in the sunshine—deep bayous—running in among wild forests that shoot their branches, and half prostrate trunks athwart.

In some places as we skirt the shore the cattle gaze for a time in astonish[ment] and then gallop into the woods.

Stop at Crawford Court House—a few log houses on high bank.[9] Justice runs wild in this part of the country—She uses the sword more than the scales.

Find at Crawford Court House a keel boat with freight belonging to M[r] Mapes, of N[ew] York—one of the proprietors of the steam boat—stop about 3 hours to take it on board. M[r] Mapes embarks also and M[r] Nolan his horse—Gen[era]l Montgomery,[10] his negro servants, a half grown bear—

[8] The town of Van Buren began as a post office established at Phillips' Landing, five miles below Fort Smith, in 1831. It was made the county seat of Crawford County in 1836.

[9] Crawford County was formed in 1820. The county seat at first was Fort Smith and then, until 1836, Crawford Court House, and finally Van Buren. Crawford Court House was a few miles below the present Webb City, Franklin County. The town has long since disappeared.

[10] Charles Mapes (possibly), who in December, 1832, was postmaster at the mouth of Arkansas River. The name in the Journal may be *Mayes*. Charles

Mrs. Trimble two other ladies of the place dine on board.[11]
Resume our course about 2 oclock & go on till dark, when
we stop at Clarke's Agency.[12]

Tuesday. Nov 13. Set off about daybreak—pass high,
broken ridge of rock coloured with iron &c called the Dardanelles[13]—here Pension Braily [word illegible][14]—great
gambling place formerly. It used to be said if a dollar could
get by the Dardanelles there was some chance of your carrying
it up the river.

Between 11 & 12 pass along mount[ain]s of Petit Jean.[15]
½ past twelve stop at Lewisburgh to take on wood—seat
of justice of the county. Hard work for Justice to get seated
as the seat has been changed every session of the Legislature.
Stop after dusk at Little Rock[16]—in the ev[enin]g Capt.
Brown, agent for settling the Indians, comes on board—also
Mr. ——— editor of the Gazette.[17]

Fenton Mercer Noland (possibly) (1808–58), originally of Virginia, and resident
of Batesville, Arkansas, from 1829 to 1840. Noland was, among other things,
the "Pete Whetstone" of *Scenes and Characters in Arkansas*. William Montgomery was born in Tennessee in 1790. About 1818 he settled at Arkansas Post
and three years later moved to the mouth of White River; the new location soon
became known as Montgomery's Point or Montgomery's Landing. He was appointed brigadier general in the Arkansas militia by Jackson, and died in 1835.

[11] Possibly the wife of Judge William Trimble, who was born in Kentucky
about 1797, was appointed a territorial judge in Arkansas in 1825, and represented Hempstead County in the legislature in 1831.

[12] This could have been at Spadra Bluff (Johnson County).

[13] "At the Dardanelles, the river cuts through a spur of this chain [Ozarks]
of greater height than ordinary, and forms by far the most picturesque scene
found along its course" (Latrobe, *Rambler*, I, 265). Dardenelle Rock stood 280
feet above the Arkansas River. Colonel David Brearly established the Cherokee
Agency there in 1820. The town was on the right bank about midway between
Fort Smith and Little Rock.

[14] The word possibly is *lives*—if so, Pension must have been the man's
nickname.

[15] Petit Jean Creek enters the Arkansas River from the south, between Yell
and Conway Counties. Irving probably referred to Magazine Mountain, which
lay between the Arkansas River and the Petit Jean Creek.

[16] According to Pope, in *Early Days in Arkansas*, the population of Little
Rock in 1833 was 527.

Wednesday, 14ᵗʰ Went on shore to the printing office of the Gazette—breakfasted with Dʳ Cunningham—called on Dʳ Fulton—Gov. Pope. Met with Dʳ Ritchie, who begged to be remem[bere]d to Mr. Peale of Missouri—his brother in Philad[elphia].

Dr. Fulton desired to be remem[bere]d to Presid[ent], Gov. Cass, & Mr. McLane.

Judge ———— & family came on board—leave Little Rock near 1 oclock.

Several ladies dine on board & accompany us a few miles to a farm.

Stop at night on account of snags &c.

Thursday. Nov. 15. Resume our course at daybreak. Pass cotton plantations. Cotton here of fine, long staple, equal to New Orleans. Pass Quawpaw settlements (tenant-at-will)— see groups in a fine, lofty grove.

Pass Quipaw hunting camps on woody banks of the river.

¹⁷ The men mentioned in this paragraph and the two following may be identified as follows:

Captain Jacob Brown, Sixth Infantry, Jefferson Barracks, was appointed superintendent of the removal and subsistence of Indians at Little Rock on September 9, 1831.

William E. Woodruff (1795–1885) was born in Suffolk County, New York; he established the *Gazette* at Arkansas Post in 1819, and moved it to Little Rock two years later.

Probably Dr. John T. Fulton, who in 1832 was an assistant agent for the removal and subsistence of the Choctaw. He was a brother of William S. Fulton of Florence, Alabama, (originally of Cecil County, Maryland), who was appointed secretary of Arkansas Territory in 1829, and was governor of it from 1835 to 1841.

John Pope of Kentucky was the third territorial governor of Arkansas (1829–35).

The reference, of course, is to the well-known family of artists, but the identity of these specific men is quite uncertain. Titian Ramsey Peale, the naturalist (1799–1885), had been in the West with Long's Expedition, but at this time, according to the *DAB* (IV, 351–52) he was collecting specimens in Colombia. The brother in Philadelphia might be Rembrandt Peale (1778–1860).

Lewis Cass, secretary of war.

Louis McLane, lately minister to England, and at this time secretary of the treasury. Irving was to spend the winter in Washington with him; see Introduction, page 40.

Put Lieut. Dawson[18] on shore at Col. Dallas cotton plantation.

Ev[enin]g about sunset, stop at the Post of Arkansas—to land Mr. & Mrs. Cumming[19] & to take on freight.

Friday. Nov 16. Get underway at day break—at 9 oclock enter the cut leading to White River. In a few miles enter White River—clear water with yellow, turbid stream of the Arkansas boiling up in it.[20] After some miles, with cypress & cotton wood groves on each side, come to the Mississippi—sweep round a large island and go up to Montgomerys Point.[21]

Pass the day at the point shifting cargo.

Point—naked table of land with woods in rear—three or four disconsolate houses—negroes—half dressed—oxen—dogs—bear tied to stake—drinkers—boatmen.

Leave the Point about 4.

Stop at mouth of Arkansas after dark & leave Mr. Mapes —sail all night.

[18] James Low Dawson of Maryland was appointed second lieutenant in the Seventh Infantry in 1821. He was promoted three years later, and received his captaincy in 1833. He resigned from the service in 1835 and died in 1879.

[19] William Cummins, a lawyer of Little Rock, on January 18, 1831, married Francine, the daughter of Colonel Frederick Notrebe of Arkansas Post.

[20] "In the afternoon [we] turned into what is called the *Cut-off*, a natural passage or canal which connects the Arkansas with the waters of *White River*. It is more convenient to take this Cut-off to reach the Mississippi, as it is a clear canal-like navigation about 250 feet broad, without any snags or sawyers. To the right lies a considerable island cut off from the main land, upon which we saw two miserable cabins, on each side of which lofty canes about 25 feet high were growing. There was no current in this Cut-off, the Arkansas rushing past it at the south end, and the White River at the north end, damming up its waters as if it were a millpond; we therefore soon got into the current of White River itself, which is here a powerful stream, and at night to our great joy we reached the Mississippi River, and brought up for a short time at Montgomery's, a notorious place" (Featherstonhaugh, *Excursion*, II, 245).

[21] "Montgomery's Point did not . . . rank either in fact or in courtesy above a small hamlet, and was apparently merely of importance as the point where goods might be deposited" (Latrobe, *Rambler*, I, 272). Featherstonhaugh did not have a good opinion of Montgomery or his Point. The settlement at Montgomery's Point, in Mississippi township, Desha County, disappeared fifty years ago.

MOUTH OF THE ARKANSAS RIVER
from a drawing by Henry Lewis, 1846–47

Reproduced from Henry Lewis,
Das Illustrirte Mississippithal, *1857*

Saturday Nov 17. Last night ran repeatedly ag[ain]st driftwood—this morng 8 oclock passed thro Stack Island[22]— reach a beautiful broad & long reach of the river.

Here about 20 years since was a formidable gang of river pirates 30 or 40 in number. Kept on an island under the eastern shore called Stack Island & sometimes Robbers' Harbour —ring leader named Mason. The band consisted of outcast Kentuckians, Spaniards, French &c. &c. &c.—well armed— resolute—had boats on the river—horses on the mainland— boarded arks & defenceless boats—noted the cargo—took what they wanted—no resisting them. Some of the keel boats & barges had crews of 40 men well armed—these the robbers dared not attack. The robbers have often been seen by these barges lurking about this island. They could descry boats at a great distance both up & down the river—they had spies in New Orleans. The boatmen & traders had to return by land, by an Indian trail thro the country of the Choctaw natives— several hundred miles—had to cash their merchandise & carry the money on pack horses. The robbers had trails leading to the great Indian trail. They would way lay the traders & rob them. Seldom killed them unless they fought in defence of their goods. Sometimes when they surprised poor travellers thro mistake they would give them money.

The terror of these robbers spread far & wide. In those days people looked upon an expedition down the Mississippi & Ohio as a fearful undertaking—country wild & unsettled —little known—Indians—river pirates—alligators &c &c &c Long voyage—required hardy and enterprising men— & then the long journey back thro savage tribes & robber hordes—

At length the authorities offered a large reward for Mason's head. He wished to divide his spoil—he had a rival ringleader—they quarrelled about division of spoil. The rival

[22] Stack Island was about 120 miles below the Arkansas River according to Cumings in *Western Pilot* (101).

killed him—carried his head to Natchez & claimed reward—
a man present who had been robbed on the Indian trail recognized his buttons on the coat of the robber & recognized the
latter for one of those who had robbed him. The robber was
seized, tried, & hung, and the band was broken up—

The very island has since been washed away by the floods
of the river & no trace of the robbers remains, but the pilot
who told me this story said he had no doubt that thousands of
dollars of the robbers money lay buried about the shore and on
the old Indian trail and could be digged up as the country became settled & cultivated.[23]

Just below this reach we begin to see neat white painted
houses and a look of some advanced civilisation—cotton plantation.

[*The following undated notes are found when this Journal is reversed.*]

Clermont, a late chief of the Osages[24]—shrewd, intelligent, wary—difficult to be brought to a point. He & Col.
Arbuckle had a great regard for each other, but often disputed
about Indian matters; both were prone to beat around the
bush. One evening he & the Col had a long talk in which Clermont played shy as usual. At length Col. Arb[u]c[k]le got out
of patience: ["]Well,["] said he, ["]you have talked now
for two hours and have said nothing.["]—["]Brother,["]
replied Clermont, ["]you have talked about as much and said
about as little, so as it is growing late, I think["] (wrapping
himself in his blanket) ["]I'll go home.["]

Gov. Hunter, tall, large, well formed, fresh-looking man
—low crowned, large brimmed white beaver—boots with

[23] For Samuel Mason and his career see Rothert, *Outlaws of Cave-in-Rock,*
157–266. Mason was killed by his confederates in 1804. Irving may have been
drawing upon Nuttall, for the latter mentioned a gang at Stack Island in 1811
in his *Travels into the Arkansas Territory* (227–28).
[24] Clermont II died in 1828. He was a favorite with Arbuckle, Chouteau,
and the missionaries.

[word illegible] eagle spurs—given to grandiloquence, a large & military mode of expressing himself. I encamped last night at ———, for I slept last night.

Old Genl Nix used to say God made him two drinks scant.

Little, thick, short legged Dutchman at Little Rock— great coward—at time when he was held up as candidate used to go with three pistols & two dirks belted round him—one of the pistols being long, used to get the muzzle filled with dirt. A swaggering man called at his house & abused him all to naught. His wife, who had been widow of a very spirited fellow, exclaimed, ["]Oh, if my first husband was alive you would not dare to do so in my house. Ah, then I had a husband! ["]

Tour of two old Dutch burghers [two words illegible] —&c to look for names of old sturdies—find 60—[line illegible]²⁵ give names and histories of the old sturdies they met with.

Choctaws—much attached to the whites—boast that they have never killed a white man—call the whites [word illegible]²⁶ the Beloved, supposing them to be peculiar favourites of the deity. The Choctaws are the most honest of Indians.

Chickasaws—amalgamated with the Choctaws—their language nearly the same—their women handsome. They came from the upper parts of the Missouri. Their tradition is that they followed a chief who had a pole of supernatural virtues. He set it up occasionally and as long as it remained perpendicular they remained in that place—when it inclined they travelled in the direction it inclined. In this way they travelled from place to place until they came to their present residence.²⁷

²⁵ It is very difficult to make anything of this line. It seems to read: "[?] themselves that there is [?] will yet in [?]."

²⁶ The marks in the Journal seem to be "(& E.)."

²⁷ Their earliest known residence was the upper portion of the present state of Mississippi.

The Quipaws a small remnant of a tribe below Little Rock —they once sold out & removed to Texas but were drawn back by their love to their native place.[28]

The bravest and finest race is the Delawares.[29] They are called the *fathers*—all the others give them preference. They used to war with the Osages, who stand in awe of their fearlessness. ["]Look at these Delawares,["] say the Osages, ["]dey got short legs—no can run—must stand fight a great heap.["] (The Delawares really are short-legged—& the Osages long.)

Delawares—all their equipments of the best—their camp kettles of brass. They are clean, neat, civil, generously obliging, light hearted, gay, fearless—go to the Rocky Mountains in bands of 20 men—have frequent skirmishes. Excellent hunters—when they go out to kill a deer you may be sure of their succeeding.

Pawnees—when they attack in the prairies it is necessary —to tie your horses head to head in circle. They come round you with feathers, mantles, &c fluttering—great whoops & yells that strike a panic into the horses.

Pawnees keep in the Praries—will not follow into the thickets.

Old Osage looked at our steamboat at the Agency with wonder—came aboard, gazed at machinery, &c.—said, ["]God must have helped to make it.["]

Ralph Izard[30] & another toper fell asleep on a bed in an

[28] Hodge says that there were about 500 Quapaw in 1829 (*Handbook*, II, 335). After the treaty of 1824 they were moved from Arkansas to the Red River country, but returned in 1828. For an interesting document concerning them, see Dallas T. Herndon, "When the Quapaws Went to Red River—a Translation," *Arkansas Historical Publications*, IV (1917), 326–31.

[29] The Commissioners West declared that the Osage were the adopted grandchildren of the Delaware.

[30] Ralph Izard (1742–1804) of South Carolina.

inn where there was a ball & supper—woke after the company had gone—called lustily for supper—waiter told them it was over. "We paid 3$ for ball & supper & must have it.["]—["]Impossible—none in the house.["]—["]Well, give us a candle & we will go home." Waiter gave them a sperm [part of word illegible] light—they sallied forth—the night was rainy—they were too tipsy to keep their legs—sat down in public square—stuck the light on end between them—thot themselves still at table. The day broke & showed them still seated toe to toe with the light burning between them.

Arkansas—continual succession of gentle, fertile, wooded scenery—graceful woods—thickets—embowered shores and islands—long winding bayous—willowed banks—yellow sands—cattle feeding peacefully along the shore—every thing peaceful but man—land of the *bloody hand.*

Petit Jean Mountain[31] on the Arkansas—a picturesque line of waving highlands, of mingled rock & cliff & wood, with far bottom below—opposite these, rich [word illegible] bottoms with hills beyond—river winds among groves, yellow sand bars, etc.—mount[ain]s with their autumnal tint & dusky haze. Log house among groves with children about it— Long vistas of river between woody points—wild geese on sand bars.

When Sarazin chief of the Quawpaws returnd with his tribe from their abode at Cadeau,[32] called on Gov. Pope— spread a white deer skin under his feet and another on his shoulder as emblem that they had never shed the blood of a white man. The old man made a speech about them, remark-[in]g he had lost a son, and when he told of his wrath the tears streamed down his cheeks. ["]When I went to that country,["] said he, ["]the sun did not seem to shine—everything

---

[31] See page 158, n. 15, above.
[32] The name was commonly spelled *Caddo.*

was strange and forlorn, but when I returned to this country of my youth where are the tombs of our fathers, the sun shone bright and everything was again cheerful.["]

Arkansas—settlers like to live apart when they can have good range—raise corn for bread—cattle which feed on prarie on pea vine or canebrake—hogs which find mast in plenty—depend on their rifles occasionally—work one day out of seven.

Quapaws—much intermarried with the French—a great part of them half breeds—honest—liked & helped by the whites.

In general the frontiersmen seem to think themselves imposed upon by the Indians, because the latter, having lost nearly all their property, seek to hold on to what is left.

They have got the Indians' coat & now begrudge them the fringe.

Post of the Arkansas—About here the speculator Law founded his colony.

Old Spanish and French settlers—retain their characteristics.

They were accustomed to be governd by commandants whose will was law. One who was capricious would exact all kind of services from those under him & bother them in a thousand ways, & another who was avaricious would squeeze them. Tho the govt is now changed & they have equal rights with their meddlesome, quarrelsome, litigious, electioneering fellow citizens of the U. S., they retain their old, passive acquiescence in the despotism of public affairs. Do not intermeddle or distress themselves in elections or worry themselves about public affairs—have not the enterprise of the Yankees—nor their eagerness for growth & conquest. If an American cultivates 20 acres and has 40 uncultivated, the next year he cultivates 10 more. If he has 3 negroes, gets 6 more, and so with his stock. The old Spanish & French cultivate the same number of acres, have the same number of negroes &c &c year in and year out—content to live within their income & not eager to increase it—simple in appearance & habits—remarkably honest and punctual. Kind and neighbourly among themselves—more civil and courteous than the Americans—dress in their best on Sundays—dance—sing—polite to the women—never quarrel but with the tongue. When one has been about and returns, great rejoicing, embracing throughout the family.

Qu.—How do they treat their negroes?

A.—Work them hard—feed & clothe them poorly. It is proverbial in this part of the country that a Frenchman is hard upon his horse and his negroes.

Qu.—Do they wear old dresses—white nightcaps—pipe—songs?

There are but two or three families at present at the fort—most of them are at a settlement below frontier on river where they retain French language—keep apart from Americans.

They have nothing of the public spirit that makes itself uneasy & unhappy about public men and public manners & sinks in sorrow through the newspapers—nothing of that spirit that sets up two newspapers in the little village of Little Rock & sets neighbours by the ears calling each other hard names and reviling each other because they differ on abstract points.

They have given up competing with the Am[ericans] who have too much enterprise & industry for them.

A few old fellows exert a patriarchal sway over the community. Their word & opinion is law.

Very fond of holidays—they dance & pass their time merrily.

All vote for Co¹ Desha[33]—

---

[33] Ben Desha came to Arkansas in 1824 and died there in 1835.

They do not like Americans; [who, they say] trouble themselves with cares beyond their horizon & impart sorrow thro newspapers from every point of the compass.

Mr. Cummings[34] married daughter of Mons. ———, the great man of the place—worth 40 or 50,000$. She inherits french vivacity of temperament and it is said rules her husband with the slipper. She is pretty, dark, black-eyed woman. Her father when he travels affects the Don—on board steam boat has his own serv[an]t—his own wine—cannot drink steam boat wine.[35]

Judge ———, very official—over mindful dignity of his office—rather slow, but upright and amicable.[36]

At the Post—old fashioned French looking houses.

Abundance of dogs—whenever you hear of poor people in this part of country you may be sure to find abundance of dogs.

Old negro with a long good humoured horse face and a straw hat smashed back from it like a mandarin cap.

This day pass Quipaw hunting camps on the border of the river.

Put Lieut. Dawson on shore at Col. Dallas cotton plantation.

After sunset stop at the Post of Arkansas—a century old.

[34] Irving traveled from Little Rock to Arkansas Post with the Cummins. See page 160, n. 19, above. This, and a few other paragraphs that follow, Irving chose to expand into the fanciful sketch he called "The Creole Village."

[35] Frederick Notrebe, who had served as an officer under Napoleon during the Consulate, came to America about 1810. Albert Pike called him "the princely old Frenchman" and declared he "was a man who ought not to be forgotten, for he was a very noble and generous man. I often dined at his houses at the Post of Arkansas, and on his plantation below that place, where I met his wife's father and mother, Mr. and Madame Encimè" (Hallum, *History of Arkansas*, 82, 108). "The great man of the place is a Monsieur Notrébe, a French emigrant, who is said to have accumulated a considerable fortune here. His house appears to be a comfortable one, and has a store attached to it, where the principal business of this part of the country is transacted. . . . he has contrived to secure a monopoly of almost all the business of the country. . . ." (Featherstonhaugh, *Excursion*, II, 234).

[36] Apparently the Judge who came aboard at Little Rock (page 159 above).

Originally a Spanish post—then French.[37] A decayed, ruinous place—old Spanish wooden building, with piazza—out houses—French buildings, with casement—piazzas—remains of stockade—at present surrounding garden & house of Mons. ————, the principal merch[an]t. Near the old Spanish house are two large ruins—neglected kitchen garden. Town stands on the abrupt end of a flat prarie that extends 70 miles—French town & American town—the former on the site of the Spanish post—the latter two or three hundred yards off—melancholy silent deserted look of the place—commands a bend and winding of the river. Old French merch[an]t large, strong built man with strong features—tall sons—French jabbered about the place. Young mons[ieur] in blanket surtout.

German merch[an]t at Little Rock who came there a Pedlar—set up store *for cash* at 25 per cent under the others—never trusted except to sure people—in 5 years has made a little fortune—chuckles at it—Ask him how he invests it.—["]Oh—most proke—tinks I must puy a steam boat.["]

Choctaws—believe in witches—one Choctaw set up for a doctor,—his father, mother, & other relatives died. It was suspected he was a wizard & had practised spells on them—several of the old men who were not wizards held a council upon it & determined he was a wizard. He heard of it and cleared out. His own brother set off in pursuit of him, tracked him for two days and killed him with a rifle. In such cases they do not attempt to resist or to defend themselves when overtaken.

A small burg—flourishing village—which published two rival newspapers, had three hotels and the usual number of Judges, Generals, and Colonels, not to speak of lawyers and Doctors.[38]

[37] Arkansas Post, of course, was of French origin, not Spanish. Tonty, lieutenant of La Salle, founded a trading post there in 1686.
[38] Little Rock, perhaps.

The Creole Village

A Sketch from a Steamboat[1]

I N travelling about our motley country, I am often reminded of Ariosto's account of the moon, in which the good
paladin Astolpho found everything garnered up that had
been lost on earth. So I am apt to imagine that many things
lost in the Old World are treasured up in the New; having
been handed down from generation to generation, since the
early days of the colonies. A European antiquary, therefore,
curious in his researches after the ancient and almost obliterat-
ed customs and usages of his country, would do well to put
himself upon the track of some early band of emigrants, follow
them across the Atlantic, and rummage among their descendants on our shores.

In the phraseology of New England might be found many
an old English provincial phrase long since obsolete in the parent country, with some quaint relics of the Roundheads; while
Virginia cherishes peculiarities characteristic of the days of
Elizabeth and Sir Walter Raleigh.

[1] From *The Adventures of Captain Bonneville* (Knickerbocker Edition),
II, 282–95. The sketch was first published in *The Magnolia*, an annual, in 1837;
Its first book publication was in the collection called *Wolfert's Roost*, 1855. It is
included here as an example of Irving's literary method, for it is based on the
few notes about Arkansas Post and Notrebe which fill the last pages of Journal V.

In the same way, the sturdy yeomanry of New Jersey and Pennsylvania keep up many usages fading away in ancient Germany; while many an honest, broad bottomed custom, nearly extinct in venerable Holland, may be found flourishing in pristine vigor and luxuriance in Dutch villages, on the banks of the Mohawk and the Hudson.

In no part of our country, however, are the customs and peculiarities imported from the Old World by the earlier settlers kept up with more fidelity than in the little, poverty-stricken villages of Spanish and French origin, which border the rivers of ancient Louisiana. Their population is generally made up of the descendants of those nations, married and interwoven together, and occasionally crossed with a slight dash of the Indian. The French character, however, floats on top, as, from its buoyant qualities, it is sure to do, whenever it forms a particle, however small, of an intermixture.

In these serene and dilapidated villages, art and nature stand still, and the world forgets to turn round. The revolutions that distract other parts of this mutable planet, reach not here, or pass over without leaving any trace. The fortunate inhabitants have none of that public spirit which extends its cares beyond its horizon, and imports trouble and perplexity from all quarters in newspapers. In fact, newspapers are almost unknown in these villages; and, as French is the current language, the inhabitants have little community of opinion with their republican neighbors. They retain, therefore, their old habits of passive obedience to the decrees of government, as though they still lived under the absolute sway of colonial commandants, instead of being part and parcel of the sovereign people, and having a voice in public legislation.

A few aged men, who have grown gray on their hereditary acres, and are of the good old colonial stock, exert a patriarchal sway in all matters of public and private import; their opinions are considered oracular, and their word is law.

The inhabitants, moreover, have none of that eagerness for gain, and rage for improvement, which keep our people continually on the move, and our country towns incessantly in a state of transition. There the magic phrases, "town lots," "water privileges," "railroads," and other comprehensive and soul-stirring words from the speculator's vocabulary, are never heard. The residents dwell in the houses built by their fore-fathers, without thinking of enlarging or modernizing them, or pulling them down and turning them into granite stores. The trees under which they have been born, and have played in infancy, flourish undisturbed; though, by cutting them down, they might open new streets, and put money in their pockets. In a word, the almighty dollar, that great object of universal devotion throughout our land, seems to have no genuine devotees in these peculiar villages; and unless some of its missionaries penetrate there, and erect banking-houses and other pious shrines, there is no knowing how long the in-habitants may remain in their present state of contented pov-erty.

In descending one of our great western rivers in a steam-boat, I met with two worthies from one of these villages, who had been on a distant excursion, the longest they had ever made, as they seldom ventured far from home. One was the great man, or Grand Seigneur of the village; not that he en-joyed any legal privileges or power there, everything of the kind having been done away when the province was ceded by France to the United States. His sway over his neighbors was merely one of custom and convention, out of deference to his family. Beside, he was worth full fifty thousand dollars, an amount almost equal, in the imagination of the villagers, to the treasures of King Solomon.[2]

---

[2] The "Grand Seigneur" was evidently Frederick Notrebe, who was a nineteenth-century immigrant and not the representative of the fourth or fifth generation of his family in this country. The reference to the fortune of fifty thousand dollars is indisputable. See Journal V, n. 19 and 35.

This very substantial old gentleman, though of the fourth or fifth generation in this country, retained the true Gallic feature and deportment, and reminded me of one of those provincial potentates that are to be met with in the remote parts of France. He was of a large frame, a ginger-bread complexion, strong features, eyes that stood out like glass knobs, and a prominent nose, which he frequently regaled from a gold snuff-box, and occasionally blew with a colored handkerchief, until it sounded like a trumpet.

He was attended by an old negro, as black as ebony, with a huge mouth, in a continual grin; evidently a privileged and favorite servant, who had grown up and grown old with him. He was dressed in creole style, with white jacket and trousers, a stiff shirt-collar, that threatened to cut off his ears, a bright Madras handkerchief tied round his head, and large gold ear-rings. He was the politest negro I met with in a western tour, and that is saying a great deal, for, excepting the Indians, the negroes are the most gentlemanlike personages to be met with in those parts. It is true they differ from the Indians in being a little extra polite and complimentary. He was also one of the merriest; and here, too, the negroes, however we may deplore their unhappy condition, have the advantage of their master. The whites are, in general, too free and prosperous to be merry. The cares of maintaining their rights and liberties, adding to their wealth, and making presidents engross all their thoughts and dry up all the moisture of their souls. If you hear a broad, hearty, devil-may-care laugh, be assured it is a negro's.

Besides this African domestic, the seigneur of the village had another no less cherished and privileged attendant. This was a huge dog, of the mastiff breed, with a deep, hanging mouth, and a look of surly gravity. He walked about the cabin with the air of a dog perfectly at home, and who had paid for his passage. At dinner-time he took his seat beside his master, giving him a glance now and then out of a corner of his eye, which bespoke perfect confidence that he would not be forgotten. Nor was he. Every now and then a huge morsel would be thrown to him, peradventure the half-picked leg of a fowl, which he would receive with a snap like the springing of a steel trap,—one gulp, and all was down; and a glance of the eye told his master that he was ready for another consignment.

The other village worthy, travelling in company with the seigneur, was of a totally different stamp. Small, thin, and weazen-faced, as Frenchmen are apt to be represented in caricature, with a bright, squirrel-like eye, and a gold ring in his ear. His dress was flimsy, and sat loosely on his frame, and he had altogether the look of one with but little coin in his pocket. Yet, though one of the poorest, I was assured he was one of the merriest and most popular personages in his native village.

Compère Martin,[3] as he was commonly called, was the factotum of the place—sportsman, schoolmaster, and land-surveyor. He could sing, dance, and above all, play the fiddle, an invaluable accomplishment in an old French creole village, for the inhabitants have a hereditary love for balls and *fêtes*. If they work but little, they dance a great deal; and a fiddle is the joy of their heart.

What had sent Compère Martin travelling with the Grand Seigneur I could not learn. He evidently looked up to him with great deference, and was assiduous in rendering him petty attentions; from which I concluded that he lived at home upon the crumbs which fell from his table. He was gayest when out of his sight, and had his song and his joke when forward among the deck passengers; but, altogether, Compère Martin was out of his element on board of a steamboat. He was quite another being, I am told, when at home in his own village.

Like his opulent fellow-traveler, he too had his canine follower and retainer,—and one suited to his different for-

---

[3] No trace of this character is to be found in the Journals.

tunes,—one of the civilest, most unoffending little dogs in the world. Unlike the lordly mastiff, he seemed to think he had no right on board of the steamboat; if you did but look hard at him, he would throw himself upon his back, and lift up his legs, as if imploring mercy. At table he took his seat a little distance from his master; not with the bluff, confident air of the mastiff, but quietly and diffidently; his head on one side, with one ear dubiously slouched, the other hopefully cocked up; his under-teeth projecting beyond his black nose, and his eye wistfully following each morsel that went into his master's mouth.

If Compère Martin now and then should venture to abstract a morsel from his plate, to give to his humble companion, it was edifying to see with what diffidence the exemplary little animal would take hold of it, with the very tip of his teeth, as if he would almost rather not, or was fearful of taking too great a liberty. And then with what decorum would he eat it! How many efforts would he make in swallowing it, as if it stuck in his throat; and with what daintiness would he lick his lips; and then with what an air of thankfulness would he resume his seat, with his teeth once more projecting beyond his nose, and an eye of humble expectation fixed upon his master.

It was late in the afternoon when the steamboat stopped at the village which was the residence of these worthies. It stood on the high bank of the river, and bore traces of having been a frontier trading-post. There were the remains of stockades that once protected it from the Indians, and the houses were in the ancient Spanish and French colonial taste, the place having been successively under the domination of both those nations prior to the cession of Louisiana to the United States.[4]

The arrival of the seigneur of fifty thousand dollars, and his humble companion, Compère Martin, had evidently been looked forward to as an event in the village. Numbers of men,

[4] Arkansas Post. See Journal V, n. 37.

women, and children, white, yellow, and black, were collected on the river bank; most of them clad in old-fashioned French garments, and their heads decorated with colored handkerchiefs, or white nightcaps. The moment the steamboat came within sight and hearing, there was a waving of handkerchiefs, and a screaming and bawling of salutations and felicitations, that baffle all description.

The old gentleman of fifty thousand dollars was received by a train of relatives, and friends, and children, and grandchildren, whom he kissed on each cheek, and who formed a procession in his rear, with a legion of domestics, of all ages, following him to a large, old-fashioned French house, that domineered over the village.

His black *valet de chambre*, in white jacket and trousers, and gold ear-rings, was met on the shore by a boon, though rustic companion, a tall negro fellow, with a long good-humored face, and the profile of a horse, which stood out from beneath a narrow-rimmed straw hat, stuck on the back of his head. The explosions of laughter of these two varlets on meeting and exchanging compliments, were enough to electrify the country round.

The most hearty reception, however, was that given to Compère Martin. Everybody, young and old, hailed him before he got to land. Everybody had a joke for Compère Martin, and Compère Martin had a joke for everybody. Even his little dog appeared to partake of his popularity, and to be caressed by every hand. Indeed, he was quite a different animal the moment he touched the land. Here he was at home; here he was of consequence. He barked, he leaped, he frisked about his old friends, and then would skim round the place in a wide circle, as if mad.

I traced Compère Martin and his little dog to their home. It was an old ruinous Spanish house, of large dimensions, with verandas overshadowed by ancient elms. The house had probably been the residence, in old times, of the Spanish commandant. In one wing of this crazy, but aristocratical abode, was nestled the family of my fellow-traveller; for poor devils are apt to be magnificently clad and lodged, in the cast-off clothes and abandoned palaces of the great and wealthy.

The arrival of Compère Martin was welcomed by a legion of women, children, and mongrel curs; and, as poverty and gayety generally go hand-in-hand among the French and their descendants, the crazy mansion soon resounded with loud gossip and light-hearted laughter.

As the steamboat paused a short time at the village, I took occasion to stroll about the place. Most of the houses were in the French taste, with casements and rickety verandas, but most of them in flimsy and ruinous condition. All the wagons, ploughs, and other utensils about the place were of ancient and inconvenient Gallic construction, such as had been brought from France in the primitive days of the colony. The very looks of the people reminded me of the villages of France.

From one of the houses came the hum of a spinning-wheel, accompanied by a scrap of an old French *chanson,* which I have heard many a time among the peasantry of Languedoc, doubtless a traditional song, brought over by the first French emigrants, and handed down from generation to generation.

Half a dozen young lasses emerged from the adjacent dwellings, reminding me, by their light step and gay costume, of scenes in ancient France, where taste in dress comes natural to every class of females. The trim bodice and colored petticoat, and little apron, with its pockets to receive the hands when in an attitude for conversation; the colored kerchief wound tastefully round the head, with a coquettish knot perking above one ear; and the neat slipper and tight-drawn stocking, with its braid of narrow ribbon embracing the ankle where it peeps from its mysterious curtain. It is from this ambush that Cupid sends his most inciting arrows.

While I was musing upon the recollections thus accidentally summoned up, I heard the sound of a fiddle from the mansion of Compere Martin, the signal, no doubt, for a joyous gathering. I was disposed to turn my steps thither, and witness the festivities of one of the very few villages I had met with in my wide tour that was yet poor enough to be merry; but the bell of the steamboat summoned me to re-embark.

As we swept away from the shore, I cast back a wistful eye upon the moss-grown roofs and ancient elms of the village, and prayed that the inhabitants might long retain their happy ignorance, their absence of all enterprise and improvement, their respect for the fiddle, and their contempt for the almighty dollar.[5] I fear, however, my prayer is doomed to be of no avail. In a little while the steamboat whirled me to an American town, just springing into bustling and prosperous existence.[6]

The surrounding forest had been laid out in town lots; frames of wooden buildings were rising from among stumps and burnt trees. The place already boasted a court-house, a jail, and two banks, all built of pine boards, on the model of Grecian temples. There were rival hotels, rival churches, and rival newspapers; together with the usual number of judges and generals and governors; not to speak of doctors by the dozen, and lawyers by the score.

The place, I was told, was in an astonishing career of improvement, with a canal and two railroads in embryo. Lots doubled in price every week; everybody was speculating in

[5] "This phrase, used for the first time in this sketch, has since passed into current circulation, and by some has been questioned as savoring of irreverence. The author, therefore, owes it to his orthodoxy to declare that no irreverence was intended even to the dollar itself; which he is aware is daily becoming more and more an object of worship."—Irving. *The Dictionary of American English* cites Irving's sketch for this phrase, but gives also a quotation from the Philadelphia *Public Ledger* of December 2, 1836: "The 'Almighty Dollar' is the only object of worship."

[6] Probably Montgomery's Point, the next settlement below Arkansas Post; but it certainly did not, at this time or any time, justify such a description. See Journal V, n. 21.

land; everybody was rich; and everybody was growing richer. The community, however, was torn to pieces by new doctrines in religion and in political economy; there were camp-meetings, and agrarian meetings; and an election was at hand, which, it was expected, would throw the whole country into a paroxysm.

Alas! with such an enterprising neighbor, what is to become of the poor little creole village![7]

[7] It is clear that the description of this American town is not of Montgomery's Point but is of an imaginary place, a hodge-podge of Little Rock and other places he saw in Arkansas. Irving was merely following his usual practice of presenting fanciful material in the guise of seeming fact.

Roster of Bean's Rangers

August 25—October 31, 1832[1]

No.	Name	Rank	Date of Enlistment	Place of Enlistment
1	Jesse Bean	Capt.		
2	Joseph Pentecost	1st. Lt.		
3	Robert King	2nd. Lt.		
4	George Caldwell	3rd. Lt.		
1	Edward W. Scruggs	1st. Sergt.	July 30	Batesville[2]
2	Robert A. Gibson	2nd. Sergt.	August 25	Batesville
3	Morfet E. Trimble[3]	3rd. Sergt.	July 30	Batesville
4	Isaac Bean	4th. Sergt.	August 25	Batesville
5	Furgus S. Morrison	5th. Sergt.	July 30	Batesville
1	John W. Patrick[4]	1st. Corpl.	August 16	Spadra[5]
2	Annanias Erwin	2nd. Corpl.	August 25	Batesville
3	James Elms	3rd. Corpl.	July 30	Batesville

[1] This roster is made from the first muster roll of Bean's company dated at Fort Gibson September 26, 1832; supplementary information in the notes is from this or from the roll of October 31 (Canadian River). Both rolls are from the Records of the War Department in the National Archives. Many of the family names in this list are to be found in Robert Neill's "Reminiscences of Independence County," *Arkansas Historical Publications*, III (1911), 332-56.

[2] Batesville was established as the county seat of Independence County, Arkansas, in 1821.

[3] Sick (September 26, 1832).

[4] "Absent at Fort Gibson on detached service" (October 31, 1832).

[5] Spadra Bluff on the Arkansas River in Johnson County, Arkansas.

4	Jarret Wayland[6]	4th. Corpl.	August 25	Batesville
5	John England	5th. Corpl.	August 15	Clark's Store
1	Elijah G. Shrum	Musician[7]	July 30	Batesville
2	Alexander C. Childers	"	August 25	Batesville
13	Aikin, Eli V.[8]	Private	July 30	Batesville
14	Allen, Washington	"	August 10	Batesville
15	Archer, Andrew B.	"	August 25	Batesville
16	Alston, James	"	August 16	Spadra
17	Allen, Westly[9]	"	July 30	Batesville
18	Bennett, James H.[10]	"	July 30	Batesville
19	Barr, James	"	August 13	Bayou Curi[11]
20	Baird, Benjamin H.	"	August 7	Red River
21	Brounts, Joshua	"	August 15	McClane's Bottom[12]
22	Bayles, Caleb	"	August 21	Batesville
23	Compton, John B.[13]	"	July 30	Batesville
24	Clements, Jeremiah C.[14]	"	July 30	Batesville
25	Caldwell, James[15]	"	August 3	Batesville
26	Caldwell, Abiram	"	August 14	Batesville
27	Dupuy, David	"	August 13	Bayou Curi
28	Davis, Abner	"	August 11	Batesville
29	Dudley, William[16]	"	August 9	Red River
30	Darter, Hezekiah	"	August 25	Batesville

[6] Reported sick (September 26, 1832). "Absent at Fort Gibson on detached service" (October 31, 1832).

[7] Both musicians were buglers.

[8] Also spelled Aken.

[9] "Horse strayed" (September 26, 1832)

[10] "Horse not present, but seen by the appraisers, the day after muster and since strayed" (September 26, 1832). "Absent at Fort Gibson on detached service" (October 31, 1832).

[11] In the first muster roll this name is illegible; in the second the first word is clearly *Bayou* and the second appears to be *Curi*.

[12] Probably McLean's Bottom, Crawford County (now Logan County), Arkansas.

[13] "Absent at Fort Gibson on detached service" (October 31, 1832). The name here is written Crumpton.

[14] "Sick. Horse on duty in search of stray horses" (September 26, 1832).

[15] "Sick. Horse on duty in search of stray horses" (September 26, 1832). "Absent at Fort Gibson on detached service" (October 31, 1832).

[16] "Absent at Fort Gibson on detached service" (October 31, 1832). The name is here spelled Dudly.

31	Davis, Johnson	Private	August 25	Batesville
32	Dennis, John	"	August 25	Batesville
33	Dillard, John[17]	"	August 25	Batesville
34	Elms, Garrett	"	August 14	Batesville
35	Elms, David M.	"	July 30	Batesville
36	Fulbright, William	"	July 30	Batesville
37	Gill, Addison	"	August 3	Batesville
38	Guist, Isaac[18]	"	August 6	Batesville
39	Griggs, Samuel[19]	"	August 25	Batesville
40	Griggs, Mayes[20]	"	August 3	Batesville
41	Garner, John C.	"	August 25	Batesville
42	Hammon, John[21]	"	July 30	Batesville
43	Hammon, James M.[22]	"	July 30	Batesville
44	Hulsey, William B.[23]	"	July 30	Batesville
45	Hogan, John W.	"	August 15	McClane's Bottom
46	Hyles, David	"	August 16	Spadra
47	Hyde, Ezekial	"	August 25	Batesville
48	Howell, Harvey B.[24]	"	August 25	Batesville
49	Ivy, Thomas G.[25]	"	August 25	Batesville
50	Johnson, Samuel[26]	"	August 14	Batesville
51	Johnson, Marbree[27]	"	August 10	Batesville
52	King, Drury[28]	"	August 13	Bayou Curi
53	Kister, John[29]	"	August 25	Batesville

[17] "Absent at Fort Gibson on detached service" (October 31, 1832).

[18] "Absent at Fort Gibson on detached service" (October 31, 1832). The name here is spelled Guest.

[19] "Absent at Fort Gibson on detached service" (October 31, 1832).

[20] "Absent at Fort Gibson on detached service" (October 31, 1832).

[21] "Absent at Fort Gibson on detached service" (October 31, 1832). The name is here spelled Hammond.

[22] Spelled Hammond in other lists.

[23] Sick (September 26, 1832).

[24] Given name is possibly Harry. "Absent at Fort Gibson on detached service" (October 31, 1832).

[25] Sick (September 26, 1832).

[26] "Absent at Fort Gibson on detached service" (October 31, 1832).

[27] "Absent at Fort Gibson on detached service" (October 31, 1832).

[28] Sick. (September 26, 1832). "Absent at Fort Gibson on detached service" (October 31, 1832).

[29] Or Kester. Sick (September 26, 1832). Died October 30 at Fort Gibson (October 31, 1832). Kester and John Palmer (No. 85) were replaced by Dolson Howell and Phillip Howell who were enlisted at Fort Gibson on October 22 and were numbered 49 and 50 in the muster roll of October 31; they were there entered as "absent at Fort Gibson on detached service."

54	Kellet, William[30]	Private	August 25	Batesville
55	Kavanaugh, John[31]	"	August 25	Batesville
56	Litchfield, Samuel	"	August 2	Batesville
57	Labass, John[32]	"	August 25	Batesville
58	Logan, Massa[33]	"	August 25	Batesville
59	Logan, Bennett T.	"	August 16	Spadra
60	Lee, John[34]	"	August 25	Horsehead
61	McClenden, Willis	"	July 30	Batesville
62	McKinney, Clark S.	"	July 30	Batesville
63	McCloud, Neil[35]	"	August 16	Spadra
64	Meacham, James A.	"	July 30	Batesville
65	Meacham, Christopher[36]	"	August 3	Batesville
66	Murphy, Mark[37]	"	August 25	Batesville
67	Markham, Thomas Sr.[38]	"	August 25	Batesville
68	Markham, Thomas Jr.[39]	"	August 25	Batesville
69	Manson, William	"	August 25	Batesville
70	Martin, James	"	August 15	McClane's Bottom
71	Nipper, Solomon	"	August 2	Batesville
72	Newcomb, Thomas[40]	"	August 25	Batesville
73	Newman, John	"	August 21	Batesville
74	Nelson, Charles	"	August 24	Batesville
75	Osburn, James	"	August 2	Batesville
76	Oneal, John[41]	"	August 25	Batesville
77	Powers, Simmeon[42]	"	August 25	Batesville
78	Palmer, David M.[43]	"	August 20	Batesville

[30] "Absent at Fort Gibson on detached service" (October 31, 1832).
[31] "In pursuit of his horse in A. T." (September 26, 1832).
[32] The name in other lists is written LaBass. "Absent at Fort Gibson on detached service" (October 31, 1832).
[33] Sick (September 26, 1832). "Absent at Fort Gibson on detached service" (October 31, 1832).
[34] Sick (September 26, 1832).
[35] "Absent at Fort Gibson on detached service" (October 31, 1832).
[36] "In pursuit of his horse in A. T." (September 26, 1832).
[37] "Absent at Fort Gibson on detached service" (October 31, 1832).
[38] Variously spelled Markam, Markum, Markham. Sick (September 26, 1832).
[39] Variously spelled Markam, Markum, Markham. Sick (September 26, 1832). "Absent at Fort Gibson on detached service" (October 31, 1832).
[40] Sick (September 26, 1832).
[41] "Absent at Fort Gibson on detached service" (October 31, 1832).
[42] "Absent at Fort Gibson on detached service" (October 31, 1832).
[43] Sick (September 26, 1832).

79	Palmer, King L.[44]	Private	July 30	Batesville
80	Penter, Martin	"	July 30	Batesville
81	Peel, Richard[45]	"	July 30	Batesville
82	Peel, John	"	July 31	Batesville
83	Peel, William[46]	"	July 31	Batesville
84	Pool, Washington[47]	"	July 30	Batesville
85	Palmer, John J.[48]	"	August 2	Batesville
86	Price, Jacob	"	August 23	Batesville
87	Peryhouse[?], Nelson	"	August 25	Batesville
88	Ryan, John	"	August 14	Horsehead
89	Russell, Samuel[49]	"	August 20	Batesville
90	Raney, David J.[50]	"	August 15	McClane's Bottom
91	Ryan, William	"	August 14	Horsehead
92	Stokes, James	"	August 25	Batesville
93	Shaddon, Lewis[51]	"	August 8	Batesville
94	Sawyers, William	"	August 16	Spadra
95	Turley, Thomas S.[52]	"	July 30	Batesville
96	Tate, William C.	"	July 30	Batesville
97	Turney, Isham[53]	"	August 2	Batesville
98	Taylor, Wiley[54]	"	August 13	Batesville
99	Vickers, William[55]	"	August 25	Batesville
100	Wilson, John S.	"	July 30	Batesville
101	Wilson, Absolom	"	August 2	Batesville
102	Wilson, Edward[56]	"	August 2	Batesville

[44] Sick (September 26, 1832). "Absent at Fort Gibson on detached service" (October 31, 1832).

[45] Sick (September 26, 1832). "Absent at Fort Gibson on detached service" (October 31, 1832).

[46] Sick (September 26, 1832).

[47] Sick (September 26, 1832). "Absent at Fort Gibson on detached service" (October 31, 1832).

[48] Sick (September 26, 1832). Died September 27 at Fort Gibson (October 31, 1832).

[49] Sick (September 26, 1832).

[50] Sick (September 26, 1832).

[51] Also Shadden.

[52] "Horse strayed" (September 26, 1832).

[53] The given name may be Joshua. "Absent at Fort Gibson on detached service" (October 31, 1832).

[54] "In pursuit of a horse in A. T. strayed from Company" (September 26, 1832).

[55] Sick (September 26, 1832). "Absent at Fort Gibson on detached service" (October 31, 1832).

[56] Sick (September 26, 1832).

103	Wilson, Daniel	Private	August 11	Batesville
104	Wilson, Joseph[57]	"	August 25	Batesville
105	Wyatt, Joseph S.	"	August 3	
106	Wilson, William[58]	"	August 11	Batesville
107	Wayland, James	"	August 25	Batesville
108	Welborne, Melton	"	August 15	McClane's Bottom
109	Young, Harvey K.[59]	"	August 21	Batesville
110	Zeachsa, Burr H.[60]	"	August 7	Red River

[57] "Absent at Fort Gibson on detached service" (October 31, 1832).

[58] "Absent at Fort Gibson on detached service" (October 31, 1832).

[59] The given name may be Harry. Sick (September 26, 1832). "Absent at Fort Gibson on detached service" (October 31, 1832).

[60] So the name appears, but on the other rolls it seems to be Zachry. "Absent at Fort Gibson on detached service" (October 31, 1832).

Bibliography

MANUSCRIPTS

Adjutant General's Office, War Department, The National Archives, Washington, D. C.

Clark Papers, Kansas Historical Society, Topeka.

Clark Papers, Missouri Historical Society, St. Louis.

Duyckinck Collection, New York Public Library.

Office of Indian Affairs, Department of the Interior, The National Archives, Washington, D. C.

Records of the American Board of Commissioners of Foreign Missions, Harvard-Andover Theological Library, Cambridge.

St. Louis Probate Court Records.

Surgeon General's Office, War Department, The National Archives, Washington, D. C.

Washington Irving, Western Travel Journals, 5 vols., New York Public Library.

CONGRESSIONAL DOCUMENTS

Senate Documents, Twenty-third Congress, first session, 5–12; second session, 1. *House Report,* Twenty-third Congress, first session, 474.

BOOKS AND MAGAZINES

Arkansas Historical Association Publications, I–IV (1903–1917).
Atkeson, W. O. *History of Bates County, Missouri.* Topeka and Cleveland, 1918.
Atwater, Caleb. *The Writings of Caleb Atwater.* Columbus, 1833.
Bache, Richard. *View of the Valley of the Mississippi: or the Emigrant's and Traveller's Guide to the West.* Philadelphia, 1832.
Bates, Frederick. *The Life and Papers of Frederick Bates.* Edited by Thomas Maitland Marshall. 2 vols. St. Louis, Missouri Historical Society, 1926.
Billon, Frederic L. *Annals of St. Louis in Its Early Days Under the French and Spanish Dominations* [1764–1804]. St. Louis, 1886.
Biographical and Historical Memoirs of Western Arkansas. Chicago, 1891.
Brackenridge, Henry Marie. *Views of Louisiana.* Second edition, Baltimore, 1817.
Bryant, William Cullen. "Illinois Fifty Years Ago," in *Prose Writings of William Cullen Bryant.* Edited by Parke Godwin (2 vols. New York, Appleton, 1884), II, 3–22.
Catlin, George. *Letters and Notes on the Manners, Customs, and Condition of the North American Indians.* Seventh edition, 2 vols. London, 1848.
Collins, Lewis. *History of Kentucky.* 2 vols. Louisville, 1882.
Cullum, George W. *Biographical Register of the Officers and Graduates of the U. S. Military Academy at West Point.* 2 vols. New York, 1868.
Cumings, Samuel. *The Western Pilot.* Cincinnati, 1834.
Dale, Harrison Clifford. *The Ashley-Smith Explorations and the Discovery of a Central Route to the Pacific, 1822–1829, With the Original Journals.* Glendale, California, Arthur H. Clark Co., 1941.
Darby, John F. *Personal Recollections.* St. Louis, 1880.
Davis, Charles B. "Judge James Hawkins Peck," *Missouri Historical Review,* XXVII (1932), 3–20.
Debo, Angie. *The Rise and Fall of the Choctaw Republic.* Norman, University of Oklahoma Press, 1934.

Dictionary of American Biography (DAB).

Dictionary of National Biography (DNB).

Donaldson, Thomas. *The George Catlin Indian Gallery in the U. S. National Museum [Smithsonian Institution] with Memoir and Statistics.* Smithsonian Institution, *Annual Report for 1885.*

Dorrance, Ward Allison. *The Survival of French in Old District of Sainte Genevieve. University of Missouri Studies,* X (April 1, 1935), No. 2.

Ellsworth, Henry Leavitt. *Washington Irving on the Prairie, or a Narrative of a Tour of the Southwest in the Year 1832.* Edited by Stanley T. Williams and Barbara D. Simison. New York, American Book Company, 1937.

Featherstonhaugh, G. W. *A Canoe Voyage up the Minnay Sotor.* 2 vols. London, Richard Bentley, 1847.

———. *Excursion through the Slave States, From Washington on the Potomac to the Frontier of Mexico.* 2 vols. London, 1844.

Ferrall, S. A. *A Ramble of Six Thousand Miles Through the United States of America.* London, 1832.

Ferris, W. A. *Life in the Rocky Mountains . . . 1830 . . . 1835.* Edited by Paul C. Phillips. Denver, Old West Publishing Company, 1940.

Flagg, Edmund. *The Far West, or a Tour beyond the Mountains.* 2 vols. New York, 1838. In Thwaites *(q.v.), Early Western Travels,* XXVI, XXVII.

Flint, Timothy. *A Condensed Geography and History of the Western States or the Mississippi Valley.* 2 vols. Cincinnati, 1828.

Foreman, Grant. *Advancing the Frontier, 1830–1860.* Norman, University of Oklahoma Press, 1933.

———. *The Five Civilized Tribes.* Norman, University of Oklahoma Press, 1934.

———. *Indians and Pioneers.* New Haven, Yale University Press, 1930.

———. *Indian Removal.* Norman, University of Oklahoma Press, 1932.

———. *Pioneer Days in the Early Southwest.* Cleveland, Arthur H. Clark Co., 1926.

Garraghan, Gilbert J., S. J. *Saint Ferdinand de Florissant*. Chicago, Loyola University Press, 1923.

Gregg, Josiah. *Commerce of the Prairies*. 2 vols. New York, 1844.

Gregg, Kate L. "The Boonslick Road in St. Charles County," *Missouri Historical Review*, XXVII (1933), 307–14; XXVIII (1933), 9–16.

Hall, Basil. *Travels in North America in the Years 1827 and 1828*. 3 vols. Edinburgh, 1829.

Hall, Mrs. Basil. *The Aristocratic Journey 1827–1828*. Prefaced and edited by Una Pope-Hennessy. New York, Putnams, 1931.

Hallum, John. *Biographical and Pictorial History of Arkansas*. Albany, 1887.

Heitman, Francis B. *Historical Register and Dictionary of the United States Army*. 2 vols. Washington, 1903 (57 Cong., 2 sess., *House Doc.* 446).

Hempstead, Fay. *A Pictorial History of Arkansas from Earliest Times to the Year 1890*. St. Louis, 1890.

Herndon, Dallas T. *Why Little Rock Was Born*. Little Rock, 1933.

The History of Cass and Bates Counties, Missouri. St. Joseph, 1883.

The History of Jackson County, Missouri. Kansas City, Missouri, 1881.

History of Vernon County, Missouri. St. Louis, 1887.

Hodge, Frederick Webb. *Handbook of American Indians North of Mexico. Bulletin 30*, Bureau of American Ethnology. 2 vols. Washington, 1907.

Hoffman, Charles F. *A Winter in the West by a New–Yorker*. 2 vols. New York, 1835.

Houck, Louis. *A History of Missouri*. 3 vols. Chicago, 1908.

——. *The Spanish Régime in Missouri*. 2 vols. Chicago, 1909.

Irving, John Treat. *Indian Sketches, Taken During an Expedition to the Pawnee Indians*. New York, Putnams, 1888.

Irving, Pierre M. *The Life and Letters of Washington Irving*. Hudson Edition, 3 vols. New York, Putnams, 1857.

Irving, Washington. "The Creole Village," in *The Adventures of Captain Bonneville*, II, 282–95. Knickerbocker Edition, New York, Putnams, 1895.

Irving, Washington. *Journals.* Edited by William P. Trent and George S. Hellman. 3 vols. Boston, Bibliophile Society, 1919.

Irving, Washington. *A Tour on the Prairies.* Knickerbocker Edition, New York, Putnams, 1895.

Irwing [*sic*], Washington. *Un Tour dans les Prairies à l'ouest des Etats-Unis traduit de l'anglais . . . par Ernest W***.* Tours, 1846.

James, Edwin. *Account of an Expedition from Pittsburgh to the Rocky Mountains . . . from the Notes of Major S. H. Long,* in Thwaites *(q.v.), Early Western Travels,* XIV, XV, XVI, XVII.

James, Marquis. *The Raven, A Biography of Sam Houston.* New York, Blue Ribbon Books, 1929.

James, Thomas. *Three Years Among the Indians and Mexicans.* Edited by Walter B. Douglas. St. Louis, Missouri Historical Society, 1916.

Johnston, J. Stoddard. *Memorial of Louisville from Its First Settlement to the Year 1896.* 2 vols. Chicago (n. d.)

La Flesche, Francis. *A Dictionary of the Osage Language. Bulletin 109,* Bureau of American Ethnology. Washington, 1932.

Langfeld, William R. and Philip C. Blackburn. *Washington Irving— A Bibliography.* New York, New York Public Library, 1933.

Latrobe, Charles Joseph. *The Rambler in North America 1832–1833.* Second edition, 2 vols. London, 1836.

McCoy, Isaac. *History of Baptist Indian Missions.* Washington, 1840.

McDermott, John Francis (ed.). "Audubon's Journrney Up the Mississippi," *Illinois State Historical Society Journal,* XXXV (1942), 148–73.

McDermott, John Francis (ed.) and Albert J. Salvan (trans.) *Tixier's Travels on the Osage Prairies.* Norman, University of Oklahoma Press, 1940.

McKenney, Thomas L. and James Hall. *The Indian Tribes of North America.* New edition, edited by Frederick Webb Hodge. 3 vols. Edinburgh, John Grant, 1933.

Martzoff, Clement L. "Caleb Atwater," *Ohio Archaeological and Historical Quarterly,* XIV (1905), 247–71.

Mason, E. G. "Pierre Menard," *Chicago Historical Society Publications,* IV (1890), 142-48.

Maximilian, Prince of Wied. *Travels in the Interior of North America*, in Thwaites *(q.v.)*, *Early Western Travels*, XXII, XXIII, XXIV, XXV.

Merrill, William Stetson. "Pierre Menard of Illinois," *Mid-America*, XIV (1931), 15–38.

Missionary Herald, XXI, XXVI–XXX (1825, 1830–34).

Missionary Register, V (1824).

Morrison, William Brown. *Military Posts and Camps in Oklahoma*. Oklahoma City, Harlow Publishing Company, 1936.

Murphy, Edmund Robert. *Henry de Tonty, Fur Trader of the Mississippi*. Institut Français de Washington, Baltimore, Johns Hopkins Press, 1941.

Murray, Charles Augustus. *Travels in North America During the years 1834, 1835, and 1836 Including a Summer Residence With the Pawnee Tribe of Indians, in the Remote Prairies of the Missouri, and on a Visit to Cuba and the Azore Islands.* 2 vols. London, Richard Bentley, 1839.

Niles Register, XLIII (1832).

Pelzer, Louis. *Marches of the Dragoons in the Mississippi Valley, 1833–1850.* Iowa City, State Historical Society of Iowa, 1917.

Peterson, Charles E. "Early Ste. Genevieve and Its Architecture," *Missouri Historical Review*, XXXV (January, 1941), 207–32.

"Pierre Menard Papers," *Chicago Historical Society Publications*, IV (1890), 162–80.

Pope, William F. *Early Days in Arkansas Being for the Most Part the Personal Recollections of an Old Settler*. Arranged and edited by his son, Dunbar H. Pope. Little Rock, 1895.

Quaife, Milo Milton (edi.). *Life of Ma-ka-tai-me-she-kia-kiak or Black Hawk. . . . Dictated by Himself.* (Boston, 1834). Chicago, The Lakeside Press, 1916.

"Review of A Tour on the Prairies," *North American Review*, XLI (July, 1835), 1–28.

Rothert, Otto A. *The Outlaws of Cave-in-Rock*. Cleveland, Arthur H. Clark Co., 1924.

The St. Louis Directory for the Year 1836–7. St. Louis, C. Keemle, 1836.

Scharf, J. Thomas. *History of St. Louis, City and County.* 2 vols. Philadelphia, Everts, 1883.

Schoolcraft, H. R. "Remarks on the Prints of Human Feet, Observed in the Secondary Limestone of the Mississippi Valley," *American Journal of Science,* V (1822), 223–31.

Schultz, Gerard. "Steamboat Navigation on the Osage River Before the Civil War," *Missouri Historical Review,* XXIX (April, 1935), 175–85.

Shinn, Josiah H. *Pioneers and Makers of Arkansas.* Little Rock, 1908.

Stuart, James. *Three Years in North America.* Second edition, revised. 2 vols. Edinburgh, 1833.

Thoburn, Joseph B. "Centennial of the Town on the Prairies by Washington Irving (1832–1932)," *Chronicles of Oklahoma,* X (September 1930), 426–33.

Thwaites, R. G. (ed.). *Original Journals of the Lewis and Clark Expedition, 1804–1806.* 7 vols. and atlas, New York, Dodd, Mead and Co., 1904.

———— (ed). *Early Western Travels.* 32 vols. Cleveland, Arthur H. Clark Co., 1904–1907.

————. "William Clark: Soldier, Explorer, Statesman," *Missouri Historical Society Collections,* No. 7, 11 (October, 1906), 1–24.

Townsend, John K. *Narrative of a Journey Across the Rocky Mountains to the Columbia River,* in Thwaites *(q.v.),* *Early Western Travels,* XXI.

Trent, William P. and George S. Hellman (editors). *The Journals of Washington Irving.* 3 vols. Boston, Bibliophile Society, 1919.

Trollope, Frances. *Domestic Manners of the Americans.* Fifth edition, London, 1839.

Wetmore, Alphonso. *Gazetteer of the State of Missouri.* St. Louis, C. Keemle, 1837.

Williams, Stanley T. *The Life of Washington Irving.* 2 vols. New York, Oxford University Press, 1935.

———— and Barbara D. Simison (editors). *Washington Irving on the Prairie, or A Narrative of a Tour of the Southwest in the Year 1832,* by Henry Leavitt Ellsworth. New York, American Book Company, 1937.

Young, William. *History of Lafayette County, Missouri.* 2 vols. In-dianapolis, Bowen, 1910.

Yealy, Francis J., S. J. *Sainte Genevieve, The Story of Missouri's Oldest Settlement.* Ste. Genevieve, The Bicentennial Historical Committee, 1935.

NEWSPAPERS

Arkansas Gazette. Little Rock, 1832, 1833, 1834.

Missouri Intelligencer and Boon's Lick Advertiser. Columbia, 1832.

Missouri Republican. St. Louis, 1832.

Index

American Fur Company: 14, 16

Anderson, William E.: 9

Arbuckle, Matthew: 23, 24, 25, 30, 31, 33, 111, 150, 151; opinion of Choctaws, 135; conversation with Clermont, 162

————, letters quoted: to Col. R. Jones regarding Bean's Rangers, 31; to Capt. Bean regarding conduct of expedition to Indian country, 31–33

Arkansas Advocate: 156n

Arkansas Gazette: quoted regarding Bean, 28, 28n, 30; interview with Irving reported, 38–39

Arkansas Post: *see* Post of Arkansas

Arkansas River: 38, 111, 115, 117, 123, 126, 127, 130, 148, 156, 156n, 160, 160n, 165

Arrow Rock Ferry: 19

Ashley, William Henry: 82, 82n

Ashtabula: 12

Atkinson: Henry: 81, 81n

Atwater, Caleb: 79, 79n

Austin, Daniel H.: 95n

Austin, John: 95, 95n

Austin, Moses: 79n

Bates, Edward: 80, 80n

Bean, Isaac: 132; describes adventure in forest, 128

Bean, Jesse: 28n, 29, 30, 31, 33, 34, 111n, 114, 119, 120, 121, 124, 125, 126, 129, 132, 139, 140, 146, 147, 149, 150; estimate of character, 28, 118n; conversation of reported, 122, 123, 127, 128

Bean's Rangers: 111n; history of, 28–31; expedition with described, 118–33, 139–50; roster of, 181–86

Beatte, Pierre: 27, 27n, 34n, 52, 53, 55, 59, 61, 117n, 118n, 121, 125, 126, 127, 130, 131, 140, 140n, 141, 142, 144, 145, 146, 147, 147n, 148, 149, 152n; character of, 138; conversation of, 122, 123

Bee hunt: 119–20

Bee hunters: 92, 124, 128

Berryhill, Mr.: 112n, 113

Bertrand, Charles P.: 156n

Billet: *see* Beatte, Pierre

Black Hawk (river dandy) 72, 73

Black Hawk (Sauk chief): 15–16, 16n, 83, 83n, 84, 84n

Bliss, John H.: quoted regarding Pourtalès and Latrobe, 5n

Boon's Lick: 19

Boonslick Road: 17

Boudinot Mission: 23, 90, 99n; story of Indians at, 105

Bradley, Madam: serves dinner to Irving, 149–50, 150n

Brailey, Mr. (A. P. Chouteau's clerk): 34, 37, 38, 114, 114n, 118, 119

Bright, Samuel B.: 94, 94n

Broken Hoof: 95, 97

Brown (*possibly* David): 155

Brown, Jacob: 158, 159n

Bucklin, John C.: 70, 70n

Buffaloes: 123, 140; habits of, 136

Bull-boat, adventure of: 61, 125, 126, 126n

Cabin Creek: 130n, 107n

Cabin de Planch Creek: *see* Cabin Creek

Cadeau: 165

Cairns, Mr.: *see* Carnes, Peter A.

Caldwell, George: 30

Caledonia: 76, 76n

Campbell, John: 111, 111n

Canadian River: 139 140n

Carnes, Peter A.: 156, 156n

Carondelet: 15, 84, 84n, 133, 134

Carroll, William: 9

Cass, Lewis: 9, 159

Castlereagh, Viscount: 75, 75n

Catlin, George: describes Black Hawk, 84n

Cave-In-Rock: 73n, 74, 74n

Chambers, Capt. (of the *Illinois*): 70

Chilhowee Mts.: 135

Chouteau, Auguste Pierre: 9, 16, 20, 23, 24, 24n, 27, 28, 80n, 90, 91, 94, 95, 96, 98, 114n; his agency on the Verdigris River, 28, 38, 111–12, 111n, 150; quotes Indian superstitions, 100, 101, 102; Indian describes visit to him, 103; his Grand Saline establishment, 108–109; his opinion of effect of missions on half bloods, 135

Chouteau, Paul Liguest: 100n

Chouteau, Pierre (père): 80, 80n

Cimarron River: *see* Red Fork of Arkansas

Cincinnati: 12, 13, 69

Clark's agency: 158

Clark, Isaac: 151, 151n

Clark, Marston G. (Kansa Indian agent): 24, 90, 90n

Clark, Meriwether Lewis: 81n

Clark, William: 15, 81, 81n, 82, 87n, 134; visited by Indian, 103

Clermont (Osage chief): 162

Cleveland: 11, 12

Columbia (Mo.): 18

Courtois, Julien Louis: 133–35, 133n

Crawford Court House: 157, 157n

Creasing: method of capturing wild horses, 143n

Cross Timbers: 37, 140n, 141n

Cumberland Mountains: 84

Cumberland River: 74

Cummins, Francine: 160, 160n, 168

Cummins, Richard W. (Delaware and Shawnee agent): 24, 24n

Cummins, William: 160, 160n, 168

Cunningham, Matthew: 156, 156n, 159

Dallas, Col.: 168

Dardanelles: 158, 158n

Dawson, James Low: 160, 160n, 168

Dean, Capt. (*misspelling for* Bean): *see* Bean, Jesse

Deep Fork of Canadian River: 146

Desha, Ben: 167, 167n

Deshetres, Antoine: 16, 17, 34n, 35, 93, 96–97, 98, 99, 110, 126, 126n, 127, 138, 140n, 144, 145; contrast between real character and Irving's presentation in *Tour*, 49–59; described by Latrobe, 57, 58; by Ellsworth, 58, 59; by Duyckinck, 60–62; his opinion of Irving, 61; tells story of white deer, 152–53

Destroyer of Cities: *see* Tuer du Village

Devil's Elbow: 156

Diamond Island: 72

Dodge, Nathaniel B.: 89, 89n, 99, 99n, 100, 105
Dodge, Sally Gale: 89n, 99
Dog Island: 74n
Drake, Mrs.: 12
Duyckinck, Evert A.: letter to W. A. Jones describing visit to Antoine Deshetres, 60–62

Education: college at Ste Genevieve, 78; school at Harmony Mission, 94, 95; at Grand Saline, 109; at Union Mission, 110, 110n
Ellsworth, Henry Leavitt: 8, 20, 25, 26, 26n, 27, 33, 34, 90, 92, 94, 110, 115n, 117, 127, 140, 147, 150; appointed Indian commissioner, 9; character of, 10–11; instructed about travel, 24n
————, letter: to Lewis Cass regarding western expedition, 24–25
————, *Irving on the Prairies, or a Narrative of a Tour of the Southwest in the Year 1832*, quoted regarding: Latrobe, 4; arrival at Fort Gibson, 23; filling tooth, 35; alarm in camp, 36; Irving's style of writing, 44; Tonish, 59; Irving's preparation for work, 63n; Irving's attitude toward writing, 64; Dr. O'Dwyer, 90n; Bean's lieutenants, 111n; Mr. Bailey, 114n; Dr. Holt, 119n; corn drink, 124n; adventure of the bull-boat, 126n; remedy for Irving's illness, 129n; washing clothes, 133n; Creek tree pictures, 143n; crossing river on logs, 147n; meal at Madam Bradley's, 150n

Faux Ouachita (False Washita): 32, 141n
Flint, Timothy: 13; *Mississippi Valley* quoted regarding limestone foot prints, 84–85; regarding cypress, 85
Florissant: 17, 60
Footprints in limestone: 84–85, 85n

Fort Gibson: 9, 23, 26, 110, 111, 111n, 150, 151n
Fort Jefferson: 15, 83, 83n
Fort Smith: 156, 156n
Fort Snelling: 5n
French settlers: in St. Louis, 80, 83; character of, 84, 167, 174, 175, 180, 181; character of villages, 78n, 167, 172–73, 178, 179–80, treatment of slaves, 84, 167; attitude toward government, 166, 167, 172; amusements, 80, 84, 167, 178,
Frontier life: 18, 20, 21, 43, 70, 71–72, 73, 74, 75, 76, 77, 78, 85, 104, 156, 157, 166; style of dwelling, 18, 43, 77, 113, 157; hospitality, 17, 18, 62; amusements, 73, 74, 91; 158; manners, 74, 75; lack of education, 74, 85; religion, 78; attitude toward Indians, 166
Fulton (*probably* John T.): 159, 159n
Fuller, Mr.: 94

Galt House (in Louisville): 70n
Globe Hotel (in Independence): 89
Grand River: *see* Neosho River
Grand Saline: *see* Salines
Grand Saline establishment of A. P. Chouteau: see Chouteau, Auguste Pierre
Gratiot, General: 9, 24n

Hamilton ("Nullifying Governor" of South Carolina): 39–40
Hardage Mr.: 113n
Harmony Mission: 89n, 94–95, 94n, 99
Heard, John J.: 19, 19n
Henry Clay (Chouteau's greyhound): 91, 96
Herculaneum: 79, 79n
Holt, David: 34n, 118, 119, 119n, 120, 121, 126, 129n, 130, 140n
Hopefield Mission: 23, 107, 107n
Houston, Sam: 24, 33, 111
Hullabuloo, Princess: 72

Hunter, Governor: 162–63

Illinois: 87
Illinois River: 78
Independence (Mo.): 16, 20, 21, 89; described, 89n
Indians: 95, 102; characteristics of, 87; ability of children to learn, 95; legends of, 101, 102, 102n, 105, 135, 153–54; ideas of happiness, 103–104; hunting customs of, 138
——, Cherokee: 87, 109, 156; criticize McCoy, 104; desire for education, 110
——, Chickasaw: tradition of, 163
——, Choctaw: 156; character of, 135–36; friendly to white man, 163; belief in witchcraft, 169
——, Comanche: 31, 32
——, Creek: 26, 149, 151; appearance of, 111, 112, 113; tree pictures, 143
——, Delaware: as mediators, 87; desire for education, 110; superior character of, 164
——, Kickapoo: once enemies of Cherokees, 87
——, Osage: 45, 46, 47, 48, 97, 99, 108, 112, 113, 114, 116, 123, 127, 137, 137n, 152, 164, 164n; manner of singing, 34, 117–18; habits when on hunting expeditions, 98; deserted war camp, 115; village scene, 117; importance of cook, 135; burial and mourning customs of, 99, 100, 101; character of, 136
——, Pawnee: 32, 97, 108, 110, 137, 152; hostility against, 25; fierce character of, 26; children at Chouteau's agency, 102; manner of attacking, 164
——, Piankishaw: 95n
——, Quapaw: 159, 164, 164n, 166
Irving, Washington: manners, 19; interest in adventures, 26, 36, 36, 130–31; style of writing, 44; romantic attitude toward life, 38, 41–

44; preparations for writing, 63n; interest in people and sharpness of observation, 64–65
——, travels: returns to America, 3–7; joins Latrobe and Pourtalès for travel, 7; meets Ellsworth and decides on western tour, 9–10; goes across Ohio to Cincinnati, 11–12; leaves Cincinnati, 12, 69; arrives Louisville, 70; visits Judge Ormsby, 70–71; travels on Ohio and Mississippi rivers to St. Louis, 13–14, 71–80; visits Clark's farm, 15, 81–82; sees Black Hawk at Fort Jefferson, 15–16, 83; leaves St. Louis, 17; joins Chouteau at Independence and passes west into Osage country, 20, 89, 90; stops at Harmony Mission, 94–95; Boudinot Mission, 23, 99; Hopefield Mission, 23, 107; Chouteau's Grand Saline, 23, 108–109; Union Mission, 23, 110; arrives Fort Gibson, 23, 111; made secretary to commission by Ellsworth, 25; leaves for expedition with Bean's Rangers, 28, 111; visits Osage village, 117; meets Bean, 34, 118; engages in bee hunt, 119–20; crosses Arkansas in bull-boat, 125–26; hunts with Bean, 129–33; returns to Fort Gibson, 37–38; 139–50; makes river journey to Post of Arkansas, 151–66; stops at New Orleans and turns north to Washington, 39–40
——, letters, excerpts from, describing: emotions upon arrival in America, 6; beginning of travels, 7, 8; meeting with Ellsworth, 10; journey across Ohio, 11–13; steamboat accident, 14; visit to Black Hawk, 15–16; western travel, 20, 22n; plans for expedition with Rangers, 26–27; life with Rangers, 35–36; difficulties faced, 37; stay at New Orleans and journey north, 39–40; scenery in Missouri, 42
——, *Tour on the Prairies:* con-

temporary reviews of, 41; merit contrasted with that of *Western Journals*, 41–66
Izard, Ralph: 164–65

Jay, William: 9
Jefferson Barracks: *see* Fort Jefferson
Jones, Amasa: 94, 94n, 95
Joseph (half blood): 97, 103

Kaskaskia: 79n
Kaskaskia River: 78
Kemble, Gouvernour: 7
Kemmel, Mr.: 77
Kentucky: nature of land and reason for name, 153
King, Robert: 30, 140n

Labette Creek: 100, 100n, 101n
Latrobe, Charles Joseph: 6, 7, 8, 11, 20, 27, 33, 34, 36, 38, 90, 92, 93, 94, 114, 119, 126n, 133, 141, 145, 150, 151; character described, 4–5; buys supplies for tour, 21–22
————, *Rambler in North America, The*, quoted regarding: plans to join western tour, 9–10; Ohio River scenery, 13–14; hiring of Tonish, 16, 17; frontier travel and hospitality, 17, 18; trappers from Santa Fé, 19–20; Independence, 21; manner of travel, 22; frontier farm, 43; Tonish, 57, 58; canal on Ohio, 71n; accident to *Illinois*, 73n; Dr. O'Dwyer, 90n; journey from Independence, 92n; western scenery, 93n; arrival of Tuer du Village, 97n; Antoine Lombard, 115n; Dr. Holt and Ryan, 119n; Uncle Sam's gun, 125n; Sawyer, 141n; making bridge, 146n
Lewis, Meriwether: 134
Lewisburgh: 158
Lexington (Mo.): 9
Licking River: 153
Little Osage River: 95–96, 96n
Little River: 139, 140n

Little Rock: 38, 158, 169, 182n
Lombard, Antoine: 34n, 129, 130, 132, 133, 140; described, 115n
Louisiana: 172
Louisville: 13, 70
Lower Blue Lick Springs Hotel: 70n
Lucas, Frederick: 75, 75n, 77

McCoy, Isaac: 25, 90, 90n, 91n, 101n; Cherokee's estimate of, 104
McCoy, John Calvin: 90n, 92
McCoy, Rice: 90n
McLane, Louis: 39, 159, 159n
McNeill, John: 79n
Madison (Indiana): 69, 69n
Magazin Mt.: 158n
Mapes, Charles: 157, 157n, 160
Martin, Compère: 175, 176, 177, 178, 179
Mason, Samuel: 161–62
Menard, Pierre: 79, 79n
Mississippi River: 76, 85, 86, 160
Missouri Intelligencer and Boon's Lick Advertiser: quoted regarding Irving's visit to Columbia, 19
Missouri River: 19, 86, 86n
Mongrain, Baptiste: 98n
Montgomery, William: 157, 158n
Montgomery's Point: 158n, 160, 160n, 179n
Mounds, prehistoric: 12, 12n, 82

Negroes: 18, 90, 112, 156, 157, 160, 168, 174, 177; character of, 43, 86, 176; steward described, 69–70, 71; manner of living, 70, 71; boatmen, 71, 156; condition of, 72, 77, 86; merchant, 77–78; Clark's slaves, 81, 82; attitude of French toward, 84, 167; at Grand Saline, 108
Neosho Mission: 99n
Neosho River: 23, 92, 98n, 100, 102, 107, 107n, 108n, 111n
New Orleans: 39
Nicks, John: 151n, 163
Nicks, Widow: 150–51
Nix, General: *see* Nicks, John

Nix, Widow: *see* Nicks, Widow
Noland *(possibly* Charles Fenton Mercer): 157, 158n
North Fork of Canadian River: 144
Notrebe, Frederick: 168, 168n, 171n, 173n

O'Dwyer, Thomas: 16, 20, 80, 80n, 83n, 90, 90n, 91, 92, 99
Ohio: beauties of, 12
Ohio River: 13, 14, 71, 73, 76, 85
Ormsby, Stephen: 70, 70n, 71
Osage River: 95, 95n, 96, 100

Paducah: 75, 75n
Paulding, James: 7
Pawnee Creek: 98, 98n
Pawnee Hill: 97
Peale family: 159, 159n
Pecan Creek: 148n
Peck, James Hawkins: 80, 80n, 83
Penticost, Joseph: 30, 111, 111n, 125, 126, 132, 140, 148
Petit Jean Creek: 158n
Petit Jean Mts.: 158, 165
Pitcher, Zina: 119n, 151, 151n
Plank Cabin Creek: *see* Cabin Creek
Pope, John: 159, 159n, 165
Post of Arkansas: 158n, 160, 166, 168, 169, 171n
Pourtalès, Albert-Alexandre de: 7, 11, 20, 27, 33, 36, 38, 47, 73, 90, 93, 94, 100, 114, 118, 121, 130, 149, 151; character described, 5–6; imitates Indian song, 34; loses boots, 113; fails to get Osage wife, 118n
Prairie dogs: 104, 105, 105n
Preston, William C.: 39
Prophet, The: *see* Winnebago Prophet

Quakers: frontier treatment of, 74

Redfield, Abraham: 110n
Red Fork of Arkansas River: 35, 37, 121, 122, 123, 125, 125n, 130, 140n, 141n
Red River: 132, 141n

Requa, Susan Comstock: 107–108
Requa, William C.: 23n, 94, 107, 107n
Ritchie, Dr.: 159
Robb, John: gives instructions to Ellsworth as to route to be followed west, 24n
Robber's Harbour: *see* Stack Island
Robertson, Felix: 9
Rock Cave: *see* Cave-In-Rock
Rogers, John (Cherokee): 109, 109n, 151n
Rogers, John (merchant of Fort Smith): 156, 156n
Ryan (hunter): 119n, 128, 132

St. Charles: 17, 57
St. Louis: 9, 15, 16, 17, 80n; mixed character of, 80, 83
Ste Genevieve: 78, 78n
Salines: Grand Saline, 109, 109n, 110; Rock Saline, 137
Salt Plain: 137n
Salt Rock: 137n
Sarazin (Chief of the Quapaws): speech to Gov. Pope, 165–66
Sawyer, Mr.: 141, 141n
Schermerhorn: John F.: 9
Sewaculty (Spirit of the Mountain): 153, 154
Shawnee Agency: 90n
Shot tower (at Herculaneum): 79
Showboat: 73
Smith, B. H. (teacher at Chouteau's Grand Saline): 109
Smithland: 74, 75n
Stack Island: 161
Stambaugh, Samuel: 11n, 23n, 25, 26n
Steamboats: *Messenger*, 13, 69; *Illinois*, 13, 14, 70, 73n, 74n; *Yellowstone*, 14, 80, 80n; *Winnebago*, 83n; *Little Rock*, 38, 151, 155
Stokes, Montfort: 9, 11, 24
Summers, Allen: 95, 95n

Thirty Mile Prairie: 18

Throckmorton, Aris: 70, 70n
Tonish: *see* Deshetres, Antoine
Trappers from Santa Fé: 19–20
Trimble, William: 158n
Trollope, Mrs.: *Domestic Manners* read in Cincinnati, 13; quoted regarding American scenery, 85, 85n
Tuer du Village (Indian warrior): 97, 97n, 98

Union Hotel: 80
Union Mission: 23, 110, 110n

Vaill, Asenath Selden: 110, 110n
Vaill, William F.: 110, 110n, 151n; preaches to Indians, 103
Van Buren (Ark.): 156, 157, 157n
Vaux, Roberts: 9
Verdigris River: 27, 37, 111, 111n, 112n, 136n, 150, 151, 152, 155
Verdigris Trading Post: *see* Chouteau, Auguste Pierre
Vuide (Vide) Poche: *see* Carondelet

Wabash Island: 72
Wabash River: 72, 73
Walnut Creek: 98n
Whetstone, Pete: see Noland, Charles Fenton Mercer
Whirling Thunder (Nah-se-us-kuk), elder son of Black Hawk: 83n
White Cloud (Wabokieshiek): *see* Winnebago Prophet
White deer: story of, 152–53
White Hair's Town: 100, 100n
White River: 160, 160n
Wild horses: 136, 137, 140, 142–43
William (Chouteau's Negro boy): 91, 110
Winnebago Prophet (brother-in-law of Black Hawk): 16, 83, 83n, 84n
Wolf hunt: 96
Wood, Mr.: 69
Woodruff, William E.: 159n

York (body servant of William Clark): 82

The American Exploration and Travel Series

of which *The Western Journals of Washington Irving* is Number 8, was started in 1939 by the University of Oklahoma Press. It follows rather logically the Press's program of regional exploration. Behind the story of the gradual and inevitable recession of the American frontier lie the accounts of explorers, traders, and travelers, which individually and in the aggregate present one of the most romantic and fascinating chapters in the development of the American domain. The following list is complete as of the date of printing of this volume.

1. Captain Randolph B. Marcy and Captain George B. McClellan. *Adventures on Red River:* Report on the Exploration of the Headwaters of the Red River. Edited by Grant Foreman.

2. Grant Foreman. *Marcy and the Gold Seekers:* The Journal of Captain R. B. Marcy, with an Account of the Gold Rush over the Southern Route.

3. Pierre-Antoine Tabeau. *Tabeau's Narrative of Loisel's Expedition to the Upper Missouri.* Edited by Annie Heloise Abel. Translated from the French by Rose Abel Wright.

4. Victor Tixier. *Tixier's Travels on the Osage Prairies.* Edited by John Francis McDermott. Translated from the French by Albert J. Salvan.

5. Teodoro de Croix. *Teodoro de Croix and the Northern Frontier of New Spain, 1776–1783.* Translated from the Spanish and edited by Alfred Barnaby Thomas.

6. A. W. Whipple. *A Pathfinder in the Southwest:* The Itinerary of Lieutenant A. W. Whipple During His Explorations for a Railway Route from Fort Smith to Los Angeles in the years 1853 & 1854. Edited and annotated by Grant Foreman.

7. Josiah Gregg. *Diary & Letters.* Two volumes. Edited by Maurice Garland Fulton. Introductions by Paul Horgan.

8. Washington Irving. *The Western Journals of Washington Irving.* Edited and annotated by John Francis McDermott.

9. Edward Dumbauld. *Thomas Jefferson, American Tourist:* Being an Account of His Journeys in the United States of America, England, France, Italy, the Low Countries, and Germany. Out of print.

10. Victor Wolfgang von Hagen. *Maya Explorer:* John Lloyd Stephens and the Lost Cities of Central America and Yucatán.

11. E. Merton Coulter. *Travels in the Confederate States:* A Bibliography.

12. W. Eugene Hollon. *The Lost Pathfinder:* Zebulon Montgomery Pike.

13. George Frederick Ruxton. *Ruxton of the Rockies.* Collected by Clyde and Mae Reed Porter. Edited by LeRoy R. Hafen. Out of print.

14. George Frederick Ruxton. *Life in the Far West.* Edited by LeRoy R. Hafen. Foreword by Mae Reed Porter.

15. Edward Harris. *Up the Missouri with Audubon:* The Journal of Edward Harris. Edited by John Francis McDermott.

16. Robert Stuart. *On the Oregon Trail:* Robert Stuart's Journey of Discovery (1812–1813). Edited by Kenneth A. Spaulding.

17. Josiah Gregg. *Commerce of the Prairies.* Edited by Max L. Moorhead.

18. John Treat Irving, Jr. *Indian Sketches.* Taken During an Expedition to the Pawnee Tribes (1833). Edited and annotated by John Francis McDermott.

19. Thomas D. Clark (ed.). *Travels in the Old South, 1527–1860:* A Bibliography. Three Volumes. Volume One and Two issued as a set (1956); Volume Three (1959). Out of print.

20. Alexander Ross. *The Fur Hunters of the Far West.* Edited by Kenneth A. Spaulding.

21. William Bollaert. *William Bollaert's Texas.* Edited by W. Eugene Hollon and Ruth Lapham Butler. Out of print.

22. Daniel Ellis Conner. *Joseph Reddeford Walker and the Arizona Adventure.* Edited by Donald J. Berthrong and Odessa Davenport.

23. Matthew C. Field. *Prairie and Mountain Sketches.* Collected by Clyde and Mae Reed Porter. Edited by Kate L. Gregg and John Francis McDermott.

24. Ross Cox. *The Columbia River:* Scenes and Adventures During a Residence of Six Years on the Western Side of the Rocky Mountains Among Various Tribes of Indians Hitherto Unknown; Together with a Journey Across the American Continent. Edited by Edgar I. and Jane R. Stewart.

25. Noel M. Loomis. *The Texan–Santa Fé Pioneers.*

26. Charles Preuss. *Exploring with Frémont:* The Private Diaries of Charles Preuss, Cartographer for John C. Frémont on His First, Second, and Fourth Expeditions to the Far West. Translated and edited by Erwin G. and Elisabeth K. Gudde.

27. Jacob H. Schiel. *Journey Through the Rocky Mountains and the Humboldt Mountains to the Pacific Ocean.* Translated from the German and edited by Thomas N. Bonner.

28. Zenas Leonard. *Adventures of Zenas Leonard, Fur Trader.* Edited by John C. Ewers.

29. Matthew C. Field. *Matt Field on the Santa Fe Trail.* Collected by Clyde and Mae Reed Porter. Edited and with an introduction and note by John E. Sunder.

30. James Knox Polk Miller. *The Road to Virginia City:* The Diary of James Knox Polk Miller. Edited by Andrew F. Rolle.

31. Benjamin Butler Harris. *The Gila Trail:* The Texas Argonauts and the California Gold Rush. Edited and annotated by Richard H. Dillon.

32. Lieutenant James H. Bradley. *The March of the Montana Column:* A prelude to the Custer Disaster. Edited by Edgar I. Stewart.

33. Heinrich Lienhard. *From St. Louis to Sutter's Fort, 1846.* Translated and edited by Erwin G. and Elisabeth K. Gudde.

34. Washington Irving. *The Adventures of Captain Bonneville.* Edited and with an introduction by Edgeley W. Todd.

35. Jean-Bernard Bossu. *Jean-Bernard Bossu's Travels in the Interior of North America, 1751–1762.* Translated and edited by Seymour Feiler.

36. Thomas D. Clark (ed.). *Travels in the New South, 1865–1955:* A Bibliography. Two volumes.
37. John Lloyd Stephens. *Incidents of Travel in Yucatán.* Edited and with an introduction by Victor Wolfgang von Hagen. Two volumes.
38. Richard A. Bartlett. *Great Surveys of the American West.*
39. Gloria Griffen Cline. *Exploring the Great Basin.*
40. Francisco de Miranda. *The New Democracy in America:* Travels of Francisco de Miranda in the United States, 1783–84. Translated by Judson P. Wood. Edited by John S. Ezell.
41. Col. Joseph K. F. Mansfield. *Mansfield on the Condition of the Western Forts, 1853–54.* Edited by Robert W. Frazer.
42. Louis Antoine de Bougainville. *Adventure in the Wilderness:* The American Journals of Louis Antoine de Bougainville, 1756–1760. Translated and edited by Edward P. Hamilton.
43. James H. Simpson. *Navaho Expedition:* Journal of a Military Reconnaissance from Santa Fe, New Mexico, to the Navaho Country Made in 1849. Edited by Frank McNitt.
44. Washington Irving. *Astoria: or, Anecdotes of an Enterprise Beyond the Rocky Mountains.* Edited and with an introduction by Edgeley W. Todd.
45. Robert Brewster Stanton. *Down the Colorado.* Edited and with an introduction by Dwight L. Smith.
46. David Meriwether. *My Life in the Mountains and on the Plains:* The Newly Discovered Autobiography. Edited by Robert A. Griffen.
47. Charles W. Cook, David E. Folsom, and William Peterson. *The Valley of the Upper Yellowstone.* Edited and with an introduction by Aubrey L. Haines.
48. *The Journals and Papers of Zebulon Montgomery Pike.* Two volumes. Edited and annotated by Donald Jackson.
49. Abraham N. Nasatir and Noel M. Loomis. *Pedro Vial and the Roads to Santa Fe.*

UNIVERSITY OF OKLAHOMA PRESS

NORMAN